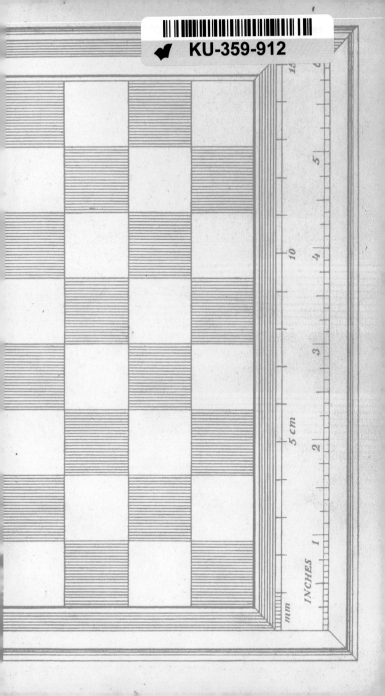

THE WEEK-END BOOK

THE
WEEK-END
BOOK

THE NONESUCH PRESS
16 GREAT JAMES STREET
BLOOMSBURY
1931

Printed and made in England by
William Brendon & Son, Ltd.

BIBLIOGRAPHY

T H E Week-End Book was first published in June 1924. It then contained 332 pages without illustration. With various additions and alterations it was reprinted in England seventeen times, to a total of more than fifty thousand copies. Other impressions were printed in the United States of America. In October 1928 was issued an enlarged edition (illustrated by Albert Rutherston), twice reprinted. This in turn is enlarged, and redecorated by T. L. Poulton, for the edition for 1931, of which this copy is an example.

SECOND IMPRESSION . . .	JUNE, 1924
THIRD IMPRESSION . . .	JULY, 1924
FOURTH IMPRESSION . . .	JULY, 1924
FIFTH IMPRESSION . .	SEPTEMBER, 1924
SIXTH IMPRESSION . .	DECEMBER, 1924
SEVENTH IMPRESSION .	DECEMBER, 1924
EIGHTH IMPRESSION (ENLARGED AND REVISED) . . .	MARCH, 1925
NINTH IMPRESSION (INDIA PAPER)	APRIL, 1925
TENTH IMPRESSION . . .	JUNE, 1925
ELEVENTH IMPRESSION .	NOVEMBER, 1925
TWELFTH IMPRESSION .	JANUARY, 1926
THIRTEENTH IMPRESSION .	APRIL, 1926
FOURTEENTH IMPRESSION (ENLARGED) . . .	JULY, 1926
FIFTEENTH IMPRESSION (INDIA PAPER) . . .	SEPTEMBER, 1926
SIXTEENTH IMPRESSION .	OCTOBER, 1926
SEVENTEENTH IMPRESSION .	APRIL, 1927
EIGHTEENTH IMPRESSION .	OCTOBER, 1927
NEW EDITION (15,000 COPIES) .	OCTOBER, 1928
REPRINTED (12,000 COPIES) .	JANUARY, 1929
REPRINTED (10,000 COPIES)	SEPTEMBER, 1929
NEW EDITION (15,000 COPIES) .	OCTOBER, 1930

BIBLIOGRAPHY

THE *Week-End Book* was first published in June, 1924. It then contained 332 pages without illustration. With various additions and alterations it was reprinted in England seventeen times to a total of more than fifty thousand copies. Other impressions were printed in the United States of America. In October 1924 there was issued an enlarged edition, illustrated by Albert Rutherston, twice reprinted. This in turn is enlarged, and redecorated by Th. L. Poulton, for the edition for 1931, of which this copy is an example.

SECOND IMPRESSION	JUNE, 1924
THIRD IMPRESSION	JULY, 1924
FOURTH IMPRESSION	JULY, 1924
FIFTH IMPRESSION	SEPTEMBER, 1924
SIXTH IMPRESSION	DECEMBER, 1924
SEVENTH IMPRESSION	DECEMBER, 1924
EIGHTH IMPRESSION (ENLARGED AND REVISED)	MARCH, 1925
NINTH IMPRESSION (INDIA PAPER)	APRIL, 1925
TENTH IMPRESSION	JUNE, 1925
ELEVENTH IMPRESSION	NOVEMBER, 1925
TWELFTH IMPRESSION	JANUARY, 1926
THIRTEENTH IMPRESSION	APRIL, 1926
FOURTEENTH IMPRESSION (ENLARGED)	JULY, 1926
FIFTEENTH IMPRESSION (INDIA PAPER)	SEPTEMBER, 1926
SIXTEENTH IMPRESSION	OCTOBER, 1926
SEVENTEENTH IMPRESSION	APRIL, 1927
EIGHTEENTH IMPRESSION	OCTOBER, 1927
NEW EDITION (15,000 COPIES)	OCTOBER, 1924
REPRINTING (12,000 COPIES)	JANUARY, 1925
REPRINTED (10,000 COPIES)	SEPTEMBER, 1929
NEW EDITION (15,000 COPIES)	OCTOBER, 1931

WEEK-END

The train! The twelve o'clock for paradise.
Hurry, or it will try to creep away.
Out in the country everyone is wise:
We can be only wise on Saturday.
There you are waiting, little friendly house:
Those are your chimney-stacks with you between,
Surrounded by old trees and strolling cows,
Staring through all your windows at the green.
Your homely floor is creaking for our tread;
The smiling tea-pot with contented spout
Thinks of the boiling water, and the bread
Longs for the butter. All their hands are out
To greet us, and the gentle blankets seem
Purring and crooning: " Lie in us, and dream."

Harold Monro.

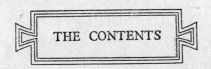

THE CONTENTS

THE CONTENTS

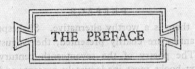

THE PREFACE

"THE WEEK-END BOOK explains itself. A preface can but italicise the anthological principles of the editors. The first of these is the axiom that there are no good anthologies, always excepting the one which every man would like to make himself—with a newly revised, abridged and amplified edition every five years or so. We have accordingly attempted to meet every man halfway and to compile a book of clues to good life and reading for week-end pairs and parties, which each in his fashion may follow up. We hope to have as many collaborators as readers; and to make it easy for them to amplify our design we have included a section of blank pages of writing paper."

The "five years or so" of the above paragraph, with which we introduced the first edition of this book, have now passed; and the collaboration of many ingenious and well-disposed readers who have filled in the manu-script pages has been continuously forthcoming. This new edition, theirs scarcely less than ours, is the result.

We repeat now with much greater confidence the hope we expressed five years ago that the poetry sections of this book will, in the main, satisfy the Georgian version of the "Open Road" public. For, after all, there is a consensus of opinion between generations, called taste: not to speak of fashion, that even closer coincidence of appreciation within generations. As it is designed to supplement and balance the Oxford Book of English Verse (carried in the opposite pocket) we have sought out the less familiar of the great poems, poets and periods. The anthology pieces of any author have been avoided wherever there is a worthy alternative. Shakespeare and the Romantics are charily presented, the Augustans not at all. The poetry of the seventeenth century, which school text-books most inadequately present, and that of the twentieth century, which older anthologies perforce ignore, is most amply represented.

The section of GREAT POEMS is arranged in chronological order and takes no account of subjects. Love poetry and Nature poetry must take so large a place in any general collection of great poems that lovers and land-lovers need no separate provision. But some pleasant and some poignant verse sprung from the mood of Hate has been grouped together for the specific enjoyment of that almost as widely felt emotion. The State poems need no comment. They provide an outlet for yet another mood, not uncommon in hours of sociable relaxation. A section of Epigrams provides a collection of poems which, left out from the run of anthologies because of their scale or subject, well deserve a place for their combination of brevity with beauty or wit. The " Zoo " should appeal to the collector's temperament. Those who take up the pleasant hobby of zoological literature will find material among the poets for building a handsome collection around this nuclear section. We have once more printed the titles, first lines and authors only, of those great poems which our pastors and masters in infancy and our poetic enthusiasms in adolescence have already made sufficiently, if not excessively, familiar. These may be transcribed on the blank pages at the end of the book, or recited or banished from memory, according to individual taste and ability.

The SONGS are ransacked from all ages, countries and moods, the only " unity " observed by the compiler being that of fitness for purpose—the sociable week-ender's purpose. They are some of the best available tunes for unaccompanied chorus singing, only occasionally and effectively to be varied by a solo and chorus rendering. Moreover, they are all folk-songs, in the spirit of the word—and the letter too if, as we may fairly contend, the term covers such newer equivalents as "shanties," "spirituals" and the spontaneous effusions of the British Expeditionary Force.

The Prose sections, now eight in number, contain the most useful hints which we have been able to gather from our own experience and from that of our many helpers on such mysteries as the prognostication of the weather, the making of camp fires and beds and improvised paper cups, and the food, drink, diversions and damages (legal as well as medical) of week-enders. By diagram and picture as well as by word the attempt is made to answer the city dweller's curiosity as to which star saw him to bed (for has not our system of weather-forecast made his sky rain-proof for him?) and what bird called him in the morning. The new section on Architecture may soften many arguments between Man and his Donkey; may enable them, even, to keep their end up if the fabric-proud Vicar surprises them in the church and insists on acting as their guide to its historical and monumental features. The Receipts are for the cookless cottage, the campfire and the restricted resources of the village public-house and store, as well as for the more expert or more elaborately provided cook. As time is usually the chief consideration, menus have been drawn up on a speed-basis. The suggestions contained in the Play section involve no more than that two or three be gathered together with such readily accessible or improvised implements as a stick and ball, or a pencil and paper. (Let those who think they know all the good ball-games try their hand at Tishy-Toshy or the Roof Game, or which our rules create an official code.) A practising barrister is responsible for counsel's opinion that the best way with the

Law is the avoidance of it, with help thereto. The Medical Prescriptions are contributed by a physician; they contain only such ingredients and doses as may be supplied by a chemist without recourse to a personal prescription.

VERA MENDEL

FRANCIS MEYNELL

General Editors.

JOHN GOSS

Music Editor.

INDEX OF POEMS (FIRST LINES)

xvii

INDEX OF POEMS

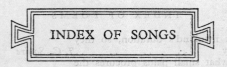

INDEX OF SONGS

INDEX OF SONGS

xxx

GREAT POEMS

OFT, IN THE PUBLIC ROADS
YET UNFREQUENTED, WHILE THE MORNING LIGHT
WAS YELLOWING THE HILL TOPS, I WENT ABROAD
WITH A DEAR FRIEND, AND FOR THE BETTER PART
OF TWO DELIGHTFUL HOURS WE STROLLED ALONG
BY THE STILL BORDERS OF THE MISTY LAKE,
REPEATING FAVOURITE VERSES WITH ONE VOICE.

William Wordsworth.

B

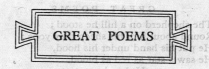

GREAT POEMS

O WESTERN WIND

O WESTERN wind, when wilt thou blow,
  That the small rain down can rain?
Christ, that my love were in my arms
  And I in my bed again!

Anonymous.

HEY NONNY NO

HEY nonny no!
Men are fools that wish to die!
Is't not fine to dance and sing
When the bells of death do ring?
Is't not fine to swim in wine,
And turn upon the toe,
And sing hey nonny no!
When the winds blow and the seas flow?
Hey nonny no!

Anonymous.

JOLY JOLY WAT

THE shepherd upon a hill he sat;
He had on him his tabard and his hat,
His tarbox, his pipe, and his flagat;
His name was called Joly Joly Wat,
For he was a good herdes boy
      Ut hoy!
  For in his pipe he made so much joy.

The shepherd upon a hill was laid;
His dog to his girdle was tied;
He had not slept but a little braid,
But "*Gloria in excelsis*" was to him said.
      Ut hoy!
  For in his pipe he made so much joy.

3

The shepherd on a hill he stood ;
Round about him his sheep they yode ;
He put his hand under his hood,
He saw a star as red as blood.
                    Ut hoy !
    For in his pipe he made so much joy.

The shepherd said anon right,
" I will go see yon farly sight,
Whereas the angel singeth on height,
And the star that shineth so bright."
                    Ut hoy !
    For in his pipe he made so much joy.

" Now farewell, Moll, and also Will !
For my love go ye all still
Unto I come again you till,
And evermore, Will, ring well thy bell."
                    Ut hoy !
    For in his pipe he made so much joy.

" Now must I go there Christ was born ;
Farewell ! I come again to morn.
Dog, keep well my sheep from the corn,
And warn well ' Warroke ' when I blow my horn ! "
                    Ut hoy !
    For in his pipe he made so much joy.

When Wat to Bethlehem come was,
He sweat, he had gone faster than a pace ;
He found Jesu in a simple place,
Between an ox and an ass.
                    Ut hoy !
    For in his pipe he made so much joy.

" Jesu, I offer to thee here my pipe,
My skirt, my tarbox, and my scrip ;
Home to my fellows now will I skip,
And also look unto my sheep."
                    Ut hoy !
    For in his pipe he made so much joy.

4

"Now farewell, mine own herdsman Wat!"
"Yea, for God, lady, even so I hight;
Lull well Jesu in thy lap,
And farewell, Joseph, with thy round cape!"
      Ut hoy!
  For in his pipe he made so much joy.

"Now may I well both hope and sing,
For I have been at Christ's bearing;
Home to my fellows now will I fling,
Christ of heaven to his bliss us bring!"
      Ut hoy!
  For in his pipe he made so much joy.

                              Anonymous.

I SING OF A MAIDEN

    I SING of a maiden
      That is makeless.
    King of all kinges
      To her son she chose.

    He came all so stille
      There his mother was
    As dew in Aprille
      That falleth on grass.

    He came all so stille
      To his mother's bower,
    As dew in Aprille
      That falleth on the flower,

    He came all so stille
      There his mother lay,
    As dew in Aprille
      That falleth on the spray.

    Mother and maiden
      Was never none but she;
    Well may such a lady
      Godes mother be.

                              Anonymous.

5

JOLLY GOOD ALE AND OLD

I CANNOT eat but little meat,
   My stomach is not good ;
But sure I think that I can drink
   With him that wears a hood.
Though I go bare, take ye no care,
   I nothing am a-cold ;
I stuff my skin so full within
   Of jolly good ale and old.
      Back and side go bare, go bare ;
      Both foot and hand go cold ;
      But, belly, God send thee good ale enough,
      Whether it be new or old.

I love no roast but a nut-brown toast,
   And a crab laid in the fire ;
A little bread shall do me stead ;
   Much bread I not desire.
No frost nor snow, no wind, I trow,
   Can hurt me if I wold ;
I am so wrapped and thoroughly lapped
   Of jolly good ale and old.
      Back and side go bare, go bare, etc.

And Tib, my wife, that as her life
   Loveth well good ale to seek,
Full oft drinks she till ye may see
   The tears run down her cheek :
Then doth she trowl to me the bowl
   Even as a maltworm should,
And saith, " Sweetheart, I took my part
   Of this jolly good ale and old."
      Back and side go bare, go bare, etc.

Now let them drink till they nod and wink,
   Even as good fellows should do ;
They shall not miss to have the bliss
   Good ale doth bring men to ;
And all poor souls that have scoured bowls
   Or have them lustily trolled,
God save the lives of them and their wives,
   Whether they be young or old.

Back and side go bare, go bare ;
Both foot and hand go cold ;
But, belly, God send thee good ale enough,
Whether it be new or old.
    John Still (Bishop of Bath and Wells).

WALY, WALY

O WALY, waly, up the bank,
    And waly, waly, doun the brae,
And waly, waly, yon burn-side,
    Where I and my Love wont to gae !
I lean'd my back unto an aik,
    I thocht it was a trustie tree ;
But first it bow'd and syne it brak—
    Sae my true love did lichtlie me.

O waly, waly, gin love be bonnie
    A little time while it is new !
But when 'tis auld it waxeth cauld,
    And fades awa' like morning dew.
O wherefore should I busk my heid,
    Or wherefore should I kame my hair ?
For my true Love has me forsook,
    And says he'll never lo'e me mair.

Now Arthur's Seat sall be my bed,
    The sheets sall ne'er be 'filed by me ;
Saint Anton's well sall be my drink,
    Since my true Love has forsaken me ;
Marti'mas wind, when wilt thou blaw,
    And shake the green leaves aff the tree ?
O gentle Death, when wilt thou come ?
    For of my life I am wearie.

'Tis not the frost, that freezes fell,
    Nor blawing snaw's inclemencie,
'Tis not sic cauld that makes me cry ;
    But my Love's heart grown cauld to me.
When we cam in by Glasgow toun,
    We were a comely sicht to see ;
My Love was clad in the black velvet,
    And I mysel in cramasie.

7

But had I wist, before I kist,
   That love had been sae ill to win,
I had lock'd my heart in a case o' gowd,
   And pinn'd it wi' a siller pin.
And O ! if my young babe were born,
   And set upon the nurse's knee ;
And I mysel were dead and gane,
   And the green grass growing over me !

                    Anonymous.

HELEN OF KIRCONNELL

I WISH I were where Helen lies,
Night and day on me she cries ;
O that I were where Helen lies,
   On fair Kirconnell lea !

Curst be the heart that thought the thought,
And curst the hand that fired the shot,
When in my arms burd Helen dropt,
   And died to succour me !

O think na ye my heart was sair,
When my Love dropp'd and spak nae mair !
There did she swoon wi' meikle care,
   On fair Kirconnell lea.

As I went down the water side,
None but my foe to be my guide,
None but my foe to be my guide,
   On fair Kirconnell lea ;

I lighted down my sword to draw,
I hacked him in pieces sma',
I hacked him in pieces sma',
   For her sake that died for me.

O Helen fair, beyond compare !
I'll mak a garland o' thy hair,
Shall bind my heart for evermair,
   Until the day I die !

8

O that I were where Helen lies !
Night and day on me she cries ;
Out of my bed she bids me rise,
   Says, " Haste, and come to me ! "

O Helen fair ! O Helen chaste !
If I were with thee, I'd be blest,
Where thou lies low and taks thy rest,
   On fair Kirconnell lea.

I wish my grave were growing green,
A winding-sheet drawn owre my e'en,
And I in Helen's arms lying,
   On fair Kirconnell lea.

I wish I were where Helen lies !
Night and day on me she cries ;
And I am weary of the skies,
   For her sake that died for me.

Anonymous.

THE BONNY EARL OF MORAY

YE Highlands and ye Lawlands,
   O where hae ye been ?
They hae slain the Earl of Moray,
   And hae laid him on the green.

Now wae be to thee, Huntley !
   And whairfore did ye sae !
I bade you bring him wi' you,
   But forbade you him to slay.

He was a braw gallant,
   And he rid at the ring ;
And the bonny Earl of Moray,
   O he might hae been a king !

He was a braw gallant,
   And he play'd at the ba' ;
And the bonny Earl of Moray
   Was the flower amang them a' !

He was a braw gallant,
　And he play'd at the gluve;
And the bonny Earl of Moray,
　O he was the Queen's luve!

O lang will his Lady
　Look owre the Castle Downe,
Ere she see the Earl of Moray
　Come sounding through the town!

Anonymous.

THE QUEEN'S MARIE

MARIE HAMILTON'S to the kirk gane,
　Wi' ribbons in her hair;
The King thought mair o' Marie Hamilton
　Than ony that were there.

Marie Hamilton's to the kirk gane
　Wi' ribbons on her breast;
The King thought mair o' Marie Hamilton
　Than he listen'd to the priest.

Marie Hamilton's to the kirk gane,
　Wi' gloves upon her hands;
The King thought mair o' Marie Hamilton
　Than the Queen and a' her lands.

She hadna been about the King's court
　A month but barely one,
Till she was beloved by a' King's court
　And the King the only man.

She hadna been about the King's court
　A month, but barely three,
Till frae the King's court Marie Hamilton,
　Marie Hamilton durstna be.

The King is to the Abbey gane,
　To pu' the Abbey tree,
To scale the babe frae Marie's heart;
　But the thing it wadna be.

O she has row'd it in her apron,
    And set it on the sea—
" Gae sink ye or swim ye, bonny babe,
    Ye'se get nae mair o' me."

Word is to the kitchen gane,
    And word is to the ha',
And word is to the noble room
    Amang the ladies a',
That Marie Hamilton's brought to bed,
    And the bonny babe's miss'd and awa'.

Scarcely had she lain down again,
    And scarcely fa'en asleep,
When up and started our gude Queen
    Just at her bed-feet ;
Saying—" Marie Hamilton, where's your babe ?
    For I am sure I heard it greet."

" O no, O no, my noble Queen !
    Think no sic thing to be ;
'Twas but a stitch into my side,
    And sair it troubles me ! "

" Get up, get up, Marie Hamilton :
    Get up and follow me ;
For I am going to Edinburgh town,
    A rich wedding for to see."

O slowly, slowly rase she up,
    And slowly put she on ;
And slowly rade she out the way
    Wi' mony a weary groan.

The Queen was clad in scarlet,
    Her merry maids all in green ;
And every town that they cam to,
    They took Marie for the Queen.

" Ride hooly, hooly, gentlemen,
    Ride hooly now wi' me !
For never, I am sure, a wearier burd
    Rade in your companie."—

But little wist Marie Hamilton,
    When she rade on the brown,
That she was gaen to Edinburgh town
    And a' to be put down.

" Why weep ye so, ye burgess wives,
    Why look ye so on me ?
O I am going to Edinburgh town,
    A rich wedding to see."

When she gaed up the tolbooth stairs,
    The corks frae her heels did flee ;
And lang or e'er she cam down again,
    She was condemn'd to die.

When she cam to the Netherbow port,
    She laugh'd loud laughters three ;
But when she came to the gallows foot
    The tears blinded her e'e.

" Yestreen the Queen had four Maries.
    The night she'll hae but three ;
There was Marie Seaton, and Marie Beaton,
    And Marie Carmichael, and me.

" O often have I dress'd my Queen
    And put gowd upon her hair ;
But now I've gotten for my reward
    The gallows to be my share.

" Often have I dress'd my Queen
    And often made her bed ;
But now I've gotten for my reward
    The gallows tree to tread.

" I charge ye all, ye mariners,
    When ye sail owre the faem,
Let neither my father nor mother get wit
    But that I'm coming hame.

" I charge ye all, ye mariners,
    That sail upon the sea,
That neither my father nor mother get wit
    The dog's death I'm to die.

" For if my father and mother got wit,
   And my bold brethren three,
O mickle wad be the gude red blude
   This day wad be spilt for me !

" O little did my mother ken,
   The day she cradled me
The lands I was to travel in
   Or the death I was to die ! "

Anonymous.

CLERK SAUNDERS

CLERK SAUNDERS and may Margaret
   Walk'd owre yon garden green ;
And deep and heavy was the love
   That fell thir twa between.

" A bed, a bed," Clerk Saunders said,
   " A bed for you and me ! "
" Fye na, fye na," said may Margaret,
   " Till anes we married be ! "

" Then I'll take the sword frae my scabbard
   And slowly lift the pin ;
And you may swear, and save your aith,
   Ye ne'er let Clerk Saunders in.

" Take you a napkin in your hand,
   And tie up baith your bonnie e'en,
And you may swear, and save your aith,
   Ye saw me na since late yestreen."

It was about the midnight hour,
   When they asleep were laid,
When in and came her seven brothers,
   Wi' torches burning red ;

When in and came her seven brothers,
   Wi' torches burning bright :
They said, " We hae but one sister,
   And behold her lying with a knight ! "

13

Then out and spake the first o' them,
"I bear the sword shall gar him die."
And out and spake the second o' them,
"His father has nae mair but he."

And out and spake the third o' them,
"I wot that they are lovers dear."
And out and spake the fourth o' them,
"They hae been in love this mony a year."

Then out and spake the fifth o' them,
"It were great sin true love to twain."
And out and spake the sixth o' them,
"It were shame to slay a sleeping man."

Then up and gat the seventh o' them.
And never a word spake he;
But he has striped his bright brand
Out through Clerk Saunders' fair body.

Clerk Saunders he started, and Margaret she turn'd
Into his arms as asleep she lay;
And sad and silent was the night
That was atween thir twae.

And they lay still and sleepit sound
Until the day began to daw';
And kindly she to him did say,
"It is time, true love, you were awa'."

But he lay still, and sleepit sound,
Albeit the sun began to sheen;
She look'd atween her and the wa',
And dull and drowsie were his e'en.

Then in and came her father dear;
Said, "Let a' your mourning be;
I'll carry the dead corse to the clay,
And I'll come back and comfort thee."

"Comfort weel your seven sons,
For comforted I will never be:
I ween 'twas neither knave nor loon
Was in the bower last night wi' me."

The clinking bell gaed through the town,
   To carry the dead corse to the clay ;
And Clerk Saunders stood at may Margaret's
     window,
   I wot, an hour before the day.

" Are ye sleeping, Margaret ? " he says,
   " Or are ye waking presently ?
Give me my faith and troth again,
   I wot, true love, I gied to thee."

" Your faith and troth ye sall never get,
   Nor our true love sall never twin,
Until ye come within my bower,
   And kiss me cheik and chin."

" My mouth it is full cold, Marg'ret ;
   It has the smell, now, of the ground ;
And if I kiss thy comely mouth,
   Thy days of life will not be lang.

" O cocks are crowing a merry midnight ;
   I wot the wild fowls are boding day ;
Give me my faith and troth again,
   And let me fare me on my way."

" Thy faith and troth thou sallna get,
   And our true love sall never twin,
Until ye tell what comes o' women,
   I wot, who die in strong traivelling ? "

" Their beds are made in the heavens high,
   Down at the foot of our good Lord's knee,
Weel set about wi' gillyflowers ;
   I wot, sweet company for to see.

" O cocks are crowing a merry midnight ;
   I wot the wild fowls are boding day ;
The psalms of heaven will soon be sung,
   And I, ere now, will be miss'd away."

Then she has taken a crystal wand,
   And she has stroken her troth thereon ;
She has given it him out at the shot-window,
   Wi' mony a sad sigh and heavy groan.

15

" I thank ye, Marg'ret ; I thank ye, Marg'ret ;
  And ay I thank ye heartily ;
Gin ever the dead come for the quick,
  Be sure, Marg'ret, I'll come for thee."

It's hosen and shoon, and gown alone,
  She climb'd the wall, and follow'd him,
Until she came to the green forest,
  And there she lost the sight o' him.

" Is there ony room at your head, Saunders ?
  Is there ony room at your feet ?
Or ony room at your side, Saunders,
  Where fain, fain, I wad sleep ? "

" There's nae room at my head, Marg'ret,
  There's nay room at my feet ;
My bed it is fu' lowly now,
  Amang the hungry worms I sleep.

" Cauld mould is my covering now,
  But and my winding-sheet ;
The dew it falls nae sooner down
  Than my resting-place is weet.

" But plait a wand o' bonny birk,
  And lay it on my breast ;
And shed a tear upon my grave,
  And wish my saul gude rest."

Then up and crew the red, red cock,
  And up and crew the gray ;
" 'Tis time, 'tis time, my dear Marg'ret,
  That you were going away.

" And fair Marg'ret, and rare Marg'ret,
  And Marg'ret o' veritie,
Gin e'er ye love another man,
  Ne'er love him as ye did me."

Anonymous.

THE LAMENT OF DAVID OVER SAUL AND JONATHAN

T H E beauty of Israel is slain upon thy high places : how are the mighty fallen !

Tell it not in Gath, publish it not in the streets of Askelon ; lest the daughters of the Philistines rejoice, lest the daughters of the uncircumcised triumph.

Ye mountains of Gilboa, let there be no dew, neither let there be rain, upon you, nor fields of offerings : for there the shield of the mighty is vilely cast away, the shield of Saul, as though he had not been anointed with oil.

From the blood of the slain, from the fat of the mighty, the bow of Jonathan turned not back, and the sword of Saul returned not empty.

Saul and Jonathan were lovely and pleasant in their lives, and in their death they were not divided : they were swifter than eagles, they were stronger than lions.

Ye daughters of Israel, weep over Saul, who clothed you in scarlet, with other delights, who put on ornaments of gold upon your apparel.

How are the mighty fallen in the midst of the battle ! O Jonathan, thou wast slain in thine high places.

I am distressed for thee, my brother Jonathan : very pleasant hast thou been unto me : thy love to me was wonderful, passing the love of women.

How are the mighty fallen, and the weapons of war perished !

The Authorised Version.

PSALM 137

B Y the waters of Babylon we sat down and wept : when we remembered thee, O Sion.

As for our harps, we hanged them up : upon the trees that are therein.

For they that led us away captive required of us then a song, and melody, in our heaviness : Sing us one of the songs of Sion.

How shall we sing the Lord's song : in a strange land ?

If I forget thee, O Jerusalem : let my right hand forget her cunning.

If I do not remember thee, let my tongue cleave to the roof of my mouth : yea, if I prefer not Jerusalem in my mirth.

Remember the children of Edom, O Lord, in the day of Jerusalem : how they said, Down with it, down with it, even to the ground.

O daughter of Babylon, wasted with misery : yea, happy shall he be that rewardeth thee, as thou hast served us.

Blessed shall he be that taketh thy children : and throweth them against the stones.

The " Great Bible."

THE SONG OF SONGS, WHICH IS SOLOMON'S

I

LET him kiss me with the kisses of his mouth : for thy love is better than wine.

Because of the savour of thy good ointments thy name is as ointment poured forth, therefore do the virgins love thee.

Draw me, we will run after thee : the king hath brought me into his chambers : we will be glad and rejoice in thee, we will remember thy love more than wine : the upright love thee.

I am black, but comely, O ye daughters of Jerusalem, as the tents of Kedar, as the curtains of Solomon.

Look not upon me, because I am black, because the sun hath looked upon me : my mother's children were angry with me ; they made me the keeper of the vineyards ; but mine own vineyard have I not kept.

Tell me, O thou whom my soul loveth, where thou feedest, where thou makest thy flock to rest at noon : for why should I be as one that turneth aside by the flocks of thy companions ?

If thou know not, O thou fairest among women, go thy way forth by the footsteps of the flock, and feed thy kids beside the shepherds' tents.

I have compared thee, O my love, to a company of horses in Pharaoh's chariots.

Thy cheeks are comely with rows of jewels, thy neck with chains of gold.

18

We will make thee borders of gold with studs of silver.

While the king sitteth at his table, my spikenard sendeth forth the smell thereof.

A bundle of myrrh is my wellbeloved unto me; he shall lie all night betwixt my breasts.

My beloved is unto me as a cluster of camphire in the vineyards of En-gedi.

Behold, thou art fair, my love; behold, thou art fair; thou hast doves' eyes.

Behold, thou art fair, my beloved, yea, pleasant; also our bed is green.

The beams of our house are cedar, and our rafters of fir.

II

I AM the rose of Sharon, and the lily of the valleys.

As the lily among thorns, so is my love among the daughters.

As the apple tree among the trees of the wood, so is my beloved among the sons. I sat down under his shadow with great delight, and his fruit was sweet to my taste.

He brought me to the banqueting house, and his banner over me was love.

Stay me with flagons, comfort me with apples; for I am sick of love.

His left hand is under my head, and his right hand doth embrace me.

I charge you, O ye daughters of Jerusalem, by the roes, and by the hinds of the field, that ye stir not up, nor awake my love, till he please.

The voice of my beloved! behold, he cometh leaping upon the mountains, skipping upon the hills.

My beloved is like a roe or a young hart: behold, he standeth behind our wall, he looketh forth at the windows, shewing himself through the lattice.

My beloved spake, and said unto me, Rise up, my love, my fair one, and come away.

For, lo, the winter is past, the rain is over and gone;

The flowers appear on the earth; the time of the singing of birds is come, and the voice of the turtle is heard in our land;

The fig tree putteth forth her green figs, and the vines
with the tender grape give a good smell. Arise, my love,
my fair one, and come away.

O my dove, that art in the clefts of the rock, in the secret
places of the stairs, let me see thy countenance, let me
hear thy voice; for sweet is thy voice, and thy countenance is comely.

Take us the foxes, the little foxes, that spoil the vines :
for our vines have tender grapes.

My beloved is mine, and I am his : he feedeth among the
lilies.

Until the day break, and the shadows flee away, turn, my
beloved, and be thou like a roe or a young hart upon the
mountains of Bether.

III

B Y night on my bed I sought him whom my soul loveth :
I sought him but I found him not.

I will rise now, and go about the city in the streets, and in
the broad ways I will seek him whom my soul loveth : I
sought him, but I found him not.

The watchmen that go about the city found me : to whom
I said, Saw ye him whom my soul loveth ?

It was but a little that I passed from them, but I found
him whom my soul loveth : I held him, and would not
let him go, until I had brought him into my mother's
house, and into the chamber of her that conceived me.

I charge you, O ye daughters of Jerusalem, by the roes,
and by the hinds of the field, that ye stir not up, nor awake
my love, till he please.

Who is this that cometh out of the wilderness like pillars
of smoke, perfumed with myrrh and frankincense, with
all powders of the merchant ?

Behold his bed, which is Solomon's ; threescore valiant
men are about it, of the valiant of Israel.

They all hold swords, being expert in war : every man
hath his sword upon his thigh because of fear in the
night.

King Solomon made himself a chariot of the wood of
Lebanon.

He made the pillars thereof of silver, the bottom thereof

of gold, the covering of it of purple, the midst thereof being paved with love, for the daughters of Jerusalem.

Go forth, O ye daughters of Zion, and behold king Solomon with the crown wherewith his mother crowned him in the day of his espousals, and in the day of the gladness of his heart.

IV

BEHOLD, thou art fair, my love; behold, thou art fair; thou hast doves' eyes within thy locks: thy hair is as a flock of goats, that appear from mount Gilead.

Thy teeth are like a flock of sheep that are even shorn, which came up from the washing; whereof every one bear twins, and none is barren among them.

Thy lips are like a thread of scarlet, and thy speech is comely: thy temples are like a piece of a pomegranate within thy locks.

Thy neck is like the tower of David builded for an armoury, whereon there hang a thousand bucklers, all shields of mighty men.

Thy two breasts are like two young roes that are twins, which feed among the lilies.

Until the day break, and the shadows flee away, I will get me to the mountain of myrrh, and to the hill of frankincense.

Thou art all fair, my love; there is no spot in thee.

Come with me from Lebanon, my spouse, with me from Lebanon: look from the top of Amana, from the top of Shenir and Hermon, from the lion's dens, from the mountains of the leopards.

Thou hast ravished my heart, my sister, my spouse; thou hast ravished my heart with one of thine eyes, with one chain of thy neck.

How fair is thy love, my sister, my spouse! how much better is thy love than wine! and the smell of thine ointments than all spices!

Thy lips, O my spouse, drop as the honeycomb: honey and milk are under thy tongue; and the smell of thy garments is like the smell of Lebanon.

A garden inclosed is my sister, my spouse; a spring shut up, a fountain sealed.

21

Thy plants are an orchard of pomegranates, with pleasant fruits ; camphire, with spikenard,

Spikenard and saffron ; calamus and cinnamon, with all trees of frankincense ; myrrh and aloes, with all the chief spices :

A fountain of gardens, a well of living waters, and streams from Lebanon.

Awake, O north wind ; and come, thou south ; blow upon my garden, that the spices thereof may flow out. Let my beloved come into his garden, and eat his pleasant fruits.

v

I AM come into my garden, my sister, my spouse : I have gathered my myrrh with my spice ; I have eaten my honeycomb with my honey ; I have drunk my wine with my milk ; eat, O friends ; drink, yea, drink abundantly, O beloved.

I sleep, but my heart waketh : it is the voice of my beloved that knocketh, saying, Open to me, my sister, my love, my dove, my undefiled : for my head is filled with dew, and my locks with the drops of the night.

I have put off my coat ; how shall I put it on ? I have washed my feet ; how shall I defile them ?

My beloved put in his hand by the hole of the door, and my bowels were moved for him.

I rose up to open to my beloved ; and my hands dropped with myrrh, and my fingers with sweet-smelling myrrh, upon the handles of the lock.

I opened to my beloved ; but my beloved had withdrawn himself, and was gone : my soul failed when he spake : I sought him, but I could not find him ; I called him, but he gave me no answer.

The watchmen that went about the city found me, they smote me, they wounded me ; the keepers of the walls took away my veil from me.

I charge you, O daughters of Jerusalem, if ye find my beloved, that ye tell him, that I am sick of love.

What is thy beloved more than another beloved, O thou fairest among women ? what is thy beloved more than another beloved, that thou dost so charge us ?

My beloved is white and ruddy, the chiefest among ten thousand.

His head is as the most fine gold, his locks are bushy and black as a raven.

His eyes are as the eyes of doves by the rivers of waters, washed with milk, and fitly set.

His cheeks are as a bed of spices, as sweet flowers : his lips like lilies, dropping sweet smelling myrrh.

His hands are as gold rings set with the beryl : his belly is as bright ivory overlaid with sapphires.

His legs are as pillars of marble, set upon sockets of fine gold : his countenance is as Lebanon, excellent as the cedars.

His mouth is most sweet : yea, he is altogether lovely. This is my beloved, and this is my friend, O daughters of Jerusalem.

VI

WHITHER is thy beloved gone, O thou fairest among women ? whither is thy beloved turned aside ? that we may seek him with thee.

My beloved is gone down into his garden, to the beds of spices, to feed in the gardens, and to gather lilies.

I am my beloved's, and my beloved is mine : he feedeth among the lilies.

Thou art beautiful, O my love, as Tirzah, comely as Jerusalem, terrible as an army with banners.

Turn away thine eyes from me, for they have overcome me : thy hair is as a flock of goats that appear from Gilead.

Thy teeth are as a flock of sheep which go up from the washing, whereof every one beareth twins, and there is not one barren among them.

As a piece of a pomegranate are thy temples within thy locks. There are threescore queens, and fourscore concubines, and virgins without number.

My dove, my undefiled is but one ; she is the only one of her mother, she is the choice one of her that bare her. The daughters saw her, and blessed her ; yea, the queens and the concubines, and they praised her.

Who is she that looketh forth as the morning, fair as the moon, clear as the sun, and terrible as an army with banners ?

I went down into the garden of nuts to see the fruits of
the valley, and to see whether the vine flourished, and the
pomegranates budded.
Or ever I was aware, my soul made me like the chariots
of Ammi-nadib.
Return, return, O Shulamite; return, return, that we
may look upon thee. What will ye see in the Shulamite?
As it were the company of two armies.

VII

H O W beautiful are thy feet with shoes, O prince's
daughter! the joints of thy thighs are like jewels, the
work of the hands of a cunning workman.
Thy navel is like a round goblet, which wanteth not liquor:
thy belly is like an heap of wheat set about with lilies.
Thy two breasts are like two young roes that are twins.
Thy neck is as a tower of ivory; thine eyes like the fish-
pools in Heshbon, by the gate of Bath-rabbim: thy nose
is as the tower of Lebanon which looketh towards
Damascus.
Thine head upon thee is like Carmel, and the hair of thine
head like purple; the king is held in the galleries.
How fair and how pleasant art thou, O love, for delights!
This thy stature is like to a palm tree, and thy breasts to
clusters of grapes.
I said, I will go up to the palm tree, I will take hold of
the boughs thereof: now also thy breasts shall be as
clusters of the vine, and the smell of thy nose like apples;
And the roof of thy mouth like the best wine for my
beloved, that goeth down sweetly, causing the lips of
those that are asleep to speak.
I am my beloved's, and his desire is toward me.
Come, my beloved, let us go forth into the field; let
us lodge in the villages.
Let us get up early to the vineyards; let us see if the
vine flourish, whether the tender grape appear, and the
pomegranates bud forth: there will I give thee my loves.
The mandrakes give a smell, and at our gates are all
manner of pleasant fruits, new and old, which I have laid
up for thee, O my beloved.

VIII

O THAT thou wert as my brother, that sucked the breasts of my mother ! when I should find thee without, I would kiss thee ; yea, I should not be despised.

I would lead thee, and bring thee into my mother's house, who would instruct me : I would cause thee to drink of spiced wine of the juice of my pomegranate.

His left hand should be under my head, and his right hand should embrace me.

I charge you, O daughters of Jerusalem, that ye stir not up, nor awake my love, until he please.

Who is this that cometh up from the wilderness, leaning upon her beloved ? I raised thee up under the apple tree : there thy mother brought thee forth : there she brought thee forth that bare thee.

Set me as a seal upon thine heart, as a seal upon thine arm : for love is strong as death ; jealousy is cruel as the grave : the coals thereof are coals of fire, which hath a most vehement flame.

Many waters cannot quench love, neither can the floods drown it : if a man would give all the substance of his house for love, it would utterly be contemned.

We have a little sister, and she hath no breasts : what shall we do for our sister in the day when she shall be spoken for ?

If she be a wall, we will build upon her a palace of silver: and if she be a door, we will inclose her with boards of cedar.

I am a wall, and my breasts like towers : then was I in his eyes as one that found favour.

Solomon had a vineyard at Baal-hamon ; he let out the vineyard unto keepers ; everyone for the fruit thereof was to bring a thousand pieces of silver.

My vineyard, which is mine, is before me : thou, O Solomon, must have a thousand, and those that keep the fruit thereof two hundred.

Thou that dwellest in the gardens, the companions hearken to thy voice ; cause me to hear it.

Make haste, my beloved, and be thou like to a roe or to a young hart upon the mountains of spices.

The Authorised Version.

TOM OF BEDLAM'S SONG

FROM the hag and hungry goblin
That into rags would rend ye,
All the spirits that stand
By the naked man
In the book of moons, defend ye,

That of your five sound senses
You never be forsaken,
Nor wander from
Yourselves with Tom
Abroad to beg your bacon.

With a thought I took for Maudlin,
And a cruse of cockle pottage,
With a thing thus tall,
Sky bless you all,
I befell into this dotage.

I slept not since the Conquest,
Till then I never wakéd,
Till the roguish boy
Of love where I lay
Me found and stript me naked.

The moon's my constant mistress,
And the lonely owl my marrow;
The flaming drake
And the night-crow make
Me music to my sorrow.

I know more than Apollo,
For oft, when he lies sleeping,
I see the stars
At mortal wars
In the wounded welkin weeping,

The moon embrace her shepherd,
And the queen of love her warrior,
While the first doth horn
The star of morn,
And the next the heavenly farrier.

With an host of furious fancies,
Whereof I am commander,
 With a burning spear
 And a horse of air
To the wilderness I wander;

By a knight of ghosts and shadows
I summoned am to tourney
 Ten leagues beyond
 The wide world's end—
Methinks it is no journey.

Anonymous.

THERE IS A LADY SWEET AND KIND

THERE is a Lady sweet and kind,
Was never face so pleas'd my mind;
I did but see her passing by,
And yet I love her till I die.

Her gesture, motion, and her smiles,
Her wit, her voice my heart beguiles,
Beguiles my heart, I know not why,
And yet I love her till I die.

Cupid is winged and doth range,
Her country so my love doth change:
But change she earth, or change she sky,
Yet will I love her till I die.

Anonymous.

LOVE NOT ME FOR COMELY GRACE

LOVE not me for comely grace,
 For my pleasing eye or face,
 Nor for any outward part,
 No, nor for a constant heart:
 For these may fail or turn to ill,
 So thou and I shall sever:
Keep, therefore, a true woman's eye,
And love me still but know not why—
 So hast thou the same reason still
 To doat upon me ever!

Anonymous.

27

THE CONCLUSION

EVEN such is Time, that takes in trust
   Our youth, our joys, our all we have,
And pays us but with earth and dust;
   Who, in the dark and silent grave,
When we have wandered all our ways,
Shuts up the story of our days.
But from this earth, this grave, this dust,
My God shall raise me up, I trust.

Walter Raleigh.

A FAREWELL TO ARMS

MY golden locks Time hath to silver turn'd;
   O Time too swift, O swiftness never ceasing!
My youth 'gainst age, and age 'gainst time, hath
   spurn'd,
   But spurn'd in vain; youth waneth by increasing:
Beauty, strength, youth, are flowers but fading seen;
Duty, faith, love, are roots, and ever green.

My helmet now shall make an hive for bees,
   And lover's sonnets turn to holy psalms;
A man-at-arms must now serve on his knees,
   And feed on prayers, which are old age his alms:
But though from court to cottage I depart,
My saint is sure of my unspotted heart.

And when I saddest sit in homely cell,
   I'll teach my swains this carol for a song,—
" Blest be the hearts that wish my sovereign well,
   Curst be the souls that think her any wrong!"
Goddess, allow this aged man his right
To be your beadsman now that was your knight.

George Peele.

THE PARTING

SINCE there's no help, come, let us kiss and part—
Nay, I have done, you get no more of me;
And I am glad, yea glad with all my heart,
That thus so cleanly I myself can free.

Shake hands for ever, cancel all our vows,
And, when we meet at any time again,
Be it not seen in either of our brows
That we one jot of former love retain.
Now at the last gasp of Love's latest breath,
When, his pulse failing, Passion speechless lies,
When Faith is kneeling by his bed of death,
And Innocence is closing up his eyes—
  Now if thou wouldst, when all have given him over,
  From death to life thou might'st him yet recover.

Michael Drayton.

SONNET

Y O U ' R E not alone when you are still alone ;
O God ! from you that I could private be !
Since you one were, I never since was one,
Since you in me, myself since out of me.
Transported from myself into your being,
Though either distant, present yet to either ;
Senseless with too much joy, each other seeing
And only absent when we are together.
Give me my self, and take your self again !
Devise some means but how I may forsake you !
So much is mine that doth with you remain,
That taking what is mine, with me I take you.
  You do bewitch me ! O that I could fly
  From my self you, or from your own self I !

Michael Drayton.

SONNET

W H E N first I ended, then I first began ;
Then more I travelled further from my rest.
Where most I lost, there most of all I won ;
Pinèd with hunger, rising from a feast.
Methinks I fly, yet want I legs to go,
Wise in conceit, in act a very sot,
Ravished with joy amidst a hell of woe,
What most I seem that surest am I not.

29

I build my hopes a world above the sky,
Yet with the mole I creep into the earth ;
In plenty I am starved with penury,
And yet I surfeit in the greatest dearth.
　　I have, I want, despair, and yet desire,
　　Burned in a sea of ice, and drowned amidst a fire.

Michael Drayton.

SPRING AND WINTER

I

WHEN daisies pied and violets blue,
　　And lady-smocks all silver-white,
And cuckoo-buds of yellow hue
　　Do paint the meadows with delight,
The cuckoo then, on every tree,
Mocks married men ; for thus sings he,
　　　　Cuckoo !
Cuckoo, cuckoo !—O word of fear.
Unpleasing to a married ear !

When shepherds pipe on oaten straws,
　　And merry larks are ploughmen's clocks,
When turtles tread, and rooks, and daws,
　　And maidens bleach their summer smocks
The cuckoo then, on every tree,
Mocks married men ; for thus sings he,
　　　　Cuckoo !
Cuckoo, cuckoo !—O word of fear,
Unpleasing to a married ear !

II

When icicles hang by the wall,
　　And Dick the shepherd blows his nail,
And Tom bears logs into the hall,
　　And milk comes frozen home in pail,
When blood is nipp'd, and ways be foul,
Then nightly sings the staring owl,
　　　　To-whit !
To-who !—a merry note,
While greasy Joan doth keel the pot.

When all aloud the wind doth blow,
    And coughing drowns the parson's saw,
And birds sit brooding in the snow,
    And Marian's nose looks red and raw,
When roasted crabs hiss in the bowl,
Then nightly sings the staring owl,
      To-whit !
To-who !—a merry note,
While greasy Joan doth keel the pot.

William Shakespeare.

SONNETS

LXV

SINCE brass nor stone, nor earth, nor boundless sea,
But sad mortality o'ersways their power,
How with this rage shall beauty hold a plea,
Whose action is no stronger than a flower ?
O, how shall summer's honey breath hold out
Against the wreckful siege of battering days,
When rocks impregnable are not so stout,
Nor gates of steel so strong, but time decays ?
O fearful meditation ! where, alack,
Shall Time's best jewel from Time's quest lie hid ?
Or what strong hand can hold his swift foot back ?
Or who his spoil of beauty can forbid ?
    O, none, unless this miracle have might,
    That in black ink my love may still shine bright.

William Shakespeare.

CXXIX

THE expense of spirit in a waste of shame
Is lust in action ; and till action, lust
Is perjured, murderous, bloody, full of blame,
Savage, extreme, rude, cruel, not to trust,
Enjoy'd no sooner but despised straight,
Past reason hunted, and no sooner had
Past reason hated, as a swallow'd bait
On purpose laid to make the taker mad ;

31

Mad in pursuit and in possession so ;
Had, having, and in quest to have, extreme ;
A bliss in proof, and proved, a very woe ;
Before, a joy proposed ; behind, a dream.
　　All this the world well knows ; yet none knows well
　　To shun the heaven that leads men to this hell.

William Shakespeare.

CXXX

MY mistress' eyes are nothing like the sun ;
Coral is far more red than her lips red ;
If snow be white, why then her breasts are dun ;
If hairs be wires, black wires grow in her head.
I have seen roses damask'd, red and white,
But no such roses see I in her cheeks ;
And in some perfumes is there more delight
Than in the breath that from my mistress reeks.
I love to hear her speak, yet well I know
That music hath a far more pleasing sound ;
I grant I never saw a goddess go ;
My mistress, when she walks, treads on the ground :
　　And yet, by heaven, I think my love as rare
　　As any she belied with false compare.

William Shakespeare.

SPRING

SPRING, the sweet Spring, is the year's pleasant king ;
Then blooms each thing, then maids dance in a ring,
Cold doth not sting, the pretty birds do sing—
　　Cuckoo, jug-jug, pu-we, to-witta-woo !

The palm and may make country houses gay,
Lambs frisk and play, the shepherds pipe all day,
And we hear aye birds tune this merry lay—
　　Cuckoo, jug-jug, pu-we, to-witta-woo !

The fields breathe sweet, the daisies kiss our feet,
Young lovers meet, old wives a-sunning sit,
In every street these tunes our ears do greet—
　　Cuckoo, jug-jug, pu-we, to-witta-woo
　　　　Spring, the sweet Spring !

Thomas Nashe.

32

IN TIME OF PESTILENCE

ADIEU, farewell earth's bliss !
This world uncertain is :
Fond are life's lustful joys,
Death proves them all but toys.
None from his darts can fly ;
I am sick, I must die—
    Lord, have mercy on us !

Rich men, trust not in wealth,
Gold cannot buy you health ;
Physic himself must fade ;
All things to end are made ;
The plague full swift goes by ;
I am sick, I must die—
    Lord, have mercy on us !

Beauty is but a flower
Which wrinkles will devour ;
Brightness falls from the air ;
Queens have died young and fair ;
Dust hath clos'd Helen's eye ;
I am sick, I must die—
    Lord, have mercy on us !

Strength stoops unto the grave,
Worms feed on Hector brave ;
Swords may not fight with fate ;
Earth still holds ope her gate ;
Come, come ! the bells do cry ;
I am sick, I must die—
    Lord, have mercy on us !

Wit with his wantonness
Tasteth death's bitterness ;
Hell's executioner
Hath no ears for to hear
What vain art can reply ;
I am sick, I must die—
    Lord, have mercy on us !

C

Haste therefore each degree
To welcome destiny;
Heaven is our heritage,
Earth but a player's stage.
Mount we unto the sky;
I am sick, I must die—
 Lord, have mercy on us!

Thomas Nashe.

KIND ARE HER ANSWERS

KIND are her answers,
 But her performance keeps no day;
Breaks time, as dancers
 From their own music when they stray:
All her free favours
And smooth words wing my hopes in vain.
O did ever voice so sweet but only feign?
 Can true love yield such delay,
 Converting joy to pain?

Lost is our freedom,
 When we submit to women so:
Why do we need them,
 When in their best they work our woe?
There is no wisdom
Can alter ends, by Fate prefixed.
O why is the good of man with evil mixed?
 Never were days yet call'd two,
 But one night went betwixt.

Thomas Campion.

JACK AND JOAN

JACK and Joan they think no ill,
But loving live, and merry still;
Do their week-days' work, and pray
Devoutly on the holy day:
Skip and trip it on the green,
And help to choose the Summer Queen;
Lash out, at a country feast,
Their silver penny with the best.

Well can they judge of nappy ale,
And tell at large a winter tale ;
Climb up to the apple loft,
And turn the crabs till they be soft.
Tib is all the father's joy,
And little Tom the mother's boy.
And all their pleasure is Content ;
And care, to pay their yearly rent.

Joan can call by name her cows,
And deck her window with green boughs ;
She can wreaths and tutties make,
And trim with plums a bridal cake.
Jack knows what brings gain or loss ;
And his long flail can stoutly toss :
Makes the hedge, which others break ;
And ever thinks what he doth speak.

Now, you courtly dames and knights,
That study only strange delights ;
Though you scorn the homespun gray,
And revel in your rich array :
Though your tongues dissemble deep,
And can your heads from danger keep ;
Yet, for all your pomp and train,
Securer lives the silly swain.

Thomas Campion.

THE TRIUMPH

SEE the Chariot at hand here of Love,
   Wherein my Lady rideth !
Each that draws is a swan or a dove,
   And well the car Love guideth.
As she goes, all hearts do duty
      Unto her beauty ;
And enamour'd do wish, so they might
      But enjoy such a sight,
That they still were to run by her side,
Through swords, through seas, whither she would ride.

35

Do but look on her eyes, they do light
    All that Love's world compriseth !
Do but look on her hair, it is bright
    As Love's star when it riseth !
Do but mark, her forehead's smoother
        Than words that soothe her ;
And from her arch'd brows such a grace
        Sheds itself through the face,
As alone there triumphs to the life
All the gain, all the good, of the elements' strife.

Have you seen but a bright lily grow
    Before rude hands have touch'd it ?
Have you mark'd but the fall of the snow
    Before the soil hath smutch'd it ?
Have you felt the wool of beaver,
        Or swan's down ever ?
Or have smelt of the bud of the brier,
        Or the nard in the fire ?
Or have tasted the bag of the bee ?
O so white, O so soft, O so sweet is she !

Ben Jonson.

THE GOOD-MORROW

I WONDER, by my troth, what thou and I
Did, till we loved ? were we not wean'd till then ?
But suck'd on country pleasures, childishly ?
Or snorted we in the Seven Sleepers' den ?
'Twas so ; but this, all pleasures fancies be ;
If ever any beauty I did see,
Which I desired, and got, 'twas but a dream of thee,

And now good-morrow to our waking souls,
Which watch not one another out of fear ;
For love all love of other sights controls,
And makes one little room an everywhere.
Let sea-discoverers to new worlds have gone ;
Let maps to other worlds on worlds have shown ;
Let us possess one world ; each hath one, and is one.

My face in thine eye, thine in mine appears,
And true plain hearts do in the faces rest ;
Where can we find two better hemispheres
Without sharp north, without declining west ?
Whatever dies, was not mix'd equally ;
If our two loves be one, or thou and I
Love so alike that none can slacken, none can die.

John Donne.

THE SUN RISING

BUSY old fool, unruly Sun,
    Why dost thou thus,
Through windows, and through curtains, call on us ?
Must to thy motions lovers' seasons run ?
        Saucy pedantic wretch, go chide
        Late school-boys and sour prentices,
    Go tell court-huntsmen that the king will ride,
    Call country ants to harvest offices ;
Love, all alike, no season knows nor clime,
Nor hours, days, months, which are the rags of time.

        Thy beams so reverend and strong
        Why shouldst thou think ?
I could eclipse and cloud them with a wink,
But that I would not lose her sight so long.
        If her eyes have not blinded thine,
        Look, and to-morrow late tell me,
    Whether both th' Indias of spice and mine
    Be where thou left'st them, or lie here with me.
Ask for those kings whom thou saw'st yesterday,
And thou shalt hear, " All here in one bed lay."

        She's all states, and all princes I ;
        Nothing else is ;
Princes do but play us ; compared to this,
All honour's mimic, all wealth alchemy.

37

Thou, Sun, art half as happy as we,
　In that the world's contracted thus ;
Thine age asks ease, and since thy duties be
To warm the world, that's done in warming us.
Shine here to us, and thou art everywhere ;
This bed thy centre is, these walls thy sphere.

John Donne.

LOVE'S DEITY

I LONG to talk with some old lover's ghost,
　Who died before the god of love was born.
I cannot think that he, who then loved most,
　Sunk so low as to love one which did scorn.
But since this god produced a destiny,
And that vice-nature, custom, lets it be,
　I must love her that loves not me.

Sure, they which made him god, meant not so much,
　Nor he in his young godhead practised it.
But when an even flame two hearts did touch,
　His office was indulgently to fit
Actives to passives.　Correspondency
Only his subject was ; it cannot be
　Love, till I love her, who loves me.

But every modern god will now extend
　His vast prerogative as far as Jove.
To rage, to lust, to write to, to commend,
　All is the purlieu of the god of love.
O ! were we waken'd by this tyranny
To ungod this child again, it could not be
　I should love her, who loves not me.

Rebel and atheist too, why murmur I,
　As though I felt the worst that love could do ?
Love might make me leave loving, or might try
　A deeper plague, to make her love me too ;

38

Which, since she loves before, I'm loth to see.
Falsehood is worse than hate ; and that must be,
   If she whom I love, should love me.

John Donne.

THE DREAM

DEAR love, for nothing less than thee
Would I have broke this happy dream ;
     It was a theme
For reason, much too strong for fantasy.
Therefore thou waked'st me wisely ; yet
My dream thou brokest not, but continued'st it.
Thou art so true that thoughts of thee suffice
To make dreams truths, and fables histories ;
Enter these arms, for since thou thought'st it best,
Not to dream all my dream, let's act the rest.

As lightning, or a taper's light,
Thine eyes, and not thy noise waked me ;
     Yet I thought thee
—For thou lov'st truth—an angel, at first sight ;
But when I saw thou saw'st my heart,
And knew'st my thoughts beyond an angel's art,
When thou knew'st what I dreamt, when thou knew'st
Excess of joy would wake me, and camest then,   [when
I must confess, it could not choose but be
Profane, to think thee any thing but thee.

Coming and staying show'd thee, thee,
But rising makes me doubt, that now
     Thou art not thou.
That love is weak where fear's as strong as he ;
'Tis not all spirit, pure and brave,
If mixture it of fear, shame, honour have ;
Perchance as torches, which must ready be,
Men light and put out, so thou deal'st with me ;
Thou cam'st to kindle, go'st to come ; then I
Will dream that hope again, but else would die.

John Donne.

LOVE'S GROWTH

I SCARCE believe my love to be so pure
    As I had thought it was,
    Because it doth endure
Vicissitude, and season, as the grass ;
Methinks I lied all winter, when I swore
My love was infinite, if spring make it more.

But if this medicine, love, which cures all sorrow
    With more, not only be no quintessence,
    But mix'd of all stuffs, vexing soul, or sense,
And of the sun his active vigour borrow,
Love's not so pure, and abstract as they use
To say, which have no mistress but their Muse ;
But as all else, being elemented too,
Love sometimes would contemplate, sometimes do.

And yet no greater, but more eminent,
    Love by the spring is grown ;
    As in the firmament
Stars by the sun are not enlarged, but shown,
Gentle love deeds, as blossoms on a bough,
From love's awaken'd root do bud out now.

If, as in water stirr'd more circles be
    Produced by one, love such additions take,
    Those like so many spheres but one heaven make,
For they are all concentric unto thee ;
And though each spring do add to love new heat,
As princes do in times of action get
New taxes, and remit them not in peace,
No winter shall abate this spring's increase.

                        John Donne.

THE ECSTACY

WHERE, like a pillow on a bed,
    A pregnant bank swell'd up, to rest
The violet's reclining head,
    Sat we two, one another's best.

Our hands were firmly cémented
    By a fast balm, which thence did spring ;
Our eye-beams twisted, and did thread
    Our eyes upon one double string.

So to engraft our hands, as yet
    Was all the means to make us one ;
And pictures in our eyes to get
    Was all our propagation.

As, 'twixt two equal armies, Fate
    Suspends uncertain victory,
Our souls—which to advance their state,
    Were gone out—hung 'twixt her and me.

And whilst our souls negotiate there,
    We like sepulchral statues lay ;
All day, the same our postures were,
    And we said nothing, all the day.

If any, so by love refined,
    That he soul's language understood,
And by good love were grown all mind,
    Within convenient distance stood,

He—though he knew not which soul spake,
    Because both meant, both spoke the same—
Might thence a new concoction take,
    And part far purer than he came.

This ecstacy doth unperplex
    (We said) and tell us what we love ;
We see by this, it was not sex ;
    We see, we saw not, what did move :

But as all several souls contain
    Mixture of things they know not what,
Love these mix'd souls doth mix again,
    And makes both one, each this and that.

A single violet transplant,
    The strength, the colour, and the size—
All which before was poor and scant—
    Redoubles still, and multiplies.

C *

When love with one another so
  Interinanimates two souls,
That abler soul, which thence doth flow,
  Defects of loneliness controls.

We then, who are this new soul, know,
  Of what we are composed and made,
For th'atomies of which we grow
  Are souls, whom no change can invade.

But, O alas! so long, so far,
  Our bodies why do we forbear?
They are ours, though they're not we; we are
  Th'intelligences, they the spheres.

We owe them thanks, because they thus
  Did us, to us, at first convey,
Yielded their forces, sense, to us,
  Nor are dross to us, but allay.

On man heaven's influence works not so,
  But that it first imprints the air;
So soul into the soul may flow,
  Though it to body first repair.

As our blood labours to beget
  Spirits, as like souls as it can;
Because such fingers need to knit
  That subtle knot, which makes us man;

So must pure lovers' souls descend
  To affections, and to faculties,
Which sense may reach and apprehend,
  Else a great prince in prison lies.

To our bodies turn we then, that so
  Weak men on love reveal'd may look;
Love's mysteries in souls do grow,
  But yet the body is his book.

And if some lover, such as we,
  Have heard this dialogue of one,
Let him still mark us, he shall see
  Small change when we're to bodies gone.

                                   John Donne.

DIVINE POEM

BATTER my heart, three personed God ; for you
As yet but knock, breathe, shine, and seek to mend.
That I may rise and stand, o'erthrow me and bend
Your force to break, blow, burn and make me new.
I, like an usurped town, to another due,
Labour to admit you, but Oh, to no end ;
Reason, your viceroy in me, me should defend,
But is captived and proves weak or untrue.
Yet dearly I love you and would be loved fain,
But am betrothed unto your enemy :
Divorce me, untie or break that knot again,
Take me to you, imprison me, for I
Except you enthrall me, never shall be free,
Nor ever chaste, except you ravish me.

John Donne.

GOD LYÆUS

GOD LYÆUS, ever young,
Ever honour'd, ever sung,
Stain'd with blood of lusty grapes,
In a thousand lusty shapes
Dance upon the mazer's brim,
In the crimson liquor swim ;
From thy plenteous hand divine
Let a river run with wine :
   God of youth, let this day here
   Enter neither care nor fear.

John Fletcher.

OBERON'S FEAST

SHAPCOT! to thee the Fairy State
I with discretion, dedicate.
Because thou prizest things that are
Curious and unfamiliar,
Take first the feast ; these dishes gone,
We'll see the Fairy Court anon.

43

A little mushroom-table spread,
After short prayers, they set on bread;
A moon-parch'd grain of purest wheat,
With some small glittering grit, to eat
His choice bits with; then in a trice
They make a feast less great than nice,
But all this while his eye is serv'd,
We must not think his ear was starv'd
But that there was in place to stir
His spleen, the chirring Grasshopper;
The merry Cricket, puling Fly,
The piping Gnat for minstrelsy.
And now, we must imagine first,
The Elves present to quench his thirst
A pure seed-pearl of infant dew,
Brought and besweetened in a blue
And pregnant violet; which done,
His kitling eyes begin to run
Quite through the table, where he spies
The horns of papery Butterflies:
Of which he eats, and tastes a little
Of that we call the cuckoo's spittle.
A little fuzz-ball pudding stands
By, yet not blessed by his hands,
That was too coarse; but then forthwith
He ventures boldly on the pith
Of sugared rush, and eats the sag
And well bestrutted Bee's sweet bag:
Gladding his palate with some store
Of Emit's eggs; what would he more?
But beards of Mice, a Newt's stew'd thigh,
A roasted Earwig, and a Fly;
With the red-capp'd Worm, that's shut
Within the concave of a nut,
Brown as his tooth. A little Moth,
Late fattened in a piece of cloth:
With wither'd cherries; Mandrake's ears;
Mole's eyes; to these, the slain Stag's tears
The unctuous dewlaps of a Snail;
The broke heart of a Nightingale
O'ercome in music; with a wine,

Ne'er ravish'd from the flattering vine,
But gently press'd from the soft side
Of the most sweet and dainty bride,
Brought in a dainty daisy, which
He fully quaffs up to bewitch
His blood to height ; this done, commended
Grace by his Priest : *The feast is ended.*

Robert Herrick.

THE ARGUMENT OF HIS BOOK

I SING of Brooks, of Blossoms, Birds, and Bowers ;
Of April, May, of June, and July-Flowers.
I sing of May-poles, Hock-carts, Wassails, Wakes,
Of Bridegrooms, Brides, and of their Bridal cakes.
I write of Youth, of Love, and have access
By these, to sing of cleanly Wantonness.
I sing of Dews, of Rains, and piece by piece
Of Balme, of Oil, of Spice, and Amber-Greece.
I sing of Time's trans-shifting ; and I write
How Roses first came red, and Lilies white.
I write of Groves, of Twilights, and I sing
The Court of Mab, and of the Fairy-King.
I write of Hell ; I sing (and ever shall)
Of Heaven, and hope to have it after all.

Robert Herrick.

EXEQUY ON HIS WIFE

ACCEPT, thou shrine of my dead saint,
Instead of dirges this complaint ;
And for sweet flowers to crown thy hearse
Receive a strew of weeping verse
From thy grieved Friend, whom thou might'st see
Quite melted into tears for thee.
    Dear loss ! since thy untimely fate,
My task hath been to meditate
On thee, on thee ! Thou art the book,
The library whereon I look,
Tho' almost blind. For thee, loved clay,
I languish out, not live, the day,

45

Using no other exercise
But what I practise with mine eyes :
By which wet glasses I find out
How lazily time creeps about
To one that mourns : this, only this,
My exercise and business is :
So I compute the weary hours,
With sighs dissolved into showers.
No wonder if my time go thus
Backward and most preposterous ;
Thou hast benighted me ; thy set
This eve of blackness did beget,
Who wast my day (tho' overcast
Before thou hadst thy noontide past) :
And I remember must in tears
Thou scarce hadst seen so many years
As day tells hours. By thy clear sun
My love and fortune first did run ;
But thou wilt never more appear
Folded within my hemisphere,
Since both thy light and motion,
Like a fled star, is fall'n and gone,
And 'twixt me and my soul's dear wish
The earth now interposed is,
Which such a strange eclipse doth make
As ne'er was read in Almanack.

I could allow thee for a time
To darken me and my sad clime ;
Were it a month, a year, or ten,
I would thy exile live till then,
And all that space my mirth adjourn—
So thou wouldst promise to return,
And putting off thy ashy shroud
At length disperse this sorrow's cloud.

But woe is me ! the longest date
Too narrow is to calculate
These empty hopes : never shall I
Be so much blest as to descry
A glimpse of thee, till that day come
Which shall the earth to cinders doom,
And a fierce fever must calcine

The body of this world—like thine,
My little world ! That fit of fire
Once off, our bodies shall aspire
To our soul's bliss : then we shall rise
And view ourselves with clearer eyes
In that calm region where no night
Can hide us from each other's sight.

    Meantime thou hast her, earth : much good
May my harm do thee ! Since it stood
With Heaven's will I might not call
Her longer mine, I give thee all
My short-lived right and interest
In her whom living I loved best :
With a most free and bounteous grief
I give thee what I could not keep.
Be kind to her, and prithee look
Thou write into thy Doomsday book
Each parcel of this rarity
Which in thy casket shrin'd doth lie :
See that thou make thy reck'ning straight,
And yield her back again by weight ;
For thou must audit on thy trust
Each grain and atom of this dust
As thou wilt answer Him that lent—
Not gave—thee my dear monument.
So close the ground, and 'bout her shade
Black curtains draw ; my bride is laid.

    Sleep on, my Love, in thy cold bed
Never to be disquieted !
My last good night ! Thou wilt not wake
Till I thy fate shall overtake :
Till age, or grief, or sickness must
Marry my body to that dust
It so much loves ; and fill the room
My heart keeps empty in thy tomb.
Stay for me there : I will not fail
To meet thee in that hollow vale,
And think not much of my delay :
I am already on the way,
And follow thee with all the speed
Desire can make, or sorrows breed.

Each minute is a short degree
And every hour a step towards thee.
At night when I betake to rest,
Next morn I rise nearer my West
Of life, almost by eight hours' sail,
Than when sleep breath'd his drowsy gale.
    Thus from the Sun my bottom steers
And my day's compass downward bears :
Nor labour I to stem the tide
Through which to thee I swiftly glide.
    'Tis true—with shame and grief I yield—
Thou, like the van, first took'st the field ;
And gotten hast the victory
In thus adventuring to die
Before me, whose more years might crave
A just precedence in the grave.
But hark ! my pulse, like a soft drum,
Beats my approach, tells thee I come ;
And slow howe'er my marches be
I shall at last sit down by thee.
The thought of this bids me go on
And wait my dissolution
With hope and comfort. Dear—forgive
The crime—I am content to live
Divided, with but half a heart,
Till we shall meet and never part.   *Henry King.*

THE SURRENDER

MY once dear Love ; hapless that I no more
Must call thee so : the rich affections store
That fed our hopes, lies now exhaust and spent,
Like sums of treasure unto bankrupts lent.

We that did nothing study but the way
To love each other, with which thoughts the day
Rose with delight to us, and with them set,
Must learn the hateful art, how to forget.

We that did nothing wish that Heav'n could give
Beyond ourselves, nor did desire to live
Beyond that wish, all these now cancel must
As if not writ in faith, but words and dust.

48

Yet witness those clear vows which lovers make,
Witness the chaste desires that never break
Into unruly heats ; witness that breast
Which in thy bosom anchor'd his whole rest,
'Tis no default in us, I dare acquit
Thy maiden faith, thy purpose fair and white
As thy pure self. Cross planets did envy
Us to each other, and Heaven did untie
Faster than vows could bind. O that the stars,
When lovers meet, should stand oppos'd in wars !

Since then some higher Destinies command,
Let us not strive, nor labour to withstand
What is past help. The longest date of grief
Can never yield a hope of our relief ;
And though we waste ourselves in moist laments,
Tears may drown us, but not our discontents.

Fold back our arms, take home our fruitless loves,
That must new fortunes try, like turtle doves
Dislodged from their haunts. We must in tears
Unwind a love knit up in many years.
In this last kiss I here surrender thee
Back to thyself, so thou again art free.
Thou in another, sad as that, resend
The truest heart that lover ere did lend.

Now turn from each. So fare our sever'd hearts
As the divorc'd soul from her body parts.

Henry King.

THE ANNIVERSE

AN ELEGY

S O soon grown old ? hast thou been six years dead ?
Poor earth, once by my Love inhabited !
And must I live to calculate the time
To which thy blooming youth could never climb,
But fell in the ascent ? yet have not I
Studied enough thy loss's history ?

How happy were mankind if Death's strict laws
Consum'd our lamentations like the cause !
Or that our grief turning to dust might end
With the dissolved body of a friend !

But sacred Heaven ! O how just thou art
In stamping death's impression on that heart
Which through thy favours would grow insolent,
Were it not physick'd by sharp discontent.
If then it stand resolv'd in thy decree
That still I must doom'd to a desert be
Sprung out of my lone thoughts, which know no path
But what my own misfortune beaten hath :
If thou wilt bind me living to a corse,
And I must slowly waste ; I then of force
Stoop to thy great appointment, and obey
That will which nought avails me to gainsay.

For whil'st in sorrow's maze I wander on,
I do but follow life's vocation.
Sure we were made to grieve : at our first birth
With cries we took possession of the earth ;
And though the lucky man reputed be
Fortune's adopted son, yet only he
Is Nature's true born child, who sums his years
(Like me) with no arithmetic but tears.

Henry King.

THE PULLEY

WHEN God at first made man,
Having a glass of blessings standing by—
Let us (said he) pour on him all we can ;
Let the world's riches, which dispersed lie,
    Contract into a span.

So strength first made a way,
Then beauty flow'd, then wisdom, honour, pleasure :
When almost all was out, God made a stay,
Perceiving that, alone of all his treasure,
    Rest in the bottom lay.

For if I should (said he)
Bestow this jewel also on my creature,
He would adore my gifts instead of me,
And rest in nature, not the God of nature :
  So both should losers be.

Yet let him keep the rest,
But keep them with repining restlessness ;
Let him be rich and weary, that at least,
If goodness lead him not, yet weariness
  May toss him to my breast.

George Herbert.

DISCIPLINE

THROW away thy rod,
Throw away thy wrath ;
    O my God,
Take the gentle path.

For my heart's desire
Unto thine is bent ;
    I aspire
To a full consent.

Not a word or look
I affect to own,
    But by book,
And thy book alone.

Though I fail, I weep ;
Though I halt in pace,
    Yet I creep
To the throne of grace.

Then let wrath remove,
Love will do the deed ;
    For with love
Stony hearts will bleed.

Love is swift of foot ;
Love's a man of war,
    And can shoot,
And can hit from far.

51

Who can 'scape his bow ?
That which wrought on thee,
        Brought thee low,
Needs must work on me.

Throw away thy rod :
Though man frailties hath,
        Thou art God ;
Throw away thy wrath.

George Herbert.

DECAY

S W E E T were the days, when thou didst lodge with Lot,
Struggle with Jacob, sit with Gideon,
Advise with Abraham, when thy power could not
Encounter Moses' strong complaints and moan.
    Thy words were then, *Let me alone.*

One might have sought and found thee presently
At some fair oak, or bush, or cave, or well :
Is my God this way ? No, they would reply :
He is to Sinai gone, as we heard tell :
    List, ye may hear great Aaron's bell.

But now thou dost thyself immure and close
In some one corner of a feeble heart :
Where yet both Sin and Satan, thy old foes,
Do pinch and straiten thee, and use much art
    To gain thy thirds and little part.

I see the world grows old, whenas the heat
Of thy great love once spread, as in an urn,
Doth closet up itself, and still retreat,
Cold sin still forcing it, till it return,
    And calling Justice, all things burn.

George Herbert.

REDEMPTION

H A V I N G been Tenant long to a rich Lord,
    Not thriving, I resolved to be bold,
    And make a suit unto him to afford
A new small-rented lease, and cancel th'old.

In Heaven at his manor I him sought,
  They told me there, that he was lately gone
    About some land, which he had dearly bought
Long since on Earth, to take possession.

I straight return'd, and knowing his great birth,
  Sought him accordingly in great resorts,
    In cities, theatres, gardens, parks, and courts :
At length I heard a ragged noise and mirth
    Of thieves and murderers. There I him espied,
    Who straight, *Your suit is granted*, said, and died.

                          George Herbert.

SONG

    A S K me no more where Jove bestows,
    When June is past, the fading rose ;
    For in your beauty's orient deep
    These flowers, as in their causes, sleep.

    Ask me no more whither do stray
    The golden atoms of the day ;
    For in pure love heaven did prepare
    Those powders to enrich your hair

    Ask me no more whither doth haste
    The nightingale when May is past ;
    For in your sweet dividing throat
    She winters and keeps warm her note.

    Ask me no more where those stars 'light
    That downwards fall in dead of night ;
    For in your eyes they sit, and there
    Fixèd become as in their sphere.

    Ask me no more if east or west
    The phœnix builds her spicy nest ;
    For unto you at last she flies,
    And in your fragrant bosom dies.

                          Thomas Carew.

A DEVOUT LOVER

I HAVE a mistress, for perfections rare
In every eye, but in my thoughts most fair.
Like tapers on the altar shine her eyes ;
Her breath is the perfume of sacrifice ;
And whersoe'er my fancy would begin,
Still her perfection lets religion in.
We sit and talk, and kiss away the hours
As chastely as the morning dews kiss flowers :
I touch her, like my beads, with devout care,
And come unto my courtship as my prayer.

Thomas Randolph.

WHY SO PALE AND WAN?

WHY so pale and wan, fond lover ?
    Prithee, why so pale ?
Will when looking well can't move her,
    Looking ill prevail ?
    Prithee, why so pale ?

Why so dull and mute, young sinner ?
    Prithee, why so mute ?
Will, when speaking well can't win her,
    Saying nothing do 't ?
    Prithee, why so mute ?

Quit, quit for shame ! This will not move ;
    This cannot take her.
If of herself she will not love,
    Nothing can make her ;
    The devil take her !

John Suckling.

UPON A WEDDING

I TELL thee, Dick, where I have been,
Where I the rarest things have seen ;
    O, things without compare !
Such sights again cannot be found
In any place on English ground,
    Be it at wake or fair.

At Charing Cross, hard by the way,
Where we, thou know'st, do sell our hay,
    There is a house with stairs;
And there did I see coming down
Such folk as are not in our town,
    Forty at least, in pairs.

Amongst the rest, one pest'lent fine
(His beard no bigger though than thine)
    Walked on before the rest:
Our landlord looks like nothing to him:
The King (God bless him) 'twould undo him,
    Should he go still so drest.

At Course-a-Park, without all doubt,
He should have first been taken out
    By all the maids i' th' town:
Though lusty Roger there had been,
Or little George upon the Green,
    Or Vincent of the Crown.

But wot you what? the youth was going
To make an end of all his wooing;
    The parson for him stay'd:
Yet by his leave, for all his haste,
He did not so much wish all past,
    Perchance, as did the maid.

The maid (and thereby hangs a tale),
For such a maid no Whitsun-ale
    Could ever yet produce:
No grape, that's kindly ripe, could be
So round, so plump, so soft as she,
    Nor half so full of juice.

Her finger was so small, the ring
Would not stay on, which they did bring,
    It was too wide a peck:
And to say truth (for out it must)
It looked like the great collar, just,
    About our young colt's neck.

Her feet beneath her petticoat,
Like little mice, stole in and out,
    As if they fear'd the light :
But O she dances such a way !
No sun upon an Easter-day
    Is half so fine a sight.

He would have kissed her once or twice,
But she would not, she was so nice,
    She would not do't in sight,
And then she looked as who should say :
I will do what I list to-day,
    And you shall do't at night.

Her cheeks so rare a white was on,
No daisy makes comparison,
    Who sees them is undone ;
For streaks of red were mingled there,
Such as are on a Catherine pear,
    The side that's next the sun.

Her lips were red, and one was thin,
Compar'd to that was next her chin
    (Some bee had stung it newly) ;
But, Dick, her eyes so guard her face ;
I durst no more upon them gaze
    Than on the sun in July.

Her mouth so small, when she does speak,
Thou'dst swear her teeth her words did break,
    That they might passage get ;
But she so handled still the matter,
They came as good as ours, or better,
    And are not spent a whit.

If wishing should be any sin,
The parson himself had guilty been,
    She look'd that day so purely ;
And did the youth so oft the feat
At night, as some did in conceit,
    It would have spoiled him surely.

Just in the nick the cook knocked thrice,
And all the waiters in a trice
    His summons did obey;
Each serving-man, with dish in hand,
Marched boldly up, like our trained band,
    Presented, and away.

When all the meat was on the table,
What man of knife or teeth was able
    To stay to be intreated?
And this the very reason was,
Before the parson could say grace,
    The company was seated.

The business of the kitchen's great,
For it is fit that men should eat,
    Nor was it there denied—
Passion o' me, how I run on!
There's that that would be thought upon,
    I trow, besides the bride.

Now hats fly off, and youths carouse;
Healths first go round, and then the house,
    The bride's came thick and thick:
And when 'twas nam'd another's health,
Perhaps he made it hers by stealth;
    And who could help it, Dick?

On the sudden up they rise and dance;
Then sit again and sigh, and glance:
    Then dance again and kiss:
Thus several ways the time did pass,
Whilst ev'ry woman wished her place,
    And every man wished his.

By this time all were stol'n aside
To counsel and undress the bride;
    But that he must not know:
But yet 'twas thought he guess'd her mind,
And did not mean to stay behind
    Above an hour or so.

57

When in he came, Dick, there she lay
Like new-fall'n snow melting away
    ('Twas time, I trow, to part)
Kisses were now the only stay,
Which soon she gave, as who would say,
    God b' w' ye, with all my heart.

But, just as Heaven would have, to cross it,
In came the bridesmaids with the posset :
    The bridegroom ate in spite ;
For had he left the women to 't,
It would have cost two hours to do 't,
    Which were too much that night.

At length the candle's out, and now
All that they had not done they do.
    What that is, who can tell ?
But I believe it was no more
Than thou and I have done before
    With Bridget and with Nell.

John Suckling.

DRINKING

T H E thirsty earth soaks up the rain,
And drinks and gapes for drink again ;
The plants suck in the earth, and are
With constant drinking fresh and fair ;
The sea itself (which one would think
Should have but little need of drink)
Drinks twice ten thousand rivers up,
So fill'd that they o'erflow the cup.
The busy Sun (and one would guess
By's drunken fiery face no less)
Drinks up the sea, and when he's done,
The Moon and Stars drink up the Sun :
They drink and dance by their own light,
They drink and revel all the night :
Nothing in Nature's sober found,
But an eternal health goes round.

Fill up the bowl, then, fill it high,
Fill all the glasses there—for why
Should every creature drink but I ?
Why, man of morals, tell me why ?

Abraham Cowley.

LOVE

I 'LL sing of Heroes, and of Kings ;
In mighty numbers, mighty things,
Begin, my Muse ; but lo, the strings
To my great song rebellious prove ;
The strings will sound of nought but Love.
I broke them all, and put on new ;
'Tis this or nothing sure will do.
These sure (said I) will me obey ;
These, sure, heroic notes will play.
Straight I began with thund'ring Jove,
And all th' immortal Powers, but Love.
Love smil'd, and from my enfeebled lyre
Came gentle airs, such as inspire
Melting love, and soft desire.
Farewell then Heroes, farewell Kings,
And mighty numbers, mighty things ;
Love tunes my heart just to my strings.

Abraham Cowley.

¶

*And she washed his feet with her tears, and
wiped them with the hairs of her head.*

THE proud Egyptian Queen, her Roman guest,
(T'express her love in height of state, and pleasure)
    With Pearl dissolv'd in Gold, did feast—
        Both Food, and Treasure.

And now (dear Lord !) thy Lover, on the fair
And silver tables of thy feet, behold !
    Pearl in her tears, and in her hair
        Offers thee gold.

Edward Sherburne.

59

TO HIS COY MISTRESS

HAD we but world enough, and time,
This coyness, lady, were no crime.
We would sit down, and think which way
To walk, and pass our long love's day.
Thou by the Indian Ganges' side
Should'st rubies find : I by the tide
Of Humber would complain. I would
Love you ten years before the Flood,
And you should, if you please, refuse
Till the conversion of the Jews.
My vegetable love should grow
Vaster than empires, and more slow.
An hundred years should go to praise
Thine eyes, and on thy forehead gaze :
Two hundred to adore each breast :
But thirty thousand to the rest ;
An age at least to every part,
And the last age should shew your heart.
For, lady, you deserve this state,
Nor would I love at lower rate.

But at my back I always hear
Time's wingèd chariot hurrying near :
And yonder all before us lie
Deserts of vast eternity.
Thy beauty shall no more be found ;
Nor, in thy marble vault, shall sound
My echoing song ; then worms shall try
That long-preserv'd virginity :
And your quaint honour turn to dust,
And into ashes all my lust.
The grave's a fine and private place,
But none, I think, do there embrace.

Now, therefore, while the youthful hue
Sits on thy skin like morning dew,
And while thy willing soul transpires
At every pore with instant fires,
Now let us sport us while we may ;
And now, like amorous birds of prey,

Rather at once our Time devour,
Than languish in his slow-chapt power.
Let us roll all our strength and all
Our sweetness up into one ball,
And tear our pleasures with rough strife
Through the iron gates of life.
Thus, though we cannot make our Sun
Stand still, yet we will make him run.

Andrew Marvell.

THE FAIR SINGER

T O make a final conquest of all me,
Love did compose so sweet an enemy,
In whom both beauties to my death agree,
Joining themselves in fatal harmony ;
That, while she with her eyes my heart does bind,
She with her voice might captivate my mind.

I could have fled from one but singly fair :
My disentangled soul itself might save,
Breaking the curled trammels of her hair.
But how should I avoid to be her slave,
Whose subtle art invisibly can wreathe
My fetters of the very air I breathe ?

It had been easy fighting in some plain,
Where victory might hang in equal choice,
But all resistance against her is vain,
Who has the advantage both of eyes and voice ;
And all my forces needs must be undone,
She having gained both the wind and sun.

Andrew Marvell.

THE GARDEN

H O W vainly men themselves amaze
To win the palm, the oak, or bays ;
And their incessant labours see
Crowned from some single herb, or tree,
Whose short and narrow-verged shade
Does prudently their toils upbraid ;
While all flow'rs and all trees do close
To weave the garlands of repose.

61

Fair Quiet, have I found thee here,
And Innocence, thy sister dear ?
Mistaken long, I sought you then
In busy companies of men.
Your sacred plants, if here below,
Only among the plants will grow ;
Society is all but rude
To this delicious solitude.

No white nor red was ever seen
So amorous as this lovely green.
Fond lovers, cruel as their flame,
Cut in these trees their mistress' name :
Little, alas ! they know or heed
How far these beauties hers exceed !
Fair trees ! wheres'e'er your barks I wound
No name shall but your own be found.

When we have run our passion's heat,
Love hither makes his best retreat.
The Gods, that mortal beauty chase,
Still in a tree did end their race ;
Apollo hunted Daphne so,
Only that she might laurel grow ;
And Pan did after Syrinx speed,
Not as a nymph, but for a reed.

What wondrous life is this I lead !
Ripe apples drop about my head ;
The luscious clusters of the vine
Upon my mouth do crush their wine;
The nectaren, and curious peach,
Into my hands themselves do reach ;
Stumbling on melons, as I pass,
Insnared with flowers, I fall on grass.

Meanwhile, the mind, from pleasure less,
Withdraws into its happiness :
The mind, that ocean where each kind
Does straight its own resemblance find ;

Yet it creates, transcending these,
Far other worlds, and other seas ;
Annihilating all that's made
To a green thought in a green shade.

Here at the fountain's sliding foot,
Or at some fruit-tree's mossy root,
Casting the body's vest aside,
My soul into the boughs does glide :
There like a bird it sits, and sings,
Then whets and claps its silver wings ;
And, till prepared for longer flight,
Waves in its plumes the various light.

Such was that happy garden-state,
While man there walked without a mate :
After a place so pure and sweet,
What other help could yet be meet !
But 'twas beyond a mortal's share
To wander solitary there :
Two paradises 'twere in one,
To live in paradise alone.

How well the skilful gardener drew
Of flowers, and herbs, this dial new ;
Where, from above, the milder sun
Does through a fragrant zodiac run ;
And, as it works, the industrious bee
Computes its time as well as we.
How could such sweet and wholesome hours
Be reckon'd but with herbs and flowers !

Andrew Marvell.

MOURNING

Y O U, that decipher out the fate
Of human offsprings from the skies,
What mean these infants which of late
Spring from the stars of *Chlora's* eyes ?

63

Her eyes confus'd, and doubled o'er,
With tears suspended ere they flow,
Seem bending upwards, to restore
To Heaven, whence it came, their woe.

When, moulding of the watery spheres,
Slow drops untie themselves away;
As if she, with those precious tears,
Would strow the ground where *Strephon* lay.

Yet some affirm, pretending art,
Her eyes have so her bosom drown'd,
Only to soften near her heart
A place to fix another wound.

And, while vain pomp does her restrain
Within her solitary bower,
She courts herself in am'rous rain;
Herself both Danäe and the shower.

Nay others, bolder, hence esteem
Joy now so much her master grown,
That whatsoever does but seem
Like grief, is from her windows thrown.

Nor that she pays, while she survives,
To her dead love this tribute due;
But casts abroad these donatives,
At the installing of a new.

How wide they dream! The Indian slaves
That sink for pearl through seas profound,
Would find her tears yet deeper waves
And not of one the bottom sound.

I yet my silent judgement keep,
Disputing not what they believe:
But sure as oft as women weep,
It is to be suppos'd they grieve.

Andrew Marvell.

64

THE DEFINITION OF LOVE

MY Love is of a birth as rare
As 'tis for object strange and high :
It was begotten by Despair
Upon Impossibility.

Magnanimous Despair alone
Could show me so divine a thing,
Where feeble Hope could ne'er have flown
But vainly flapt its tinsel wing.

And yet I quickly might arrive
Where my extended soul is fixt,
But Fate does iron wedges drive,
And always crowds itself betwixt.

For Fate with jealous eye does see
Two perfect loves ; nor lets them close :
Their union would her ruin be,
And her tyrannic power depose.

And therefore her decrees of steel
Us as the distant poles have placed,
(Though love's whole world on us doth wheel)
Not by themselves to be embraced.

Unless the giddy Heaven fall,
And earth some new convulsion tear ;
And, us to join, the world should all
Be cramped into a *planisphere*.

As lines, so loves *oblique* may well
Themselves in every angle greet :
But ours so truly *parallel*,
Though infinite can never meet.

Therefore the love which us doth bind,
But Fate so enviously debars,
Is the conjunction of the mind,
And opposition of the stars.

Andrew Marvell.

D

THE REVIVAL

UNFOLD, unfold ! take in his light,
Who makes thy cares more short than night.
The joys which with his day-star rise
He deals to all but drowsy eyes ;
And (what the men of this world miss)
Some drops and dews of future bliss.

Hark, how his winds have chang'd their note,
And with warm whispers call thee out.
The frosts are past, the storms are gone,
And backward life at last comes on.
The lofty groves in express joys
Reply unto the turtle's voice ;
And here in dust and dirt, O here
The lilies of his love appear !

Henry Vaughan

THE ECLIPSE

WHITHER, O whither didst thou fly
When I did grieve thine holy eye
When thou didst mourn to see me lost,
And all thy care and counsels crost.
O do not grieve, where'er thou art !
Thy grief is an undoing smart,
Which doth not only pain, but break
My heart, and makes me blush to speak.
Thy anger I could kiss, and will :
But O thy grief, thy grief doth kill !

Henry Vaughan.

THE WORLD

I SAW Eternity the other night,
Like a great Ring of pure and endless light,
    All calm, as it was bright ;
And round beneath it, Time in hours, days, years,
    Driven by the spheres
Like a vast shadow moved ; in which the world
    And all her train were hurled.

The doting lover in his quaintest strain
    Did there complain ;
Near him, his lute, his fancy, and his flights,
    Wit's sour delights,
With gloves, and knots, the silly snares of pleasure,
    Yet his dear treasure,
All scattered lay, while he his eyes did pour
    Upon a flower.

The darksome statesman, hung with weights and woe,
Like a thick midnight-fog, moved there so slow,
    He did not stay, nor go ;
Condemning thoughts—like sad eclipses—scowl
    Upon his soul,
And clouds of crying witnesses without
    Pursu'd him with one shout.
Yet digg'd the mole, and lest his ways be found,
    Worked under ground,
Where he did clutch his prey ; (But one did see
    That policy) ;
Churches and altars fed him ; perjuries
    Were gnats and flies ;
It rained about him blood and tears ; but he
    Drank them as free.

The fearful miser on a heap of rust
Sate pining all his life there, did scarce trust
    His own hands with the dust,
Yet would not place one piece above, but lives
    In fear of thieves.
Thousands there were as frantic as himself
    And hugged each one his pelf,
The downright epicure placed heaven in sense
    And scorn'd pretence,
While others, slipp'd into a wide excess,
    Said little less ;
The weaker sort slight, trivial wares enslave,
    Who think them brave ;
And poor, despised Truth sate counting by
    Their victory.

67

Yet some, who all this while did weep and sing,
And sing, and weep, soared up into the Ring ;
    But most would use no wing.
O fools (said I) thus to prefer dark night
    Before true light !
To live in grots and caves, and hate the day
    Because it shows the way,
The way, which from this dead and dark abode
    Leads up to God,
A way where you might tread the sun, and be
    More bright than he.
But as I did their madness so discuss,
    One whisper'd thus,
This Ring the Bridegroom did for none provide,
    But for his bride.

Henry Vaughan.

THE NIGHT

    THROUGH that pure virgin-shrine,
That sacred veil drawn o'er thy glorious noon,
That men might look and live, as glow-worms shine
    And face the moon :
    Wise Nicodemus saw such light
    As made him know his God by night.

    Most blest believer he !
Who in that land of darkness and blind eyes
Thy long-expected healing wings could see
    When thou didst rise,
    And, what can never more be done,
    Did at midnight speak with the Sun !

    O who will tell me, where
He found thee at that dead and silent hour ?
What hallowed solitary ground did bear
    So rare a flower,
    Within whose sacred leaves did lie
    The fulness of the Deity ?

No mercy-seat of gold,
No dead and dusty cherub, nor carved stone,
But his own living works did my Lord hold
        And lodge alone ;
    Where trees and herbs did watch and peep
    And wonder, while the Jews did sleep.

Dear Night ! this world's defeat ;
The stop to busy fools ; care's check and curb ;
The day of spirits ; my soul's calm retreat
        Which none disturb !
    Christ's progress, and his prayer-time ;
    The hours to which high Heaven doth chime.

God's silent, searching flight :
When my Lord's head is fill'd with dew and all
His locks are wet with the clear drops of night ;
        His still, soft call ;
    His knocking-time ; the soul's dumb watch,
    When spirits their fair kindred catch.

Were all my loud, evil days
Calm and unhaunted as is thy dark tent,
Whose peace but by some angel's wing or voice
        Is seldom rent ;
    Then I in heaven all the long year
    Would keep, and never wander here.

But living where the sun
Doth all things wake, and where all mix and tire
Themselves and others, I consent and run
        To every mire ;
    And by this world's ill-guiding light,
    Err more than I can do by night.

There is in God (some say)
A deep, but dazzling darkness ; as men here
Say it is late and dusky, because they
        See not all clear.
    O for that night ! where I in him
    Might live invisible and dim.

                                    Henry Vaughan.

69

THE DAWNING

AH! what time wilt thou come? when shall that cry
" *The Bridegroom's coming!* " fill the sky?
Shall it in the evening run
When our words and works are done?
Or will thy all-surprising light
  Break at midnight,
When either sleep, or some dark pleasure
Possesseth mad man without measure?
Or shall these early, fragrant hours
  Unlock thy bowers
And with their blush of light descry
Thy locks crowned with eternity?
Indeed, it is the only time
That with thy glory doth best chime;
All now are stirring, ev'ry field
  Full hymns doth yield,
The whole Creation shakes off night,
And for thy shadow looks the light;
Stars now vanish without number,
Sleepy planets set and slumber,
The pursy clouds disband and scatter,
All expect some sudden matter;
Not one beam triumphs, but from far
  That morning-star.
Oh at what time soever thou,
Unknown to us, the heavens wilt bow,
And with thy angels in the van,
Descend to judge poor careless man,
Grant I may not like puddle lie
In a corrupt security,
Where, if a traveller water crave,
He finds it dead, and in a grave.
But as this restless, vocal spring
All day and night doth run, and sing,
And though here born, yet is acquainted
Elsewhere, and flowing keeps untainted;
So let me all my busy age
In thy free services engage;

And though (while here) of force I must
Have commerce sometimes with poor dust,
And in my flesh, though vile and low,
As this doth in her channel, flow,
Yet let my course, my aim, my love
And chief acquaintance be above ;
So when that day and hour shall come,
In which thyself will be the sun,
Thou'lt find me dress'd and on my way,
Watching the break of thy great day.

Henry Vaughan.

ANGUISH

MY God and King ! to Thee
    I bow my knee ;
I bow my troubled soul, and greet
With my foul heart thy holy feet.
Cast it, or tread it ! it shall do
Even what thou wilt, and praise thee too.

My God, could I weep blood,
    Gladly I would,
Or if thou wilt give me that art,
Which through the eyes pours out the heart,
I will exhaust it all, and make
Myself all tears, a weeping lake.

O ! 'tis an easy thing
    To write and sing ;
But to write true, unfeigned verse
Is very hard ! O God, disperse
These weights, and give my spirit leave
To act as well as to conceive !

O my God, hear my cry ;
    Or let me die ! . . .

Henry Vaughan.

71

PHILLADA FLOUTS ME

O WHAT a plague is love !
　How shall I bear it ?
She will inconstant prove,
　I greatly fear it.
She so torments my mind
　That my strength faileth,
And wavers with the wind
　As a ship saileth.
Please her the best I may,
She loves still to gainsay ;
Alack and well-a-day !
　Phillada flouts me.

At the fair yesterday
　She did pass by me ;
She look'd another way
　And would not spy me :
I woo'd her for to dine,
　But could not get her ;
Will had her to the wine—
　He might entreat her.
With Daniel she did dance,
On me she look'd askance :
O thrice unhappy chance !
　Phillada flouts me.

Fair maid, be not so coy,
　Do not disdain me !
I am my mother's joy :
　Sweet, entertain me !
She'll give me, when she dies,
　All that is fitting :
Her poultry and her bees,
　And her goose sitting,
A pair of mattress beds,
And a bag full of shreds ;
And yet, for all these goods,
　Phillada flouts me.

She hath a clout of mine
  Wrought with blue coventry,
Which she keeps for a sign
  Of my fidelity :
But i' faith, if she flinch
  She shall not wear it ;
To Tib, my t'other wench,
  I mean to bear it.
And yet it grieves my heart
So soon from her to part :
Death strike me with his dart !
  Phillada flouts me.

Thou shalt eat crudded cream
  All the year lasting,
And drink the crystal stream
  Pleasant in tasting ;
Whig and whey whilst thou lust,
  And bramble-berries,
Pie-lid and pastry-crust,
  Pears, plums, and cherries.
Thy raiment shall be thin,
Made of a weevil's skin—
Yet all's not worth a pin !
  Phillada flouts me.

In the last month of May
  I made her posies ;
I heard her often say
  That she loved roses.
Cowslips and gillyflowers
  And the white lily
I brought to deck the bowers
  For my sweet Philly.
But she did all disdain,
And threw them back again ;
Therefore 'tis flat and plain
  Phillada flouts me.

D*

Fair maiden, have a care,
   And in time take me ;
I can have those as fair
   If you forsake me :
For Doll the dairy-maid
   Laugh'd at me lately,
And wanton Winifred
   Favours me greatly.
One throws milk on my clothes,
T'other plays with my nose ;
What wanting signs are those ?
   Phillada flouts me.

I cannot work nor sleep
   At all in season :
Love wounds my heart so deep,
   Without all reason.
I 'gin to pine away
   In my love's shadow,
Like as a fat beast may,
   Penn'd in a meadow.
I shall be dead, I fear,
Within this thousand year :
And all for that my dear
   Phillada flouts me.

Anonymous.

POVERTY

As in the house I sate
   Alone & desolate,
No creature but the fire & I,
The chimney & the stool, I lift mine eye
   Up to the wall,
   And in the silent hall
   Saw nothing mine
But some few cups & dishes shine,
The table & the wooden stools
   Where people used to dine :
   A painted cloth there was
Wherein some ancient story wrought
A little entertain'd my thought
Which light discover'd through the glass.

I wonder'd much to see
That all my wealth should be
Confin'd in such a little room,
Yet hope for more I scarcely durst presume.
It griev'd me sore
That such a scanty store
Should be my all :
For I forgot my ease & health,
Nor did I think of hands or eyes,
Nor soul nor body prize ;
I neither thought the sun,
Nor moon, nor stars, nor people, *mine*,
Tho' they did round about me shine ;
And therefore was I quite undone.

Some greater things I thought
Must needs for me be wrought,
Which till my craving mind could see
I ever should lament my poverty :
I fain would have
Whatever bounty gave ;
Nor could there be
Without, or love or deity :
For, should not he be infinite
Whose hand created me ?
Ten thousand absent things
Did vex my poor & wanting mind,
Which, till I be no longer blind,
Let me not see the King of kings.

His love must surely be
Rich, infinite, & free ;
Nor can he be thought a God
Of grace & pow'r, that fills not his abode,
His holy court,
In kind & liberal sort ;
Joys & pleasures,
Plenty of jewels, goods, & treasures,
(To enrich the poor, cheer the forlorn)
His palace must adorn,

75

And given all to me :
For till *his* works *my* wealth became,
No love, or peace, did me enflame :
But now I have a DEITY.

Thomas Traherne.

UPON NOTHING

NOTHING! thou elder brother ev'n to Shade,
Thou hadst a being e're the world was made,
And (well fixt) art alone of ending not afraid.

E'er time and place were, time and place were not,
When primitive Nothing something straight begot,
Then all proceeded from the great united—What.

Something the gen'ral attribute of all,
Sever'd from thee, its sole original,
Into thy boundless self must undistinguish'd fall.

Yet something did thy mighty pow'r command,
And from thy fruitful emptiness's hand,
Snatch'd men, beasts, birds, fire, air and land.

Matter, the wickedest off-spring of thy race,
By Form assisted, flew from thy embrace,
And rebel Light obscur'd thy reverend dusky face.

With Form, and Matter, Time and Place did join,
Body, thy foe, with thee did leagues combine,
To spoil thy peaceful realm, and ruin all thy line.

But turn-coat Time assists the foe in vain,
And, brib'd by thee, assists thy short-liv'd reign,
And to thy hungry womb drives back thy slaves again.

Tho' mysteries are barr'd from laick eyes,
And the Divine alone, with warrant, pries
Into thy bosom, where the truth in private lies,

Yet this of thee the wise may freely say,
Thou from the vertuous nothing tàk'st away,
And to be part with thee the wicked wisely pray.

Great Negative, how vainly would the wise
Enquire, define, distinguish, teach, devise,
Didst thou not stand to point their dull philosophies ?

Is, or *is not*, the two great ends of fate,
And, true or false, the subject of debate,
That perfect, or destroy, the vast designs of fate,

When they have rack'd the politician's breast,
Within thy bosom must securely rest,
And, when reduc'd to thee, are least unsafe and best.

But, Nothing, why does Something still permit.
That sacred monarchs should at council sit,
With persons highly thought, at best, for nothing.

Whilst weighty Something modestly abstains,
From prince's coffers, and from statesmen's brains,
And nothing there like stately Nothing reigns.

Nothing, who dwell'st with fools in grave disguise,
For whom they reverend shapes, and forms devise,
Lawn sleeves, and furs, and gowns, when they like
  thee look wise.

French truth, Dutch prowess, British policy,
Hibernian learning, Scotch civility,
Spaniards' dispatch, Danes' wit, are mainly seen in thee.

The great man's gratitude to his best friend,
King's promises, whores' vows, towards thee they bend,
Flow swiftly into thee, and in thee ever end.

                    John Wilmot, Earl of Rochester.

THE CHOICE

GRANT me, indulgent Heaven ! a rural seat,
  Rather contemptible than great !
Where, though I taste Life's sweets, still I may be
  Athirst for Immortality !

77

I would have business ; but exempt from strife !
    A private, but an active, life !
A Conscience bold, and punctual to his charge !
    My stock of Health ; or Patience large !
Some books I'd have, and some acquaintance too ;
    But very good, and very few !
Then (if one mortal two such grants may crave !)
    From silent life, I'd steal into my grave !

Nahum Tate.

THE SOLDIER'S DEATH

TRAIL all your pikes, dispirit every drum,
March in a slow procession from afar,
Ye silent, ye dejected men of war !
Be still the hautboys, and the flute be dumb !
Display no more, in vain, the lofty banner ;
For see ! where on the bier before ye lies
The pale, the fall'n, th' untimely Sacrifice
To your mistaken Shrine, to your false Idol Honour.

Anne, Countess of Winchilsea.

LOVE'S SECRET

NEVER seek to tell thy love,
    Love that never told can be ;
For the gentle wind does move
    Silently, invisibly.

I told my love, I told my love,
    I told her all my heart ;
Trembling, cold, in ghastly fears,
    Ah ! she did depart !

Soon as she was gone from me,
    A traveller came by,
Silently, invisibly :
    He took her with a sigh.

William Blake.

MILTON

AND did those feet in ancient time
Walk upon England's mountains green?
And was the Holy Lamb of God
On England's pleasant pastures seen?

And did the countenance divine
Shine forth upon our clouded hills?
And was Jerusalem builded here
Among these dark satanic mills?

Bring me my bow of burning gold!
Bring me my arrows of desire!
Bring me my spear! O clouds, unfold!
Bring me my chariot of fire!

I will not cease from mental fight,
Nor shall my sword sleep in my hand,
Till we have built Jerusalem
In England's green and pleasant land.

William Blake.

TO THE MUSES

WHETHER on Ida's shady brow,
 Or in the chambers of the East,
The chambers of the Sun, that now
 From ancient melody have ceased;

Whether in heaven ye wander fair,
 Or the green corners of the earth,
Or the blue regions of the air
 Where the melodious winds have birth;

Whether on crystal rocks ye rove,
 Beneath the bosom of the sea
Wandering in many a coral grove,
 Fair Nine, forsaking Poetry;

How have you left the ancient love
    That bards of old enjoyed in you !
The languid strings do scarcely move !
    The sound is forced, the notes are few !
                    William Blake.

THE DIVINE IMAGE

T O Mercy, Pity, Peace, and Love
All pray in their distress ;
And to these virtues of delight
Return their thankfulness.

For Mercy, Pity, Peace, and Love
Is God, our father dear,
And Mercy, Pity, Peace, and Love
Is Man, his child and care.

For Mercy has a human heart,
Pity a human face,
And Love, the human form divine,
And Peace, the human dress.

Then every man, of every clime,
That prays in his distress,
Prays to the human form divine,
Love, Mercy, Pity, Peace.

And all must love the human form,
In heathen, turk, or jew ;
Where Mercy, Love, & Pity dwell
There God is dwelling too.

                    William Blake.

INFANT JOY

" I H A V E no name :
" I am but two days old."
What shall I call thee ?
" I happy am,
Joy is my name."
Sweet joy befall thee

Pretty joy !
Sweet joy but two days old,
Sweet joy I call thee :
Thou dost smile,
I sing the while,
Sweet joy befall thee

William Blake.

¶

I LAID me down upon a bank
Where love lay sleeping ;
I heard among the rushes dank
Weeping, Weeping.

Then I went to the heath and the wild
To the thistles and thorns of the waste ;
And they told me how they were beguil'd,
Driven out, and compel'd to be chaste.

William Blake.

AUGURIES OF INNOCENCE

TO see a World in a Grain of Sand
And a Heaven in a Wild Flower,
Hold Infinity in the palm of your hand
And Eternity in an hour.
A Robin Red breast in a Cage
Puts all Heaven in a Rage.
A dove house fill'd with Doves & Pigeons
Shudders Hell thro' all its regions.
A dog starv'd at his Master's Gate
Predicts the ruin of the State.
A Horse misus'd upon the Road
Calls to Heaven for Human blood.
Each outcry of the hunted Hare
A fibre from the Brain does tear.
A Skylark wounded in the wing,
A Cherubim does cease to sing.
The Game Cock clip'd & arm'd for fight
Does the Rising Sun affright.

Every Wolf's & Lion's howl
Raises from Hell a Human Soul.
The wild Deer, wand'ring here & there,
Keeps the Human Soul from Care.
The Lamb misus'd breeds Public Strife
And yet forgives the Butcher's Knife.
The Bat that flits at close of Eve
Has left the Brain that won't Believe.
The Owl that calls upon the Night
Speaks the Unbeliever's fright.
He who shall hurt the little Wren
Shall never be belov'd by Men.
He who the Ox to wrath has mov'd
Shall never be by Woman lov'd.
The wanton Boy that kills the Fly
Shall feel the Spider's enmity.
He who torments the Chafer's Sprite
Weaves a Bower in endless Night.
The Caterpiller on the Leaf
Repeats to thee thy Mother's grief.
Kill not the Moth nor Butterfly,
For the Last Judgment draweth nigh.
He who shall train the Horse to War
Shall never pass the Polar Bar.
The Beggar's Dog & Widow's Cat,
Feed them & thou wilt grow fat.
The Gnat that sings his Summer's Song
Poison gets from Slander's tongue.
The poison of the Snake & Newt
Is the sweat of Envy's Foot.
The Poison of the Honey Bee
Is the Artist's Jealousy.
The Prince's Robes & Beggar's Rags
Are Toadstools on the Miser's Bags.
A Truth that's told with bad intent
Beats all the Lies you can invent.
It is right it should be so;
Man was made for Joy & Woe;
And when this we rightly know
Thro' the World we safely go.
Joy & Woe are woven fine,

A Clothing for the Soul divine;
Under every grief & pine
Runs a joy with silken twine.
The Babe is more than Swadling Bands;
Throughout all these Human Lands
Tools were made, & Born were hands,
Every Farmer understands.
Every Tear from Every Eye
Becomes a Babe in Eternity;
This is caught by Females bright,
And return'd to its own delight.
The Bleat, the Bark, Bellow & Roar
Are Waves that Beat on Heaven's Shore.
The Babe that weeps the Rod beneath
Writes Revenge in realms of Death.
The Beggar's Rags, fluttering in Air,
Does to Rags the Heavens tear.
The Soldier, arm'd with Sword & Gun,
Palsied strikes the Summer's Sun.
The poor Man's farthing is worth more
Than all the Gold on Afric's Shore.
One Mite wrung from the Lab'rer's hands
Shall buy and sell the Miser's Lands:
Or, if protected from on high,
Does the whole Nation sell & buy.
He who mocks the Infant's Faith
Shall be mock'd in Age & Death.
He who shall teach the Child to Doubt
The rotting Grave shall ne'er get out.
He who respects the Infant's faith
Triumphs over Hell & Death.
The Child's Toys & the Old Man's Reasons
Are the Fruits of the Two Seasons.
The Questioner, who sits so sly,
Shall never know how to Reply.
He who replies to words of Doubt
Doth put the Light of Knowledge out.
The Strongest Poison ever known
Came from Cæsar's Laurel Crown.
Nought can deform the Human Race
Like to the Armour's iron brace.

When Gold & Gems adorn the Plow
To peaceful Arts shall Envy Bow.
A Riddle or the Cricket's Cry
Is to Doubt a fit Reply.
The Emmet's Inch & Eagle's Mile
Make Lame Philosophy to smile.
He who Doubts from what he sees
Will ne'er Believe, do what you Please.
If the Sun & Moon should Doubt,
They'd immediately Go Out.
To be in a Passion you Good may do,
But no Good if a Passion is in you.
The Whore & Gambler, by the State
Licenc'd, build that Nation's Fate.
The Harlot's cry from Street to Street
Shall weave Old England's winding Sheet.
The Winner's Shout, the Loser's Curse,
Dance before dead England's Hearse.
Every Night & every Morn
Some to Misery are Born.
Every Morn and every Night
Some are Born to Sweet Delight.
Some are Born to Sweet Delight,
Some are Born to Endless Night.
We are led to Believe a Lie
When we see not Thro' the Eye,
Which was Born in a Night to perish in a Night,
When the Soul Slept in Beams of Light.
God appears & God is Light
To those poor Souls who dwell in Night;
But does a Human Form Display
To those who Dwell in Realms of day.

William Blake.

MUTABILITY

FROM low to high doth dissolution climb,
And sink from high to low, along a scale
Of awful notes, whose concord shall not fail;
A musical, but melancholy chime,

Which they can hear who meddle not with crime,
Nor avarice, nor over-anxious care.
Truth fails not ; but her outward forms that bear
The longest date do melt like frosty rime,
That in the morning whitened hill and plain
And is no more ; drop like the tower sublime
Of yesterday, which royally did wear
His crown of weeds, but could not even sustain
Some casual shout that broke the silent air,
Or the unimaginable touch of Time.

William Wordsworth.

HUMAN LIFE

If dead, we cease to be ; if total gloom
  Swallow up life's brief flash for ay, we fare
As summer-gusts, of sudden birth and doom,
  Whose sound and motion not alone declare,
But are their whole of being ! If the breath
Be Life itself, and not its task and tent,
If even a soul like Milton's can know death ;
  O Man ! thou vessel purposeless, unmeant,

Yet drone-hive strange of phantom purposes !
  Surplus of nature's dread activity,
Which, as she gazed on some nigh-finish'd vase,
Retreating slow, with meditative pause,
  She form'd with restless hands unconsciously !
Blank accident ! nothing's anomaly !
  If rootless thus, thus substanceless thy state,
Go, weigh thy dreams, and be thy hopes, thy fears,
The counter-weights !—Thy laughter and thy tears
  Mean but themselves, each fittest to create,

And to repay the other ! Why rejoices
  Thy heart with hollow joy for hollow good ?
  Why cowl thy face beneath the mourner's hood,
Why waste thy sighs, and thy lamenting voices,
  Image of Image, Ghost of Ghostly Elf,

85

That such a thing as thou feel'st warm or cold?
Yet what and whence thy gain, if thou withhold
   These costless shadows of thy shadowy self?
Be sad! be glad! be neither! seek, or shun!
Thou hast no reason why! Thou canst have none;
Thy being's being is contradiction.

S. T. Coleridge.

JENNY KISS'D ME

JENNY kiss'd me when we met,
   Jumping from the chair she sat in;
Time, you thief, who love to get
   Sweets into your list, put that in!
Say I'm weary, say I'm sad,
   Say that health and wealth have miss'd me,
Say I'm growing old, but add,
   Jenny kiss'd me.

Leigh Hunt.

WE'LL GO NO MORE A-ROVING

SO, we'll go no more a-roving
   So late into the night,
Though the heart be still as loving,
   And the moon be still as bright.

For the sword outwears its sheath,
   And the soul wears out the breast,
And the heart must pause to breathe,
   And love itself have rest.

Though the night was made for loving,
   And the day returns too soon,
Yet we'll go no more a-roving
   By the light of the moon.

Byron.

86

LOVE'S PHILOSOPHY

THE fountains mingle with the river
　　And the rivers with the ocean,
The winds of heaven mix for ever
　　With a sweet emotion ;
Nothing in the world is single ;
　　All things by a law divine
In one another's being mingle.
　　Why not I with thine ?

See the mountains kiss high heaven
　　And the waves clasp one another ;
No sister-flower would be forgiven
　　If it disdained its brother ;
And the sunlight clasps the earth
　　And the moonbeams kiss the sea :
What are all these kissings worth
　　If thou kiss not me ?

P. B. Shelley.

TO NIGHT

SWIFTLY walk o'er the western wave,
　　Spirit of Night !
Out of the misty eastern cave,
Where, all the long and lone day-light,
Thou wovest dreams of joy and fear,
Which make thee terrible and dear—
　　Swift be thy flight !

Wrap thy form in a mantle gray,
　　Star-inwrought !
Blind with thine hair the eyes of Day ;
Kiss her until she be wearied out,
Then wander o'er city, and sea, and land
Touching all with thine opiate wand—
　　Come, long-sought !

87

When I arose and saw the dawn,
    I sighed for thee ;
When light rode high, and the dew was gone,
And noon lay heavy on flower and tree,
And the weary day turned to his rest,
Lingering like an unloved guest,
    I sighed for thee.

Thy brother Death came, and cried,
    Wouldst thou me ?
Thy sweet child Sleep, the filmy-eyed,
Murmured like a noontide bee,
Shall I nestle near thy side ?
Wouldst thou me ?—And I replied,
    No, not thee !

Death will come when thou art dead,
    Soon, too soon—
Sleep will come when thou art fled ;
Of neither would I ask the boon
I ask of thee, belovéd Night—
Swift be thine approaching flight,
    Come soon, soon !

P. B. Shelley.

¶

A WIDOW bird sate mourning for her love
    Upon a wintry bough ;
The frozen wind crept on above,
    The freezing stream below.

There was no leaf upon the forest bare,
    No flower upon the ground,
And little motion in the air
    Except the mill-wheel's sound.

P. B. Shelley.

SONG TO THE MEN OF ENGLAND

MEN of England, wherefore plough
For the lords who lay ye low?
Wherefore weave with toil and care
The rich robes your tyrants wear?

Wherefore feed, and clothe, and save,
From the cradle to the grave,
Those ungrateful drones who would
Drain your sweat—nay, drink your blood?

Wherefore, Bees of England, forge
Many a weapon, chain, and scourge,
That these stingless drones may spoil
The forced produce of your toil?

Have ye leisure, comfort, calm,
Shelter, food, love's gentle balm?
Or what is it ye buy so dear
With your pain and with your fear?

The seed ye sow, another reaps;
The wealth ye find, another keeps;
The robes ye weave, another wears;
The arms ye forge, another bears.

Sow seed,—but let no tyrant reap;
Find wealth,—let no impostor heap;
Weave robes,—let not the idle wear;
Forge arms,—in your defence to bear.

Shrink to your cellars, holes, and cells;
In halls ye deck another dwells.
Why shake the chains ye wrought?   Ye see
The steel ye tempered glance on ye.

With plough and spade, and hoe and loom,
Trace your grave, and build your tomb,
And weave your winding-sheet, till fair
England be your sepulchre.

P. B. Shelley.

WRITTEN IN THE FIELDS

TO one who has been long in city pent,
'Tis very sweet to look into the fair
And open face of heaven,—to breathe a prayer
Full in the smile of the blue firmament.
Who is more happy, when, with heart's content,
Fatigued he sinks into some pleasant lair
Of wavy grass, and reads a debonair
And gentle tale of love and languishment?
Returning home at evening, with an ear
Catching the notes of Philomel,—an eye
Watching the sailing cloudlet's bright career,
He mourns that day so soon has glided by:
E'en like the passage of an angel's tear,
That falls through the clear ether silently.

John Keats.

DAISY'S SONG

THE sun, with his great eye,
Sees not so much as I;
And the moon, all silver, proud,
Might as well be in a cloud.

And O the spring—the spring!
I lead the life of a king!
Couched in the teeming grass,
I spy each pretty lass.

I look where no one dares,
And I stare where no one stares;
And when the night is nigh,
Lambs bleat my lullaby.

John Keats.

ON THE ELGIN MARBLES

MY spirit is too weak; mortality
    Weighs heavily on me like unwilling sleep,
    And each imagined pinnacle and steep
Of godlike hardship tells me I must die
Like a sick eagle looking at the sky.

Yet 'tis a gentle luxury to weep,
   That I have not the cloudy winds to keep
Fresh for the opening of the morning's eye.
Such dim-conceived glories of the brain,
   Bring round the heart an indescribable feud ;
So do these wonders a most dizzy pain,
   That mingles Grecian grandeur with the rude
Wasting of old Time—with a billowy main
   A sun, a shadow of a magnitude.

John Keats.

DAYS

DAUGHTERS of Time, the hypocritic Days,
Muffled and dumb like barefoot dervishes
And marching single in an endless file,
Bring diadems and faggots in their hands.
To each they offer gifts after his will—
Bread, kingdoms, stars, and sky that holds them all.
I, in my pleached garden, watch'd the pomp,
Forgot my morning wishes, hastily
Took a few herbs and apples, and the day
Turn'd and departed silent.   I, too late,
Under her solemn fillet saw the scorn.

Ralph Waldo Emerson.

A FAREWELL

FLOW down, cold rivulet, to the sea,
   Thy tribute wave deliver :
No more by thee my steps shall be,
   For ever and for ever.

Flow, softly flow, by lawn and lea,
   A rivulet then a river :
Nowhere by thee my steps shall be,
   For ever and for ever.

But here will sigh thine alder tree,
  And here thine aspen shiver;
And here by thee will hum the bee,
  For ever and for ever.

A thousand suns will stream on thee,
  A thousand moons will quiver;
But not by thee my steps shall be,
  For ever and for ever.

Tennyson.

IN MEMORIAM

L

BE near me when my light is low,
  When the blood creeps, and the nerves prick
  And tingle; and the heart is sick,
And all the wheels of Being slow.

Be near me when the sensuous frame
  Is rack'd with pangs that conquer trust;
  And Time, a maniac scattering dust,
And Life, a Fury slinging flame.

Be near me when my faith is dry,
  And men the flies of latter spring,
  That lay their eggs, and sting and sing
And weave their petty cells and die.

Be near me when I fade away,
  To point the term of human strife,
  And on the low dark verge of life
The twilight of eternal day.

Tennyson.

TWO IN THE CAMPAGNA

I WONDER do you feel to-day
  As I have felt since, hand in hand,
We sat down on the grass, to stray
  In spirit better through the land,
This morn of Rome and May?

For me, I touched a thought, I know,
  Has tantalized me many times,
(Like turns of thread the spiders throw
  Mocking across our path) for rhymes
To catch at and let go.

Help me to hold it ! First it left
  The yellowing fennel, run to seed
There, branching from the brickwork's cleft,
  Some old tomb's ruin ; yonder weed
Took up the floating weft,

Where one small orange cup amassed
  Five beetles—blind and green they grope
Among the honey-meal ; and last,
  Everywhere on the grassy slope
I traced it. Hold it fast !

The champaign with its endless fleece
  Of feathery grasses everywhere !
Silence and passion, joy and peace,
  An everlasting wash of air—
Rome's ghost since her decease.

Such life here, through such length of hours,
  Such miracles performed in play,
Such primal naked forms of flowers,
  Such letting Nature have her way
While Heaven looks from its towers !

How say you ? Let us, O my dove,
  Let us be unashamed of soul,
As earth lies bare to heaven above !
  How is it under our control
To love or not to love ?

I would that you were all to me,
  You that are just so much, no more,
Nor yours, nor mine, nor slave nor free !
  Where does the fault lie ? What the core
Of the wound, since wound must be ?

93

I would I could adopt your will,
  See with your eyes, and set my heart
Beating by yours, and drink my fill
  At your soul's springs,—your part my part
In life, for good and ill.

No. I yearn upward, touch you close,
  Then stand away. I kiss your cheek,
Catch your soul's warmth—I pluck the rose
  And love it more than tongue can speak—
Then the good minute goes.

Already how am I so far
  Out of that minute ? Must I go
Still like the thistle-ball, no bar,
  Onward, whenever light winds blow,
Fixed by no friendly star ?

Just when I seemed about to learn !
  Where is the thread now ? Off again !
The old trick ! Only I discern—
  Infinite passion, and the pain
Of finite hearts that yearn.

Robert Browning.

MAGNA EST VERITAS

HERE, in this little Bay,
Full of tumultuous life and great repose,
Where, twice a day,
The purposeless, glad ocean comes and goes,
Under high cliffs, and far from the huge town,
I sit me down.
For want of me the world's course will not fail :
When all its work is done, the lie shall rot ;
The truth is great, and shall prevail,
When none cares whether it prevail or not.

Coventry Patmore.

94

ST. VALENTINE'S DAY

WELL dost thou, Love, thy solemn Feast to hold
In vestal February ;
Not rather choosing out some rosy day
From the rich coronet of the coming May,
When all things meet to marry !
    O, quick, prævernal Power
That signall'st punctual through the sleepy mould
The Snowdrop's time to flower,
Fair as the rash oath of virginity
Which is the first-love's first cry ;
O, Baby Spring,
That flutter'st sudden 'neath the breast of Earth
A month before the birth ;
Whence is the peaceful poignancy,
The joy contrite,
Sadder than sorrow, sweeter than delight,
That burthens now the breath of everything,
Though each one sighs as if to each alone
The cherish'd pang were known ?
At dusk of dawn, on his dark spray apart,
With it the Blackbird breaks the young Day's heart ;
In evening's hush
About it talks the heavenly-minded Thrush ;
The hill with like remorse
Smiles to the Sun's smile in his westering course ;
The fisher's drooping skiff
In yonder sheltering bay ;
The choughs that call about the shining cliff ;
The children, noisy in the setting ray ;
Own the sweet season, each thing as it may ;
Thoughts of strange kindness and forgotten peace
In me increase ;
And tears arise
Within my happy, happy Mistress' eyes,
And, lo, her lips, averted from my kiss,
Ask from Love's bounty, ah, much more than bliss !
    Is't the sequester'd and exceeding sweet
    Of dear Desire electing his defeat ?

95

Is't the waked Earth now to yon purpling cope
Uttering first-love's first cry,
Vainly renouncing, with a Seraph's sigh,
Love's natural hope?
Fair-meaning Earth, foredoom'd to perjury!
Behold, all amorous May,
With roses heap'd upon her laughing brows,
Avoids thee of thy vows!
Were it for thee, with her warm bosom near,
To abide the sharpness of the Seraph's sphere?
Forget thy foolish words;
Go to her summons gay,
Thy heart with dead, wing'd Innocencies fill'd,
Ev'n as a nest with birds
After the old ones by the hawk are kill'd.
   Well dost thou, Love, to celebrate
The noon of thy soft ecstasy,
Or e'er it be too late,
Or e'er the Snowdrop die!

Coventry Patmore.

LIFE

I ASKED no other thing,
No other was denied.
I offered Being for it;
The mighty merchant smiled.

Brazil?   He twirled a button,
Without a glance my way:
" But, madam, is there nothing else
That we can show to-day? "

Emily Dickinson.

THE SHOW

THE show is not the show,
But they that go.
Menagerie to me
My neighbours be.
Fair play—
Both went to see.

Emily Dickinson.

LOVE SIGHT

WHEN do I see thee most, beloved one?
  When in the light the spirits of mine eyes
  Before thy face, their altar, solemnize
The worship of that Love through thee made known?
Or when, in the dusk hours, (we two alone,)
  Close-kissed and eloquent of still replies
  Thy twilight-hidden glimmering visage lies,
And my soul only sees thee sees its own?

O love, my love! if I no more should see
Thyself, nor on the earth the shadow of thee,
  Nor image of thine eyes in any spring,—
How then should sound upon Life's darkening slope
The ground-whirl of the perish'd leaves of Hope,
  The wind of Death's imperishable wing?

Dante Gabriel Rossetti.

THE WOODSPURGE

THE wind flapped loose, the wind was still,
  Shaken out dead from tree and hill:
  I had walk'd on at the wind's will,—
  I sat now, for the wind was still.

Between my knees my forehead was,—
  My lips, drawn in, said not Alas!
  My hair was over in the grass,
  My naked ears heard the day pass.

My eyes, wide open, had the run
  Of some ten weeds to fix upon;
  Among those few, out of the sun,
  The woodspurge flowered, three cups in one.

From perfect grief there need not be
  Wisdom or even memory:
  One thing then learnt remains to me,—
  The woodspurge has a cup of three.

Dante Gabriel Rossetti.

E

97

MODERN LOVE

XLVII

WE saw the swallows gathering in the sky,
And in the osier-isle we heard them noise
We had not to look back on summer joys,
Or forward to a summer of bright dye :
But in the largeness of the evening earth
Our spirits grew as we went side by side.
The hour became her husband and my bride.
Love that had robbed us so, thus blessed our dearth !
The pilgrims of the year waxed very loud
In multitudinous chatterings, as the flood
Full brown came from the West, and like pale blood
Expanded to the upper crimson cloud.
Love that had robbed us of immortal things,
This little moment mercifully gave,
Where I have seen across the twilight wave
The swan sail with her young beneath her wings.

George Meredith.

SEED-TIME

FLOWERS of the willow-herb are wool ;
Flowers of the briar berries red ;
Speeding their seed as the breeze may rule.
Flowers of the thistle loosen the thread.
Flowers of the clematis drip in beard,
Slack from the fir-tree youngly climbed ;
Chaplets in air, flies foliage seared ;
Heeled upon earth, lie clusters rimed.

Where were skies of the mantle stained
Orange and scarlet, a coat of frieze
Travels from North till day has waned,
Tattered, soaked in the ditch's dyes ;
Tumbles the rook under grey or slate ;
Else enfolding us, damps to the bone ;
Narrows the world to my neighbour's gate ;
Paints me Life as a wheezy crone.

Now seems none but the spider lord ;
Star in circle his web waits prey,
Silvering bush-mounds, blue brushing sward ;
Slow runs the hour, swift flits the ray.
Now to his thread-shroud is he nigh,
Nigh to the tangle where wings are sealed,
He who frolicked the jewelled fly ;
All is adroop on the down and the weald.

Mists more lone for the sheep-bell enwrap
Nights that tardily let slip a morn
Paler than moons, and on noontide's lap
Flame dies cold, like the rose late born.
Rose born late, born withered in bud !—
I, even I, for a zenith of sun
Cry, to fulfil me, nourish my blood :
O for a day of the long light, one !

Master the blood, nor read by chills,
Earth admonishes : Hast thou ploughed,
Sown, reaped, harvested grain for the mills,
Thou hast the light over shadow of cloud.
Steadily eyeing, before that wail
Animal-infant, thy mind began,
Momently nearer me : should sight fail,
Plod in the track of the husbandman.

Verily now is our season of seed,
Now in our Autumn ; and Earth discerns
Them that have served her in them that can read,
Glassing, where under the surface she burns,
Quick at her wheel, while the fuel, decay,
Brightens the fire of renewal : and we ?
Death is the word of a bovine-day,
Know you the breast of the springing To-be.

George Meredith.

MIRAGE

THE hope I dreamed of was a dream,
  Was but a dream ; and now I wake,
Exceeding comfortless, and worn, and old,
  For a dream's sake.

99.

I hang my harp upon a tree,
  A weeping willow in a lake ;
I hang my silent harp there, wrung and snapt
  For a dream's sake.

Lie still, lie still, my breaking heart ;
  My silent heart, lie still and break :
Life, and the world, and mine own self, are changed
  For a dream's sake.

Christina Rossetti.

WEATHERS

THIS is the weather the cuckoo likes,
      And so do I ;
When showers betumble the chestnut spikes,
      And nestlings fly ;
And the little brown nightingale bills his best,
And they sit outside the " Traveller's Rest,"
And maids come forth sprig-muslin drest,
And citizens dream of the South and West,
      And so do I.

This is the weather the shepherd shuns,
      And so do I :
When beeches drip in browns and duns,
      And thresh, and ply ;
And hill-hid tides throb, throe on throe,
And meadow rivulets overflow,
And drops on gate-bars hang in a row,
And rooks in families homeward go,
      And so do I.

Thomas Hardy.

I LOOK INTO MY GLASS

I LOOK into my glass,
  And view my wasting skin,
And say, " Would God it came to pass
  My heart had shrunk as thin ! "

For then, I, undistrest
By hearts grown cold to me,
Could lonely wait my endless rest
With equanimity.

But Time, to make me grieve,
Part steals, lets part abide ;
And shakes this fragile frame at eve
With throbbings of noontide.

Thomas Hardy.

THE SLEEP-WORKER

WHEN wilt thou wake, O Mother, wake and see—
As one who, held in trance, has laboured long
By vacant rote and prepossession strong—
The coils that thou hast wrought unwittingly ;

Wherein have place, unrealized by thee,
Fair growths, foul cankers, right enmeshed with wrong,
Strange orchestras of victim-shriek and song,
And curious blends of ache and ecstasy ?—

Should that morn come, and show thy opened eyes
All that Life's palpitating tissues feel,
How wilt thou bear thyself in thy surprise ?—

Wilt thou destroy, in one wild shock of shame,
Thy whole high heaving firmamental frame,
Or patiently adjust, amend, and heal ?

Thomas Hardy.

I BENDED UNTO ME

I BENDED unto me a bough of May,
That I might see and smell :
It bore it in a sort of way,
It bore it very well.
But when I let it backward sway,
Then it were hard to tell

With what a toss, with what a swing,
The dainty thing
Resumed its proper level,
And sent me to the devil.
I know it did—you doubt it ?
I turned, and saw them whispering about it.

T. E. Brown.

THE BRISTOL CHANNEL

THIS sea was Lazarus, all day
At Dives' gate he lay,
And lapped the crumbs.
Night comes ;
The beggar dies—
Forthwith the Channel, coast to coast,
Is Abraham's bosom ; and the beggar lies
A lovely ghost.

T. E. Brown.

SUNSET AT CHAGFORD

HOMO LOQUITUR

IS it ironical, a fool enigma,
This sunset show ?
The purple stigma,
Black mountain cut upon a saffron glow—
Is it a mammoth joke,
A riddle put for me to guess,
Which, having duly honoured, I may smoke,
And go to bed,
And snore,
Having a soothing consciousness
Of something red ?
Or is it more ?
Ah, is it, is it more ?

A dole, perhaps ?
The scraps
Tossed from the table of the revelling gods ?—
What odds !

I taste them—Lazarus
Was nourished thus !
But, all the same, it surely is a cheat—
Is this the stuff they eat ?
A cheat ! a cheat !
Then let the garbage be—
Some pig-wash ! let it vanish down the sink
Of night ! 'tis not for me.
I will not drink
Their draff,
While, throned on high, they quaff
The fragrant sconce—
Has Heaven no cloaca for the nonce ?
Say 'tis an anodyne—
It never shall be mine.
I want no opiates—
The best of all their cates
Were gross to balk the meanest sense ;
I want to be co-equal with their fates ;
I will not be put off with temporal pretence :
I want to be awake, and know, not stand
And stare at waving of a conjuror's hand.

But is it speech
Wherewith they strive to reach
Our poor inadequate souls ?
The round earth rolls ;
I cannot hear it hum—
The stars are dumb—
The voices of the world are in my ear
A sensuous murmur.   Nothing speaks
But man, my fellow—him I hear,
And understand ; but beasts and birds
And winds and waves are destitute of words.
What is the alphabet
The gods have set ?
What babbling ! what delusion !
And in these sunset tints
What gay confusion !
Man prints

His meaning, has a letter
Determinate.   I know that it is better
Than all this cumbrous hieroglyph—
The *For*, the *If*
Are growth of man's analysis :
The gods in bliss
Scrabble a baby jargon on the skies
For us to analyse !
Cumbrous ? nay, idiotic—
A party-coloured symbolism,
The fragments of a shivered prism :
Man gives the swift demotic.

'Tis good to see
The economy
Of poor upstriving man !
Since time began,
He has been sifting
The elements ; while God, on chaos drifting,
Sows broadcast all His stuff.
Lavish enough,
No doubt ; but why this waste ?
See ! of these very sunset dyes
The virgin chaste
Takes one, and in a harlot's eyes
Another rots.   They go by billion billions :
Each blade of grass
Ignores them as they pass ;
The spiders in their foul pavilions,
Behold this vulgar gear,
And sneer ;
Dull frogs
In bogs
Catch rosy gleams through rushes,
And know that night is near ;
Wrong-headed thrushes
Blow bugles to it ;
And a wrong-headed poet
Will strut, and strain the cogs
Of the machine, he blushes

To call his Muse, and maunder;
And, marvellous to relate!
These pseudo-messengers of state
Will wander
Where there is no intelligence to meet them,
Nor even a sensorium to greet them.
The very finest of them
Go where there's naught to love them
Or notice them: to cairns, to rocks
Where ravens nurse their young,
To mica-splints from granite-boulders wrung
By channels of the marsh, to stocks
Of old dead willows in a pool as dead.
Can anything be said
To these? The leech
Looks from its muddy lair,
And sees a silly something in the air—
Call you this *speech*?
O God, if it be speech,
Speak plainer,
If Thou would'st teach
That I shall be a gainer!
The age of picture-alphabets is gone:
We are not now so weak;
We are too old to con
The horn-book of our youth. Time lags—
O, rip this obsolete blazon into rags!
And speak! O, speak!

But, if I be a spectacle
In Thy great theatre, then do Thy will:
Arrange Thy instruments with circumspection;
Summon Thine angels to the vivisection!
But quick! O, quick!
For I am sick,
And very sad.
Thy pupils will be glad.
"See," Thou exclaim'st, "this ray!
How permanent upon the retina!
How odd that purple hue!

The pineal gland is blue.
I stick this probe
In the posterior lobe—
Behold the cerebellum
A smoky yellow, like old vellum !
Students will please observe
The structure of the optic nerve.
See ! nothing could be finer—
That film of pink
Around the hippocampus minor.
Behold !
I touch it, and it turns bright gold.
Again !—as black as ink.
Another lancet—thanks !
That's Manx—
Yes, the delicate pale sea-green
Passing into ultra-marine—
A little blurred—in fact
This brain seems packed
With sunsets.   Bring
That battery here ; now put your
Negative pole beneath the suture—
That's just the thing.
Now then the other way—
I say !   I say !
More chloroform !
(A little more will do no harm).
Now this is the most instructive of all
The phenomena, what in fact we may call
The most obvious justification
Of vivisection in general.
Observe (once ! twice !
That's very nice)—
Observe, I say, the incipient relation
Of a quasi-moral activity
To this physical agitation !
Of course, you see. . . ."
Yes, yes, O God,
I feel the prod
Of that dissecting knife.
Instructive, say the pupil angels *very :*

And some take notes, and some take sandwiches
   and sherry;
And some are prying
Into the very substance of my brain—
I feel their fingers!
(My life! my life!)
Yes, yes! it lingers!
The sun, the sun—
Go on! go on!
Blue, yellow, red!
But please remember that I am not dead,
Nor even dying.

SUNSET AT CHAGFORD

RESPONDET δημιουργός

Yes, it is hard, but not for you alone
You speak of cup and throne,
And all that separates Me from you.
It is not that you don't believe:
It is but that you misconceive
The work I have to do.

No throne, no cup
Nor down, but likest up,
As from a deep black shaft, I look to see
The fabric of My own immensity.
You have the temporal activity, and rejoice
In sweet, articulate voice—
Tunes, songs.
To Me no less
Belongs
The fixed, sad fashion of productiveness.
You think that I am wise,
Or cunning, clever as a man is clever.
You think all knowledge with Me lies,
From Me must flow.
I know not if I know—
But this I know, I will work on for ever.
You fret because you are not this and that,

107

And so you die ;
But I,
Who have not sat
Since first into the void I swam,
Obeying Mine own laws,
Persist, because
I am but what I am.

I am old and blind ;
I have no speech
" Wherewith to reach "
Your quick-selecting ears.
And yet I mark your tears ;
And yet I would be kind.
And so I strain
To speak, as now ;
And, in more cheerful vein,
You haply will allow
I make My meaning fairly plain.
Therefore it is I store
Such beauty in the clouds, and on the shore
Make foam-flakes glisten ; therefore you have seen
This sunset ; therefore 'tis the green
And lusty grass
Hath come to pass
And flame
Lies sparkling in the dews—
And yet I cannot choose
But do the same !

I am no surgeon,
I have no lancet, but I mingle
Sap for the buds, that they may burgeon,
And tingle
With soft sweet throes
Of parturition vegetal.
And so to all
The surfaces
I outward press,
And hold the very brink
Of speech, that I would think

Speech must come next.
But I can do no more : wherefore I am not vexed ;
But you are, being perplexed
With suppositions, scribbling o'er he text
Of natural life. And, seeing that this is so,
And that I cannot know
The innumerous ills,
Therefore I strew the hills
And vallies with delight,
That, day or night,
In sad or merry plight,
You may catch sight
Of some sweet joy that thrills
Your heart.
And what if I impart
The same to frog or newt,
What if I steep the root
Of some old stump in bright vermilion,
And if the spider in his quaint pavilion
Catches a sunbeam where he thought a fly,
Ah, why
Should I not care for such ?
I, Who make all things, know it is not much.
And, by analogy I must suppose
They have their woes
Like you :
Therefore I still must strew
Joys that may wait for centuries,
And light at last on Socrates,
Or on the frog, whose eyes
You may have noticed full of bright surprise—
Or have you not ? Ah, then
You only think of men !
But I would have no single creature miss
One possible bliss.
And this
Is certain : never be afraid !
I love what I have made.
I know this is not wit,
This is not to be clever,
Or anything whatever.

You see, I am a servant, that is it :
You've hit
The mark—a servant : for the other word—
Why, you are Lord, if any one is Lord.

T. E. Brown.

MY BODY WHICH MY DUNGEON IS

M Y body, which my dungeon is,
And yet my parks and palaces :—
    Which is so great that there I go
All the day long to and fro,
And when the night begins to fall
Throw down my bed and sleep, while all
The building hums with wakefulness—
Even as a child of savages
When evening takes her on her way,
(She having roamed a summer's day
Along the mountain-sides and scalp)
Sleeps in the antre of that alp :—
    Which is so broad and high that there,
As in the topless field of air,
My fancy soars like to a kite
And faints in the blue infinite :—
    Which is so strong, my strongest throes
And the rough world's besieging blows
Not break it, and so weak withal,
Death ebbs and flows in its loose wall
As the green sea in fishers' nets,
And tops its topmost parapets :—
    Which is so wholly mine that I
Can wield its whole artillery,
And mine so little, that my soul
Dwells in perpetual control,
And I but think and speak and do
As my dead fathers move me to :—
    If this born body of my bones
The beggared soul so barely owns,
What money passed from hand to hand,
What creeping custom of the land,
What deed of author or assign,
Can make a house a thing of mine ?

R. L. Stevenson.

TO SILENCE

"Space, the bound of a solid": silence, then, the form of a melody.

NOT, Silence, for thine idleness I raise
My silence-bounded singing in thy praise,
But for thy moulding of my Mozart's tune
Thy hold upon the bird that sings the moon,
     Thy magisterial ways.

Man's lovely definite melody-shapes are thine,
Outlined, controlled, compressed, complete, divine ;
Also thy fine intrusions do I trace,
Thy afterthoughts, thy wandering, thy grace,
     Within the poet's line.

Thy secret is the song that is to be.
Music had never stature but for thee,
Sculptor ! strong as the sculptor Space whose hand
Urged the Discobolus and bade him stand.

.   .   .   .   .

Man, on his way to Silence, stops to hear and see.
                    Alice Meynell.

THE WIND IS BLIND

"Eyeless, in Gaza, at the mill, with slaves."—Milton's *Samson.*

THE wind is blind.
The earth sees sun and moon ; the height
Is watch-tower to the dawn ; the plain
Shines to the summer ; visible light
Is scattered in the drops of rain.

The wind is blind.
The flashing billows are aware ;
With open eyes the cities see ;
Light leaves the ether, everywhere
Known to the homing bird and bee.

The wind is blind,
Is blind alone.   How has he hurled
His ignorant lash, his aimless dart,
His eyeless rush upon the world,
Unseeing, to break his unknown heart !

The wind is blind.
And the sail traps him, and the mill
Captures him ; and he cannot save
His swiftness and his desperate will
From those blind uses of the slave.

Alice Meynell.

TO THE BODY

THOU inmost, ultimate
Council of judgement, palace of decrees,
Where the high senses hold their spiritual state,
    Sued by earth's embassies,
And sign, approve, accept, conceive, create ;

Create—thy senses close
With the world's pleas.   The random odours reach
Their sweetness in the place of thy repose,
    Upon thy tongue the peach,
And in thy nostrils breathes the breathing rose.

To thee, secluded one,
The dark vibrations of the sightless skies,
The lovely inexplicit colours run ;
    The light gropes for those eyes.
O thou august ! thou dost command the sun.

Music, all dumb, hath trod
Into thine ear her one effectual way ;
And fire and cold approach to gain thy nod,
    Where thou call'st up the day,
Where thou awaitest the appeal of God.

Alice Meynell.

112

THE PRECEPT OF SILENCE

I KNOW you : solitary griefs,
Desolate passions, aching hours !
I know you : tremulous beliefs,
Agonized hopes, and ashen flowers !

The winds are sometimes sad to me ;
The starry spaces, full of fear ;
Mine is the sorrow on the sea,
And mine the sigh of places drear.

Some players upon plaintive strings
Publish their wistfulness abroad :
I have not spoken of these things,
Save to one man, and unto God.

Lionel Johnson.

FROM THE NIGHT OF FOREBEING

" In the chaos of preordination, and night of our forebeings."
Sir Thomas Browne.

" Et lux in tenebris erat, et tenebræ eam non comprehenderunt."
St. John.

CAST wide the folding doorways of the East,
For now is light increased !
And the wind-besomed chambers of the air,
See they be garnished fair ;
And look the ways exhale some precious odours,
And set ye all about wild-breathing spice,
Most fit for Paradise !
Now is no time for sober gravity,
Season enough has Nature to be wise ;
But now discint, with raiment glittering free,
Shake she the ringing rafters of the skies
With festal footing and bold joyance sweet,
And let the earth be drunken and carouse !
For lo, into her house
Spring is come home with her world-wandering feet,

113

And all things are made young with young desires ;
And all for her is light increased
In yellow stars and yellow daffodils,
And East to West, and West to East,
Fling answering welcome-fires,
By dawn and day-fall, on the jocund hills.
And ye, winged minstrels of her fair meinie,
Being newly coated in glad livery,
Upon her steps attend,
And round her treading dance, and without end
Reel your shrill lutany.
What popular breath her coming does out-tell
The garrulous leaves among !
What little noises stir and pass
From blade to blade along the voluble grass !
O Nature, never-done
Ungaped-at Pentecostal miracle,
We hear thee, each man in his proper tongue !
Break, elemental children, break ye loose
From the strict frosty rule
Of grey-beard Winter's school.
Vault, O young winds, vault in your tricksome courses
Upon the snowy steeds that reinless use
In cœrule pampas of the heaven to run ;
Foaled of the white sea-horses,
Washed in the lambent waters of the sun.
Let even the slug-abed snail upon the thorn
Put forth a conscious horn !
Mine elemental co-mates, joy each one ;
And ah, my foster-brethren, seem not sad—
No, seem not sad,
That my strange heart and I should be so little glad.
Suffer me at your leafy feast
To sit apart, a somewhat alien guest,
And watch your mirth,
Unsharing in the liberal laugh of earth ;
Yet with a sympathy
Begot of wholly sad and half-sweet memory—
The little sweetness making grief complete ;
Faint wind of wings from hours that distant beat,
When I, I too,

Was once, O wild companions, as are you,—
Ran with such wilful feet;
Wraith of a recent day and dead,
Risen wanly overhead,
Frail, strengthless as a noon-belated moon,
Or as the glazing eyes of watery heaven,
When the sick night sinks into deathly swoon.

A higher and a solemn voice
I heard through your gay-hearted noise;
A solemn meaning and a stiller voice
Sounds to me from far days when I too shall rejoice,
Nor more be with your jollity at strife.
O prophecy
Of things that are, and are not, and shall be!
The great-vanned Angel March
Hath trumpeted
His clangorous " Sleep no more " to all the dead—
Beat his strong vans o'er earth, and air, and sea.
And they have heard;
Hark to the *Jubilate* of the bird
For them that found the dying way to life!
And they have heard,
And quicken to the great precursive word;
Green spray showers lightly down the cascade of the
    larch;
The graves are riven,
And the Sun comes with power amid the clouds of
    heaven!
Before his way
Went forth the trumpet of the March;
Before his way, before his way
Dances the pennon of the May!
O Earth, unchilded, widowed Earth, so long
Lifting in patient pine and ivy-tree
Mournful belief and steadfast prophecy,
Behold now all things are made true!
Behold your bridegroom cometh in to you,
Exceeding glad and strong.
Raise up your eyes, O raise your eyes abroad!

No more shall you sit sole and vidual,
Searching, in servile pall,
Upon the hieratic night the star-sealed sense of all :
Rejoice, O barren, and look forth abroad !
Your children gathered back to your embrace
See with a mother's face.
Look up, O mortals, and the portent heed ;
In very deed,
Washed with new fire to their irradiant birth,
Reintegrated are the heavens and earth !
From sky to sod,
The world's unfolded blossom smells of God.

O imagery
Of that which was the first, and is the last !
For, as the dark profound nativity,
God saw the end should be,
When the world's infant horoscope He cast.
Unshackled from the bright Phœbean awe,
In leaf, flower, mold, and tree,
Resolved into dividual liberty,
Most strengthless, unparticipant, inane,
Or suffered the ill peace of lethargy,
Lo, the Earth eased of rule :
Unsummered, granted to her own worst smart
The dear wish of the fool—
Disintegration, merely which man's heart
For freedom understands,
Amid the frog-like errors from the damp
And quaking swamp
Of the low popular levels spawned in all the lands.
But thou, O Earth, dost much disdain
The bondage of thy waste and futile reign,
And sweetly to the great compulsion draw
Of God's alone true-manumitting law,
And Freedom, only which the wise intend,
To work thine innate end.
Over thy vacant counterfeit of death
Broods with soft urgent breath
Love, that is child of Beauty and of Awe :

To intercleavage of sharp warring pain,
As of contending chaos come again,
Thou wak'st, O Earth,
And work'st from change to change and birth to birth
Creation old as hope, and new as sight ;
For meed of toil not vain,
Hearing once more the primal fiat toll :
" Let there be light ! "
And there is light !
Light flagrant, manifest ;
Light to the zenith, light from pole to pole ;
Light from the East that waxeth to the West,
And with its puissant goings-forth
Encroaches on the South and on the North ;
And with its great approaches does prevail
Upon the sullen fastness of the height,
And summoning its levied power
Crescent and confident through the crescent hour,
Goes down with laughters on the subject vale.
Light flagrant, manifest ;
Light to the sentient closeness of the breast,
Light to the secret chambers of the brain !
And thou up-floatest, warm, and newly-bathed,
Earth, through delicious air,
And with thine own apparent beauties swathed,
Wringing the waters from thine arborous hair ;
That all men's hearts, which do behold and see,
Grow weak with their exceeding much desire,
And turn to thee on fire,
Enamoured with their utter wish of thee,
Anadyomene !
What vine-outquickening life all creatures sup,
Feel, for the air within its sapphire cup
How it does leap, and twinkle headily !
Feel, for Earth's bosom pants, and heaves her scarfing sea ;
And round and round in bacchanal rout reel the swift
        spheres intemperably !
My little-worlded self ! the shadows pass
In this thy sister-world, as in a glass,
Of all processions that revolve in thee :
Not only of cyclic Man

Thou here discern'st the plan,
Not only of cyclic Man, but of the cyclic Me.
Not solely of Mortality's great years
The reflex just appears,
But thine own bosom's year, still circling round
In ample and in ampler gyre
Toward the far completion, wherewith crowned,
Love unconsumed shall chant in his own furnace-fire.
How many trampled and deciduous joys
Enrich thy soul for joys deciduous still,
Before the distance shall fulfil
Cyclic unrest with solemn equipoise !
Happiness is the shadow of things past,
Which fools still take for that which is to be !
And not all foolishly :
For all the past, read true, is prophecy,
And all the firsts are hauntings of some Last,
And all the springs are flash-lights of one Spring,
Then leaf, and flower, and fall-less fruit
Shall hang together on the unyellowing bough ;
And silence shall be Music mute
For her surchargéd heart.   Hush thou !
These things are far too sure that thou should'st dream
Thereof, lest they appear as things that seem.

Shade within shade ! for deeper in the glass
Now other imaged meanings pass ;
And as the man, the poet there is read.
Winter with me, alack !
Winter on every hand I find :
Soul, brain, and pulses dead,
The mind no further by the warm sense fed,
The soul weak-stirring in the arid mind,
More tearless-weak to flash itself abroad
Than the earth's life beneath the frost-scorched sod.
My lips have drought, and crack,
By laving music long unvisited.
Beneath the austere and macerating rime
Draws back constricted in its icy urns
The genial flame of Earth, and there

With torment and with tension does prepare
The lush disclosures of the vernal time.
All joys draw inward to their icy urns,
Tormented by constraining rime,
And there,
With undelight and throe prepare
The bounteous efflux of the vernal time.
Nor less beneath compulsive Law
Rebukéd draw
The numbéd musics back upon my heart;
Whose yet-triumphant course I know
And prevalent pulses forth shall start,
    Like cataracts that with thunderous hoof charge the
      disbanding snow.
All power is bound
In quickening refusal so;
And silence is the lair of sound;
In act its impulse to deliver,
With fluctuance and quiver
The endeavouring thew grows rigid.   Strong
From its retracted coil strikes the resilient song.

Giver of spring,
And song, and every young new thing!
Thou only seest in me, so stripped and bare,
The lyric secret waiting to be born,
The patient term allowed
Before it stretch and flutteringly unfold
Its rumpled webs of amethyst-freaked, diaphanous gold.
And what hard task abstracts me from delight,
Filling with hopeless hope and dear despair
The still-born day and parchéd fields of night,
That my old way of song, no longer fair,
For lack of serene care,
Is grown a stony and a weed-choked plot,
Thou only know'st aright,
Thou only know'st, for I know not.
How many songs must die that this may live!
And shall this most rash hope and fugitive,
Fulfilled with beauty and with might
In days whose feet are rumorous on the air,

119

Make me forget to grieve
For songs which might have been, nor ever were ?
Stern the denial, the travail slow,
The struggling wall will scantly grow :
And though with that dread rite of sacrifice
Ordained for during edifice,
How long, how long ago !
Into that wall which will not thrive
I build myself alive,
Ah, who shall tell me will the wall uprise ?
Thou wilt not tell me, who dost only know
Yet still in mind I keep,
He that observes the wind shall hardly sow,
He that regards the clouds shall hardly reap.
Thine ancient way !   I give,
Nor wit if I receive ;
Risk all, who all would gain : and blindly. Be it so.

" And blindly," said I ?—No !
That saying I unsay : the wings
Hear I not in prævenient winnowings
Of coming songs, that lift my hair and stir it ?
What winds with music wet do the sweet storm foreshow !
Utter stagnation
Is the solstitial slumber of the spirit,
The blear and blank negation of all life :
But these sharp questionings mean strife, and strife
Is the negation of negation.
The thing from which I turn my troubled look,
Fearing the gods' rebuke ;
That perturbation putting glory on,
As is the golden vortex in the West
Over the foundered sun ;
That—but low breathe it, lest the Nemesis
Unchild me, vaunting this—
Is bliss, the hid, hugged, swaddled bliss !
O youngling Joy carest !
That on my now first-mothered breast
Pliest the strange wonder of thine infant lip,
What this aghast surprise of keenest panging,
Wherefrom I blench, and cry thy soft mouth rest ?

120

Ah hold, withhold, and let the sweet mouth slip !
So, with such pain, recoils the woolly dam,
Unused, affrighted, from her yeanling lamb :
I, one with her in cruel fellowship,
Marvel what unmaternal thing I am.

Nature, enough ! Within thy glass
Too many and too stern the shadows pass.
In this delighted season, flaming
For thy resurrection-feast,
Ah, more I think the long ensepulture cold,
Than stony winter rolled
From the unsealed mouth of the holy East ;
The snowdrop's saintly stoles less heed
Than the snow-cloistered penance of the seed.
'Tis the weak flesh reclaiming
Against the ordinance
Which yet for just the accepting spirit scans.
Earth waits, and patient heaven,
Self-bonded God doth wait
Thrice-promulgated bans
Of His fair nuptial-date.
And power is man's,
With that great word of " Wait,"
To still the sea of tears,
And shake the iron heart of Fate.
In that one word is strong
An else, alas, much-mortal song ;
With sight to pass the frontier of all spheres,
And voice which does my sight such wrong.

Not without fortitude I wait
The dark majestical ensuit
Of destiny, nor peevish rate
Calm-knowledged Fate.
I, that no part have in the time's bragged way,
And its loud bruit ;
I, in this house so rifted, marred,
So ill to live in, hard to leave ;
I, so star-weary, over-warred,
That have no joy in this your day—

Rather foul fume englutting, that of day
Confounds all ray—
But only stand aside and grieve ;
I yet have sight beyond the smoke,
And kiss the gods' feet, though they wreak
Upon me stroke and again stroke ;
And this my seeing is not weak.
The Woman I behold, whose vision seek
All eyes and know not ; t'ward whom climb
The steps o' the world, and beats all wing of rhyme,
And knows not ; 'twixt the sun and moon
Her inexpressible front enstarred
Tempers the wrangling spheres to tune ;
Their divergent harmonies
Concluded in the concord of her eyes,
And vestal dances of her glad regard.
I see, which fretteth with surmise
Much heads grown unsagacious-grey,
The slow aim of wise-hearted Time,
Which folded cycles within cycles cloak ;
We pass, we pass, we pass ; this does not pass away,
But holds the furrowing earth still harnessed to its yoke.
The stars still write their golden purposes
On heaven's high palimpsest, and no man sees,
Nor any therein Daniel ; I do hear
From the revolving year
A voice which cries :
" All dies ;
Lo, how all dies ! O seer,
And all things too arise :
All dies, and all is born ;   [Morn."
But each resurgent morn, behold, more near the Perfect

Firm is the man, and set beyond the cast
Of Fortune's game, and the iniquitous hour,
Whose falcon soul sits fast,
And not intends her high sagacious tour
Or ere the quarry sighted ; who looks past
To slow much sweet from little instant sour,
And in the first does always see the last.

Francis Thompson.

THE HEART

O NOTHING, in this corporal earth of man,
  That to the imminent heaven of his high soul
Responds with colour and with shadow, can
  Lack correlated greatness. If the scroll
Where thoughts lie fast in spell of hieroglyph
  Be mighty through its mighty habitants ;
If God be in His Name ; grave potence if
  The sounds unbind of hieratic chants ;
All's vast that vastness means. Nay, I affirm
  Nature is whole in her least things exprest,
Nor know we with what scope God builds the worm.
  Our towns are copied fragments from our breast ;
  And all man's Babylons strive but to impart
  The grandeurs of his Babylonian heart.

                                    Francis Thompson.

THE KINGDOM OF GOD

" In no Strange Land "

O WORLD invisible, we view thee,
  O world intangible, we touch thee,
  O world unknowable, we know thee,
Inapprehensible, we clutch thee !

Does the fish soar to find the ocean,
  The eagle plunge to find the air—
That we ask of the stars in motion
  If they have rumour of thee there ?

Not where the wheeling systems darken,
  And our benumbed conceiving soars !—
The drift of pinions, would we hearken,
  Beats at our own clay-shuttered doors.

The angels keep their ancient places ;—
  Turn but a stone, and start a wing !
'Tis ye, 'tis your estrangèd faces,
  That miss the many-splendoured thing.

123

But (when so sad thou canst not sadder)
Cry ;—and upon thy so sore loss
Shall shine the traffic of Jacob's ladder
Pitched betwixt Heaven and Charing Cross.

Yea, in the night, my Soul, my daughter,
Cry,—clinging Heaven by the hems ;
And lo, Christ walking on the water
Not of Gennesareth, but Thames !

Francis Thompson.

SLOW SPRING

O YEAR, grow slowly. Exquisite, holy,
    The days go on
With almonds showing the pink stars blowing,
    And birds in the dawn.

Grow slowly, year, like a child that is dear,
    Or a lamb that is mild,
By little steps, and by little skips,
    Like a lamb or a child.

Katharine Tynan.

EGYPT'S MIGHT IS TUMBLED DOWN

EGYPT'S might is tumbled down
    Down a-down the deeps of thought ;
Greece is fallen and Troy town,
Glorious Rome hath lost her crown,
    Venice' pride is nought.

But the dreams their children dreamed
    Fleeting, unsubstantial, vain,
Shadowy as the shadows seemed,
Airy nothing, as they deemed,
    These remain.

Mary Coleridge.

124

THAT THE NIGHT COME

SHE lived in storm and strife,
Her soul had such desire
For what proud death may bring
That it could not endure
The common good of life,
But lived as 'twere a king
That packed his marriage day
With banneret and pennon,
Trumpet and kettledrum,
And the outrageous cannon,
To bundle time away
That the night come.

W. B. Yeats.

EASTER, 1916

I HAVE met them at close of day
Coming with vivid faces
From counter or desk among grey
Eighteenth-century houses.
I have passed with a nod of the head
Or polite meaningless words,
Or have lingered awhile and said
Polite meaningless words,
And thought before I had done
Of a mocking tale or a gibe
To please a companion
Around the fire at the club,
Being certain that they and I
But lived where motley is worn:
All changed, changed utterly:
A terrible beauty is born.

That woman's days were spent
In ignorant good will,
Her nights in argument
Until her voice grew shrill.
What voice more sweet than hers
When young and beautiful,

125

She rode to harriers ?
This man had kept a school
And rode our wingèd horse ;
This other his helper and friend
Was coming into his force ;
He might have won fame in the end,
So sensitive his nature seemed,
So daring and sweet his thought.
This other man I had dreamed
A drunken, vain-glorious lout.
He had done most bitter wrong
To some who are near my heart,
Yet I number him in the song ;
He, too, has resigned his part
In the casual comedy :
He, too, has been changed in his turn,
Transformed utterly :
A terrible beauty is born.

Hearts with one purpose alone
Through summer and winter seem
Enchanted to a stone
To trouble the living stream.
The horse that comes from the road,
The rider, the birds that range
From cloud to tumbling cloud,
Minute by minute they change ;
A shadow of cloud on the stream
Changes minute by minute ;
A horse-hoof slides on the brim,
And a horse plashes within it
Where long-legged moor-hens dive,
And hens to moor-cocks call.
Minute by minute they live :
The stone's in the midst of all.

Too long a sacrifice
Can make a stone of the heart.
O when may it suffice ?
That is Heaven's part, our part

To murmur name upon name
As a mother names her child
When sleep at last has come
On limbs that had run wild.
What is it but nightfall ?
No, no, not night but death ;
Was it needless death after all ?
For England may keep faith
For all that is done and said.
We know their dream ; enough
To know they dreamed and are dead
And what if excess of love
Bewildered them till they died ?
I write it out in a verse—
MacDonagh and MacBride
And Connolly and Pearse
Now and in time to be,
Wherever green is worn,
Are changed, changed utterly :
A terrible beauty is born.

W. B. Yeats.

SOLOMON AND THE WITCH

A N D thus declared that Arab lady :
" Last night, where under the wild moon
On grassy mattress I had laid me,
Within my arms great Solomon,
I suddenly cried out in a strange tongue
Not his, not mine."
                              And he that knew
All sounds by bird or angel sung
Answered : " A crested cockerel crew
Upon a blossoming apple bough
Three hundred years before the Fall,
And never crew again till now,
And would not now but that he thought,
Chance being at one with Choice at last,
All that the brigand apple brought
And this foul world were dead at last.

He that crowed out eternity
Thought to have crowed it in again.
A lover with a spider's eye
Will find out some appropriate pain,
Aye, though all passion's in the glance,
For every nerve : lover tests lover
With cruelties of Choice and Chance ;
And when at last that murder's over
Maybe the bride-bed brings despair,
For each an imagined image brings
And finds a real image there ;
Yet the world ends when these two things,
Though several, are a single light,
When oil and wick are burned in one ;
Therefore a blessed moon last night
Gave Sheba to her Solomon."

" Yet the world stays " :
                              " If that be so,
Your cockerel found us in the wrong
Although he thought it worth a crow.
Maybe an image is too strong
Or maybe is not strong enough."

" The night has fallen ; not a sound
In the forbidden sacred grove,
Unless a petal hit the ground,
Nor any human sight within it
But the crushed grass where we have lain ;
And the moon is wilder every minute.
Oh, Solomon ! let us try again."

                                   W. B. Yeats.

IN THE POPPY FIELD

MAD Patsy said, he said to me,
That every morning he could see
An angel walking on the sky ;
Across the sunny skies of morn
He threw great handfuls far and nigh
Of poppy seed among the corn ;
And then, he said, the angels run
To see the poppies in the sun.

A poppy is a devil weed,
I said to him—he disagreed ;
He said the devil had no hand
In spreading flowers tall and fair
Through corn and rye and meadow land,
By garth and barrow everywhere :
The devil has not any flower,
But only money in his power.

And then he stretched out in the sun
And rolled upon his back for fun :
He kicked his legs and roared for joy
Because the sun was shining down,
He said he was a little boy
And would not work for any clown :
He ran and laughed behind a bee,
And danced for very ecstasy.

James Stephens.

THE SNARE

I HEAR a sudden cry of pain !
  There is a rabbit in a snare :
Now I hear the cry again,
  But I cannot tell from where.

But I cannot tell from where
  He is calling out for aid ;
Crying on the frightened air,
  Making everything afraid.

Making everything afraid,
  Wrinkling up his little face,
As he cries again for aid ;
  And I cannot find the place !

And I cannot find the place
  Where his paw is in the snare :
Little one ! Oh, little one !
  I am searching everywhere !

James Stephens.

F   129

LEISURE

WHAT is this life if, full of care,
We have no time to stand and stare.

No time to stand beneath the boughs
And stare as long as sheep or cows.

No time to see, when woods we pass,
Where squirrels hide their nuts in grass.

No time to see, in broad daylight,
Streams full of stars, like skies at night.

No time to turn at Beauty's glance,
And watch her feet, how they can dance.

No time to wait till her mouth can
Enrich that smile her eyes began.

A poor life this if, full of care,
We have no time to stand and stare.

W. H. Davies.

THE LIKENESS

WHEN I came forth this morn I saw
    Quite twenty cloudlets in the air ;
And then I saw a flock of sheep,
    Which told me how those clouds came there.

That flock of sheep, on that green grass,
    Well might it lie so still and proud !
Its likeness had been drawn in heaven
    On a blue sky, in silvery cloud.

I gazed me up, I gazed me down,
    And swore, though good the likeness was,
'Twas a long way from justice done
    To such white wool, such sparkling grass.

W. H. Davies.

THE TWO CHILDREN

" A H , little boy ! I see
   You have a wooden spade.
Into this sand you dig
   So deep—for what ? " I said.
" There's more rich gold," said he,
   " Down under where I stand,
Than twenty elephants
   Could move across the land."

" Ah, little girl with wool !—
   What are you making now ? "
" Some stockings for a bird,
   To keep his legs from snow."
And there those children are,
   So happy, small, and proud :
The boy that digs his grave,
   The girl that knits her shroud.

W. H. Davies.

A GREAT TIME

S W E E T Chance, that led my steps abroad,
   Beyond the town, where wild flowers grow—
A rainbow and a cuckoo, Lord,
   How rich and great the times are now !
     Know, all ye sheep
     And cows, that keep
On staring that I stand so long
   In grass that's wet from heavy rain—
A rainbow and a cuckoo's song
   May never come together again ;
     May never come
     This side the tomb.

W. H. Davies.

131

THE BELLS OF HEAVEN

'TWOULD ring the bells of Heaven
The wildest peal for years,
If Parson lost his senses
And people came to theirs,
And he and they together
Knelt down with angry prayers
For tamed and shabby tigers
And dancing dogs and bears,
And wretched, blind pit ponies,
And little hunted hares.

Ralph Hodgson.

TIME, YOU OLD GIPSY MAN

TIME, you old gipsy man,
Will you not stay,
Put up your caravan
Just for one day?

All things I'll give you
Will you be my guest,
Bells for your jennet
Of silver the best,
Goldsmiths shall beat you
A great golden ring,
Peacocks shall bow to you,
Little boys sing,
Oh, and sweet girls will
Festoon you with may,
Time, you old gipsy,
Why hasten away?

Last week in Babylon,
Last night in Rome,
Morning, and in the crush
Under Paul's dome;
Under Paul's dial
You tighten your rein—

Only a moment,
And off once again ;
Off to some city
Now blind in the womb,
Off to another
Ere that's in the tomb.

Time, you old gipsy man,
    Will you not stay,
Put up your caravan
    Just for one day ?

Ralph Hodgson.

¶

REASON has moons, but moons not hers,
    Lie mirror'd on her sea,
Confounding her astronomers,
    But, O ! delighting me.

Ralph Hodgson.

BY A BIER-SIDE

THIS is a sacred city built of marvellous earth.
Life was lived nobly here to give such beauty birth.
Beauty was in this brain and in this eager hand :
Death is so blind and dumb Death does not understand.
Death drifts the brain with dust and soils the young limbs'
    glory,
Death makes justice a dream, and strength a traveller's story.
Death drives the lovely soul to wander under the sky,
Death opens unknown doors. It is most grand to die.

John Masefield.

INVOCATION

O WANDERER into many brains
O spark the emperor's purple hides,
You sow the dusk with fiery grains
When the gold horseman rides.
    O beauty on the darkness hurled,
    Be it through me you shame the world.

John Masefield.

133

TO HIS MOTHER, C.L.M.

I N the dark womb where I began
My mother's life made me a man.
Through all the months of human birth
Her beauty fed my common earth.
I cannot see, nor breathe, nor stir,
But through the death of some of her.

Down in the darkness of the grave
She cannot see the life she gave.
For all her love, she cannot tell
Whether I use it ill or well,
Nor knock at dusty doors to find
Her beauty dusty in the mind.

If the grave's gates could be undone,
She would not know her little son,
I am so grown.   If we should meet,
She would pass by me in the street,
Unless my soul's face let her see
My sense of what she did for me.

What have I done to keep in mind
My debt to her and womankind?
What woman's happier life repays
Her for those months of wretched days?
For all my mouthless body leech'd
Ere Birth's releasing hell was reach'd?

What have I done, or tried, or said
In thanks to that dear woman dead?
Men triumph over women still,
Men trample women's rights at will,
And man's lust roves the world untamed.

          .   .

O grave, keep shut lest I be shamed.

John Masefield.

SONNETS

V

I COULD not sleep for thinking of the sky,
The unending sky, with all its million suns
Which turn their planets everlastingly
In nothing, where the fire-haired comet runs.
If I could sail that nothing, I should cross
Silence and emptiness with dark stars passing ;
Then, in the darkness, see a point of gloss
Burn to a glow, and glare, and keep amassing,
And rage into a sun with wandering planets,
And drop behind ; and then, as I proceed,
See his last light upon his last moon's granites
Die to a dark that would be night indeed :
Night where my soul might sail a million years
In nothing, not even Death, not even tears.

XIV

YOU are too beautiful for mortal eyes,
You the divine unapprehended soul ;
The red worm in the marrow of the wise
Stirs as you pass, but never sees you whole.
Even as the watcher in the midnight tower
Knows from a change in heaven an unseen star,
So from your beauty, so from the summer flower,
So from the light, one guesses what you are.
So in the darkness does the traveller come
To some lit chink, through which he cannot see
More than a light, nor hear, more than a hum,
Of the great hall where Kings in council be.
So, in the grave, the red and mouthless worm
Knows of the soul that held his body firm.

XV

IS it a sea on which the souls embark
Out of the body, as men put to sea ?
Or do we come like candles in the dark
In the rooms in cities in eternity ?

135

Is it a darkness that our powers can light ?
Is this, our little lantern of man's love,
A help to find friends wandering in the night
In the unknown country with no star above ?
Or is it sleep, unknowing, outlasting clocks
That outlast men, that, though the cockcrow ring,
Is but one peace, of the substance of the rocks ;
Is but one space in the now unquickened thing ;
Is but one joy, that, though the million tire,
Is one, always the same, one life, one fire ?

XLIV

O LITTLE self, within whose smallness lies
All that man was, and is, and will become,
Atom unseen that comprehends the skies
And tells the tracks by which the planets roam ;
That, without moving, knows the joys of wings,
The tiger's strength, the eagle's secrecy,
And in the hovel can consort with kings,
Or clothe a God with his own mystery.
O with what darkness do we cloak thy light,
What dusty folly gather thee for food,
Thou who alone art knowledge and delight,
The heavenly bread, the beautiful, the good.
O living self, O God, O morning star,
Give us thy light, forgive us what we are.

LIX

IF Beauty be at all, if, beyond sense,
There be a wisdom piercing into brains,
Why should the glory wait on impotence,
Biding its time till blood is in the veins ?
There is no beauty, but, when thought is quick,
Out of the noisy sickroom of ourselves
Some flattery comes to try to cheat the sick,
Some drowsy drug is groped for on the shelves.
There is no beauty, for we tread a scene
Red to the eye with blood of living things

Thought is but joy from murder that has been,
Life is but brute at war upon its kings.
There is no beauty, nor could beauty care
For us, this dust, that men make everywhere.

John Masefield.

ECCLESIASTES

THERE is one sin : to call a green leaf grey,
    Whereat the sun in heaven shuddereth.
There is one blasphemy : for death to pray,
    For God alone knoweth the praise of death.

There is one creed : 'neath no world-terror's wing
    Apples forget to grow on apple-trees.
There is one thing is needful—everything—
    The rest is vanity of vanities.

G. K. Chesterton.

THE PRAISE OF DUST

" WHAT of vile dust ? " the preacher said.
    Methought the whole world woke,
The dead stone lived beneath my foot,
    And my whole body spoke.

" You, that play tyrant to the dust,
    And stamp its wrinkled face,
This patient star that flings you not
    Far into homeless space,

" Come down out of your dusty shrine
    The living dust to see,
The flowers that at your sermon's end
    Stand blazing silently.

" Rich white and blood-red blossom ; stones,
    Lichens like fire encrust ;
A gleam of blue, a glare of gold,
    The vision of the dust.

F*

137

"Pass them all by : till, as you come
  Where, at a city's edge,
Under a tree—I know it well—
  Under a lattice ledge,

"The sunshine falls on one brown head.
  You, too, O cold of clay,
Eater of stones, may haply hear
  The trumpets of that day

"When God to all his paladins
  By his own splendour swore
To make a fairer face than heaven,
  Of dust and nothing more."

G. K. Chesterton.

WINE AND WATER

OLD Noah he had an ostrich farm and fowls on the
  largest scale,
He ate his egg with a ladle in an egg-cup big as a pail,
And the soup he took was Elephant Soup, and the fish he
  took was Whale,
But they all were small to the cellar he took when he set
  out to sail,
And Noah he often said to his wife when he sat down to dine,
"I don't care where the water goes if it doesn't get into
  the wine."

The cataract of the cliff of heaven fell blinding off the brink
As if it would wash the stars away as suds go down a sink,
The seven heavens came roaring down for the throats of
  hell to drink,
And Noah he cocked his eye and said, "It looks like rain,
  I think,
The water has drowned the Matterhorn as deep as a
  Mendip mine,
But I don't care where the water goes if it doesn't get
  into the wine."

138

But Noah he sinned, and we have sinned; on tipsy feet
  we trod,
Till a great big black teetotaller was sent to us for a rod,
And you can't get wine at a P.S.A., or chapel, or Eisteddfod.
For the Curse of Water has come again because of the
  wrath of God,
And water is on the Bishop's board and the Higher
  Thinker's shrine,
But I don't care where the water goes if it doesn't get into
  the wine.

G. K. Chesterton.

THE DANIEL JAZZ

*Let the leader train the audience to roar like lions, to join in the refrain,
  " Go chain the lions down," before he begins to lead them in this jazz.*

DARIUS the Mede was a king and a wonder.   *Beginning*
His eye was proud, and his voice was thunder.   *with a*
He kept bad lions in a monstrous den.   *strain of*
He fed up the lions on Christian men.   *" Dixie."*

Daniel was the chief hired man of the land.   *With a touch*
He stirred up the jazz in the palace band.   *of*
He whitewashed the cellar. He shovelled in   *"Alexander's*
  the coal.   *Ragtime*
And Daniel kept a-praying : " Lord, save my soul." *Band."*
Daniel kept a-praying : " Lord, save my soul."
Daniel kept a-praying : " Lord, save my soul."

Daniel was the butler, swagger and swell.
He ran upstairs. He answered the bell.
And *he* would let in whoever came a-calling :
Saints so holy, scamps so appalling.
" Old man Ahab leaves his card.
Elisha and the bears are a-waiting in the yard.
Here comes Pharaoh and his snakes a-calling.
Here comes Cain and his wife a-calling.
Shadrach, Meshach and Abednego for tea.
Here comes Jonah and the whale,
And the *Sea !*

Here comes St. Peter and his fishing-pole.
Here comes Judas and his silver a-calling.
Here comes old Beelzebub a-calling."
And Daniel kept a-praying : " Lord, save my soul."
Daniel kept a-praying : " Lord, save my soul."
Daniel kept a-praying : " Lord, save my soul."

His sweetheart and his mother were Christian and meek.
They washed and ironed for Darius every week.
One Thursday he met them at the door :
Paid them as usual, but acted sore.
He said : " Your Daniel is a dead little pigeon.
He's a good hard worker, but he talks religion."
And he showed them Daniel in the lion's cage.
Daniel standing quietly, the lions in a rage.

His good old mother cried :—
" Lord, save him."
And Daniel's tender sweetheart cried :—
" Lord, save him."

And she was a golden lily in the dew.
And she was as sweet as an apple on the tree
And she was as fine as a melon in the corn-field,
Gliding and lovely as a ship on the sea,
Gliding and lovely as a ship on the sea.

And she prayed to the Lord :—
" *Send* Gabriel.   *Send* Gabriel."

King Darius said to the lions :—
" Bite Daniel.   Bite Daniel.
Bite him.   Bite him.   Bite him ! "

Thus roared the lions :—
" We want Daniel, Daniel, Daniel,
We want Daniel, Daniel, Daniel.
Grrrrrrrrrrrrrrrrrrrrrrrrrrrrrrrrrrrrrrrrrrrr   *Here the audience roars*
Grrrrrrrrrrrrrrrrrrrrrrrrrrrrrrrrrrrrrrrrrrrr "   *with the leader.*

And Daniel did not frown,
Daniel did not cry.
He kept on looking at the sky.
And the Lord said to Gabriel :—
" Go chain the lions down,
Go chain the lions down.
Go chain the lions down.
Go chain the lions down."
And *Gabriel* chained the lions,
And *Gabriel* chained the lions,
And *Gabriel* chained the lions,
And Daniel got out of the den,
And Daniel got out of the den,
And Daniel got out of the den.
And Darius said : " You're a Christian child,"
Darius said : " You're a Christian child,"
Darius said : " You're a Christian child,"
And gave him his job again,
And gave him his job again,
And gave him his job again.

The audience sings this with the leader, to the old negro tune.

Nicholas Vachel Lindsay.

HOW SAMSON BORE AWAY THE GATES OF GAZA

(*A Negro Sermon*)

ONCE, in a night as black as ink,
She drove him out when he would not drink.
Round the house there were men in wait
Asleep in rows by the Gaza gate.
But the Holy Spirit was in this man.
Like a gentle wind he crept and ran.
(" It is midnight," said the big town clock.)

He lifted the gates up, post and lock.
The hole in the wall was high and wide
When he bore away old Gaza's pride
Into the deep of the night :—
The bold Jack Johnson Israelite,—
Samson—
The Judge,
The Nazarite.

141

The air was black, like the smoke of a dragon.
Samson's heart was as big as a wagon.
He sang like a shining golden fountain.
He sweated up to the top of the mountain.
He threw down the gates with a noise like judgment.
And the quails all ran with the big arousement.

But he wept—" I must not love tough queens,
And spend on them my hard-earned means.
I told that girl I would drink no more.
Therefore she drove me from her door.
Oh sorrow !
Sorrow !
I cannot hide.
Oh Lord look down from your chariot side.
You make me Judge, and I am not wise.
I am weak as a sheep for all my size."

Let Samson
Be coming
Into your mind.

The moon shone out, the stars were gay.
He saw the foxes run and play.
He rent his garments, he rolled around
In deep repentance on the ground.
Then he felt a honey in his soul
Grace abounding made him whole.
Then he saw the Lord in a chariot blue.
The gorgeous stallions whinnied and flew.
The iron wheels hummed an old hymn-tune
And crunched in thunder over the moon.
And Samson shouted to the sky :
" My Lord, my Lord is riding high."

Like a steed, he pawed the gates with his hoof.
He rattled the gates like rocks on the roof,
And danced in the night
On the mountain top,
Danced in the deep of the night :
The Judge, the holy Nazarite,
Whom ropes and chains could never bind.

Let Samson
Be coming
Into your mind.

Whirling his arms, like a top he sped.
His long black hair flew round his head
Like an outstretched net of silky cord,
Like a wheel of the chariot of the Lord.

Let Samson
Be coming
Into your mind.

Samson saw the sun anew.
He left the gates in the grass and dew.
He went to a county-seat a-nigh.
Found a harlot proud and high :
Philistine that no man could tame—
Delilah was her lady-name.
Oh sorrow,
Sorrow,
She was too wise.
She cut off his hair,
She put out his eyes.

Let Samson
Be coming
Into your mind.

Nicholas Vachel Lindsay.

MENDING WALL

SOMETHING there is that doesn't love a wall,
That sends the frozen-ground-swell under it,
And spills the upper boulders in the sun ;
And makes gaps even two can pass abreast.
The work of hunters is another thing :
I have come after them and made repair

Where they have left not one stone on stone,
But they would have the rabbit out of hiding,
To please the yelping dogs. The gaps I mean,
No one has seen them made or heard them made,
But at spring mending-time we find them there.
I let my neighbour know beyond the hill ;
And on a day we meet to walk the line
And set the wall between us once again.
We keep the wall between us as we go.
To each the boulders that have fallen to each.
And some are loaves and some so nearly balls
We have to use a spell to make them balance :
" Stay where you are until our backs are turned ! "
We wear our fingers rough with handling them.
Oh, just another kind of out-door game,
One on a side. It comes to little more :
There where it is we do not need the wall :
He is all pine and I am apple orchard.
My apple trees will never get across
And eat the cones under his pines, I tell him.
He only says, " Good fences make good neighbours."
Spring is the mischief in me, and I wonder
If I could put a notion in his head :
" Why do they make good neighbours ? Isn't it
Where there are cows ? But here there are no cows.
Before I built a wall I'd ask to know
What I was walling in or walling out,
And to whom I was like to give offence.
Something there is that doesn't love a wall,
That wants it down." I could say " Elves " to him,
But it's not elves exactly, and I'd rather
He said it for himself.   I see him there
Bringing a stone grasped firmly by the top
In each hand, like an old-stone savage armed.
He moves in darkness as it seems to me,
Not of woods only and the shade of trees.
He will not go behind his father's saying,
And he likes having thought of it so well.
He says again, " Good fences make good neighbours."

Robert Frost.

TO A POET A THOUSAND YEARS HENCE

I WHO am dead a thousand years,
    And wrote this sweet archaic song,
Send you my words for messengers
    The way I shall not pass along.

I care not if you bridge the seas,
    Or ride secure the cruel sky,
Or build consummate palaces
    Of metal or of masonry.

But have you wine and music still,
    And statues and a bright-eyed love,
And foolish thoughts of good or ill,
    And prayers to them who sit above?

How shall we conquer? Like a wind
    That falls at eve our fancies blow,
And old Mæonides the blind
    Said it three thousand years ago.

O friend unseen, unborn, unknown,
    Student of our sweet English tongue,
Read out my words at night, alone,
    I was a poet, I was young.

Since I can never see your face,
    And never shake you by the hand,
I send my soul through time and space
    To greet you. You will understand.

                James Elroy Flecker.

THE BALLAD OF HAMPSTEAD HEATH

FROM Heaven's Gate to Hampstead Heath
    Young Bacchus and his crew
Came tumbling down, and o'er the town
    Their bursting trumpets blew.

145

The silver night was wildly bright,
   And madly shone the Moon
To hear a song so clear and strong,
   With such a lovely tune.

From London's houses, huts and flats,
   Came busmen, snobs, and Earls,
And ugly men in bowler hats
   With charming little girls.

Sir Moses came with eyes of flame,
   Judd, who is like a bloater,
The brave Lord Mayor in coach and pair,
   King Edward, in his motor.

Far in a rosy mist withdrawn
   The God and all his crew,
Silenus pulled by nymphs, a faun,
   A satyr drenched in dew,

Smiled as they wept those shining tears
   Only Immortals know,
Whose feet are set among the stars,
   Above the shifting snow.

And one spake out into the night,
   Before they left for ever,
" Rejoice, rejoice ! " and his great voice
   Rolled like a splendid river.

He spake in Greek, which Britons speak
   Seldom, and circumspectly ;
But Mr. Judd, that man of mud,
   Translated it correctly.

And when they heard that happy word,
   Policemen leapt and ambled :
The busmen pranced, the maidens danced,
   The men in bowlers gambolled.

A wistful Echo stayed behind
   To join the mortal dances,
But Mr. Judd, with words unkind,
   Rejected her advances,

146

And passing down through London Town
    She stopped, for all was lonely
Attracted by a big brass plate
    Inscribed, FOR MEMBERS ONLY.

And so she went to Parliament,
    But those ungainly men
Woke up from sleep, and turned about,
    And fell asleep again.

James Elroy Flecker.

THE BIRDS

WITHIN mankind's duration, so they say,
Khephren and Ninus lived but yesterday.
Asia had no name till man was old
And long had learned the use of iron and gold ;
And æons had passed, when the first corn was planted,
Since first the use of syllables was granted.

Men were on earth while climates slowly swung,
Fanning wide zones to heat and cold, and long
Subsidence turned great continents to sea,
And seas dried up, dried up interminably,
Age after age ; enormous seas were dried
Amid wastes of land.   And the last monsters died.

Earth wore another face.   O since that prime
Man with how many works has sprinkled time !
Hammering, hewing, digging tunnels, roads ;
Building ships, temples, multiform abodes.
How for his body's appetites, his toils
Have conquered all earth's products, all her soils ;
And in what thousand thousand shapes of art
He has tried to find a language for his heart !

Never at rest, never content or tired :
Insatiate wanderer, marvellously fired,
Most grandly piling and piling into the air
Stones that will topple or arch he knows not where.

147

And yet did I, this spring, think it more strange,
More grand, more full of awe, than all that change,
And lovely and sweet and touching unto tears,
That through man's chronicled and unchronicled years,
And even into that unguessable beyond,
The water-hen has nested by a pond,
Weaving dry flags, into a beaten floor,
The one sure product of her only lore.
Low on a ledge above the shadowed water
Then, when she heard no men, as Nature taught her,
Plashing around with busy scarlet bill
She built that nest, her nest, and builds it still.

O let your strong imagination turn
The great wheel backward, until Troy unburn,
And then unbuild, and seven Troys below
Rise out of death, and dwindle, and outflow,
Till all have passed, and none has yet been there :
Back, ever back.   Our birds still crossed the air ;
Beyond our myriad changing generations
Still built, unchanged, their known inhabitations.
A million years before Atlantis was
Our lark sprang from some hollow in the grass,
Some old soft hoof-print in a tussock's shade ;
And the wood-pigeon's smooth snow-white eggs were
    laid
High, amid green pines' sunset-coloured shafts,
And rooks their villages of twiggy rafts
Set on the tops of elms, where elms grew then,
And still the thumbling tit and perky wren
Popped through the tiny doors of cosy balls
And the blackbird lined with moss his high-built walls.
A round mud cottage held the thrush's young,
And straws from the untidy sparrow's hung.
And, skimming forktailed in the evening air,
When man first was were not the martens there ?
Did not those birds some human shelter crave,
And stow beneath the cornice of his cave
Their dry tight cups of clay ?   And from each door
Peeped on a morning wiseheads three or four.

Yes, daw and owl, curlew and crested hern,
Kingfisher, mallard, water-rail and tern,
Chaffinch and greenfinch, warbler, stonechat, ruff,
Pied wagtail, robin, fly-catcher and chough,
Missel-thrush, magpie, sparrow-hawk, and jay,
Built, those far ages gone, in this year's way.
And the first man who walked the cliffs of Rame,
As I this year, looked down and saw the same
Blotches of rusty red on ledge and cleft
With grey-green spots on them, while right and left
A dizzying tangle of gulls were floating and flying,
Wheeling and crossing and darting, crying and crying,
Circling and crying, over and over and over,
Crying with swoop and hover and fall and recover.
And below on a rock against the grey sea fretted,
Pipe-necked and stationary and silhouetted,
Cormorants stood in a wise, black, equal row
Above the nests and long blue eggs we know.

O delicate chain over all ages stretched,
O dumb tradition from what far darkness fetched :
Each little architect with its one design
Perpetual, fixed and right in stuff and line,
Each little ministrant who knows one thing,
One learned rite to celebrate the spring.
Whatever alters else on sea or shore,
These are unchanging : man must still explore.

J. C. Squire.

MORTALITY

I N the green quiet wood, where I was used,
   In summer, to a welcome calm and dark,
I found the threat of murder introduced
   By scars of white paint on the wrinkled bark.

How few old friends were to be spared ! And now
   I see my friends with new eyes here in town
—Men as trees walking, and on every brow
   A pallid scar, and all to be cut down.

Gerald Gould.

149

THE COUNTRY BEDROOM

MY room's a square and candle-lighted boat,
In the surrounding depths of night afloat.
My windows are the portholes, and the seas
The sound of rain on the dark apple-trees.

Sea monster-like beneath, an old horse blows
A snort of darkness from his sleeping nose,
Below, among drowned daisies.   Far off, hark !
Far off one owl amidst the waves of dark.

Frances Cornford.

EVERYONE SANG

EVERYONE suddenly burst out singing ;
And I was filled with such delight
As prisoned birds must find in freedom
Winging wildly across the white
Orchards and dark green fields ; on ; on ; and out
    of sight.

Everyone's voice was suddenly lifted,
And beauty came like the setting sun.
My heart was shaken with tears and horror
Drifted away . . . O but every one
Was a bird ; and the song was wordless ; the
    singing will never be done.

Siegfried Sassoon.

LOST IN FRANCE

HE had the plowman's strength
In the grasp of his hand.
He could see a crow
Three miles away,
And the trout beneath the stone.
He could hear the green oats growing,
And the sou'-west making rain ;
And the wheel upon the hill

When it left the level road.
He could make a gate, and dig a pit
And plow as straight as stone can fa
And he is dead.

THE HILL

BREATHLESS, we flung us on the windy hill,
Laughed in the sun, and kissed the lovely grass.
You said, " Through glory and ecstasy we pass ;
Wind, sun, and earth remain, the birds sing still,
When we are old, are old. . . ." " And when we die
All's over that is ours ; and life burns on
Through other lovers, other lips," said I,
" Heart of my heart, our heaven is now, is won ! "

" We are Earth's best, that learnt her lesson here.
Life is our cry. We have kept the faith ! " we said ;
" We shall go down with unreluctant tread
Rose-crowned into the darkness ! " . . . Proud we were,
And laughed, that had such brave true things to say.
—And then you suddenly cried, and turned away.

Rupert Brooke.

THE BUSY HEART

NOW that we've done our best and worst, and parted,
I would fill my mind with thoughts that will not rend.
(O heart, I do not dare go empty-hearted)
I'll think of Love in books, Love without end ;
Women with child, content ; and old men sleeping ;
And wet strong ploughlands, scarred for certain grain ;
And babes that weep, and so forget their weeping ;
And the young heavens, forgetful after rain ;
And evening hush, broken by homing wings ;
And Song's nobility, and Wisdom holy,
That live, we dead. I would think of a thousand things,
Lovely and durable, and taste them slowly,
One after one, like tasting a sweet food.
I have need to busy my heart with quietude.

Rupert Brooke.

THE DEAD

THESE hearts were woven of human joys and cares,
    Washed marvellously with sorrow, swift to mirth.
The years had given them kindness. Dawn was theirs,
    And sunset, and the colours of the earth.
These had seen movement, and heard music ; known
    Slumber and waking ; loved ; gone proudly friended ;
Felt the quick stir of wonder ; sat alone ;
    Touched flowers and furs and cheeks. All this is ended.

There are waters blown by changing winds to laughter
And lit by the rich skies, all day. And after,
    Frost, with a gesture, stays the waves that dance
And wandering loveliness. He leaves a white
    Unbroken glory, a gathered radiance,
A width, a shining peace, under the night.

Rupert Brooke.

TALKING WITH SOLDIERS

THE mind of the people is like mud,
    From which arise strange and beautiful things,
But mud is none the less mud,
    Though it bear orchids and prophesying Kings,
Dreams, trees, and water's bright babblings.

It has found form and colour and light,
    The cold glimmer of the ice-wrapped Poles ;
It has called a far-off glow Arcturus,
    And some pale weeds, lilies of the valley.

It has imagined Virgil, Helen and Cassandra ;
    The sack of Troy, and the weeping for Hector—
Rearing stark up 'mid all this beauty
    In the thick, dull neck of Ajax.

There is a dark Pine in Lapland,
    And the great, figured Horn of the Reindeer
Moving soundlessly across the snow,
    Is its twin brother, double-dreamed,
    In the mind of a far-off people.

It is strange that a little mud
Should echo with sounds, syllables, and letters,
Should rise up and call a mountain Popocatepetl,
And a green-leafed wood Oleander.

These are the ghosts of invisible things ;
There is no Lapland, no Helen and no Hector,
And the Reindeer is a darkening of the brain,
And Oleander is but Oleander.

Mary Magdalena and the vine Lachryma Christi,
Were like ghosts up the ghost of Vesuvius,
As I sat and drank wine with the soldiers,
As I sat in the Inn on the mountain,
Watching the shadows in my mind.

The mind of the people is like mud :
Where are the imperishable things,
The ghosts that flicker in the brain—
Silent women, orchids, and prophesying Kings,
Dreams, trees, and water's bright babblings !

W. J. Turner.

FIFTH PHILOSOPHER'S SONG

A MILLION million spermatozoa,
  All of them alive :
Out of their cataclysm but one poor Noah
  Dare hope to survive.

And among that billion minus one
  Might have chanced to be
Shakespeare, another Newton, a new Donne—
  But the One was Me.

Shame to have ousted your betters thus,
  Taking ark while the others remained outside !
Better for all of us, froward Homunculus,
  If you'd quietly died !

Aldous Huxley.

153

LOST LOVE

HIS eyes are quickened so with grief,
He can watch a grass or leaf
Every instant grow; he can
Clearly through a flint wall see,
Or watch the startled spirit flee
From the throat of a dead man:
Across two counties he can hear,
And catch your words before you speak,
The woodlouse or the maggot's weak
   Clamour rings in his sad ear;
And noise so slight it would surpass
Credence:—drinking sound of grass,
Worm talk, clashing jaws of moth
Chumbling holes in cloth:
The groan of ants who undertake
Gigantic loads for honour's sake,
Their sinews creak, their breath comes thin:
Whir of spiders when they spin,
And minute whispering, mumbling, sighs
Of idle grubs and flies.
This man is quickened so with grief,
He wanders god-like or like thief
Inside and out, below, above,
Without relief seeking lost love.

Robert Graves.

ILIAD

FALSE dreams, all false,
mad heart, were yours.
The word, and nought else,
in time endures.
Not you long after,
perished and mute,
will last, but the defter
viol and lute.
Sweetly they'll trouble

the listeners
with the cold dropped pebble
of painless verse.
Not you will be offered,
but the poet's false pain.
Mad heart, you have suffered,
and loved in vain.
What joy doth Helen
or Paris have
where these lie still in
a nameless grave ?
Her beauty's a wraith,
and the boy Paris
muffles in death
his mouth's cold cherries.
Aye ! these are less,
that were love's summer,
than one gold phrase
of old blind Homer !
Not Helen's wonder
nor Paris stirs,
but the bright untender
hexameters.
And thus, all passion
is nothing made,
but a star to flash in
an Iliad.
Mad heart, you were wrong !
No love of yours,
but only what is sung,
when love's over, endures.

Humbert Wolfe.

THE FIDDLE AND THE BOW

THIS is what the fiddle said to the bow :
    " No ! oh no !
You should have warned me before the touch
of music, that it hurt too much.

You should have warned me, you should have told me,
before you let the music hold me,
how this poor world were fain to melt
into the beauty it has felt.

How for one breathless note it trembles
almost on the edge of flame, then tumbles,
wounded with the sense of mortal things,
down down down down with broken wings.

It was not right to wound and wake me.
Give me my silence back, or take me
wholly, and never let me go."
This is what the fiddle said to the bow.

But the bow said, " How shall I guess
what bids me answer ' Yes, oh yes ! '
Since a greater thing than we are thus
for its blind purpose useth us ?

We did not choose our way of making,
not sleeping ours to choose, nor waking,
not ours the starry stroke of sound
to choose or fly, though ours the wound.

Though dead wood cry, ' How shall I dare it ? '
and wood reply, ' I cannot bear it,'
Yet his alone to choose, whose fingers
take the dead wood, and makes his singers.

And if of dust he shapes this brittle
life of the wings, this song's one petal
that shines and dies, is it not just
to suffer for song, oh singing dust ?

His was the choice, and if he wake us
out of the wood, but will not slake us,
thus stirred with the stars, at least we know
what pain the Stars have," says the bow.

Humbert Wolfe.

IN MEMORIAM D.O.M.

CHESTNUT candles are lit again
For the dead that died in spring :
Dead lovers walk the orchard ways,
And the dead cuckoos sing.

Is it they who live and we who are dead ?
Hardly the springtime knows
For which to-day the cuckoo calls,
And the white blossom blows.

Listen and hear the happy wind
Whisper and lightly pass :
Your love is sweet as hawthorn is,
Your hope green as the grass.

The hawthorn's faint and quickly gone,
The grass in autumn dies ;
Put by your life, and see the spring
With everlasting eyes.

William Kerr.

THE SEED SHOP

HERE in a quiet and dusty room they lie,
Faded as crumbled stone or shifting sand,
Forlorn as ashes, shrivelled, scentless, dry—
Meadows and gardens running through my hand.

In this brown husk a dale of hawthorn dreams,
A cedar in this narrow cell is thrust,
That will drink deeply of a century's streams,
These lilies shall make summer on my dust.

Here in their safe and simple house of death,
Sealed in their shells a million roses leap ;
Here I can blow a garden with my breath,
And in my hand a forest lies asleep.

Muriel Stuart.

157

THE LITTLE GHOST WHO DIED
FOR LOVE

Deborah Churchill, born 1678, was hanged 1708 for shielding her lover
after a duel in which he killed his opponent and then fled to Holland.
According to the law at the time she was hanged in his stead. It is
recorded that: " Though she died at peace with God, this malefactor
could never understand the justice of her sentence, to the last moment
of her life."

" FEAR not, O maidens, shivering
As bunches of the dew-drenched leaves
In the calm moonlight . . . it is the cold sends quivering
My voice, a little nightingale that grieves.

Now Time beats not, and dead Love is forgotten . . .
The spirit too is dead and dank and rotten,

And I forget the moment when I ran
Between my lover and the sworded man—
Blinded with terror lest I lose his heart.
The sworded man dropped, and I saw depart

Love and my lover and my life . . . he fled
And I was strung and hung upon the tree.
It is so cold now that my heart is dead
And drops through time . . . night is too dark to see

Him still. . . . But it is spring ; upon the fruit-boughs of
        your lips,
Young maids, the dew like India's splendour drips.
Pass by among the strawberry beds, and pluck the berries
Cooled by the silver moon ; pluck boughs of cherries
That seem the lovely lucent coral bough
(From streams of starry milk those branches grow)
That Cassiopeia feeds with her faint light,
Like Ethiopia ever jewelled bright.

Those lovely cherries do enclose
Deep in their hearts the silver snows,

And the small budding flowers upon the trees
Are filled with sweetness like the bags of bees.

Forget my fate . . . but I, a moonlight ghost,
Creep down the strawberry paths and seek the lost

World, the apothecary at the Fair.
I, Deborah, in my long cloak of brown
Like the small nightingale that dances down
The cherried boughs, creep to the doctor's bare
Booth . . . cold as ivy in the air,
And, where I stand, the brown and ragged light
Holds something still beyond, hid from my sight.

Once, plumaged like the sea, his swanskin head
Had wintry white quills. . . . ' Hearken to the Dead. . . .
I was a nightingale, but now I croak
Like some dark harpy hidden in night's cloak,
Upon the walls ; among the Dead, am quick.
Oh, give me medicine, for the world is sick ;
Not medicines planet-spotted like fritillaries
For country sins and old stupidities,
Nor potions you may give a country maid
When she is lovesick . . . love in earth is laid,
Grown dead and rotten ' . . . so I sank me down,
Poor Deborah in my long cloak of brown.

Though cockcrow marches crying of false dawns
Shall bury my dark voice, yet still it mourns
Among the ruins,—for it is not I
But this old world, is sick and soon must die ! "

Edith Sitwell.

PASSER MORTUUS EST

DEATH devours all lovely things ;
Lesbia with her sparrow
Shares the darkness,—presently
   Every bed is narrow.

Unremembered as old rain
   Dries the sheer libation,
And the little petulant hand
   Is an annotation.

After all, my erstwhile dear,
   My no longer cherished,
Need we say it was not love,
   Now that love is perished ?

Edna St. Vincent Millay.

159

RENASCENCE

ALL I could see from where I stood
Was three long mountains and a wood;
I turned and looked another way,
And saw three islands in a bay.
So with my eyes I traced the line
Of the horizon, thin and fine,
Straight around till I was come
Back to where I'd started from.
And all I saw from where I stood
Was three long mountains and a wood.
Over these things I could not see:
These were the things that bounded me;
And I could touch them with my hand,
Almost, I thought, from where I stand.
And all at once things seemed so small
My breath came short, and scarce at all.
But, sure, the sky is big, I said;
Miles and miles above my head;
So here upon my back I'll lie
And look my fill into the sky.
And so I looked, and, after all,
The sky was not so very tall.
The sky, I said, must somewhere stop,
And—sure enough!—I see the top!
The sky, I thought, is not so grand;
I 'most could touch it with my hand!
And reaching up my hand to try,
I screamed to feel it touch the sky.

I screamed, and—lo!—Infinity
Came down and settled over me;
Forced back my scream into my chest,
Bent back my arm upon my breast,
And, pressing of the Undefined
The definition on my mind,
Held up before my eyes a glass
Through which my shrinking sight did pass
Until it seemed I must behold
Immensity made manifold;

Whispered to me a word whose sound
Deafened the air for worlds around,
And brought unmuffled to my ears
The gossiping of friendly spheres,
The creaking of the tented sky,
The ticking of Eternity.
I saw and heard and knew at last
The How and Why of all things, past,
And present, and for evermore.
The Universe, cleft to the core,
Lay open to my probing sense
That, sick'ning, I would fain pluck thence
But could not,—nay ! But needs must suck
At the great wound, and could not pluck
My lips away till I had drawn
All venom out.—Ah, fearful pawn !
For my omniscience paid I toll
In infinite remorse of soul.
All sin was of my sinning, all
Atoning mine, and mine the gall
Of all regret. Mine was the weight
Of every brooded wrong, the hate
That stood behind each envious thrust,
Mine every greed, mine every lust.
And all the while for every grief,
Each suffering, I craved relief
With individual desire,—
Craved all in vain ! And felt fierce fire
About a thousand people crawl ;
Perished with each,—then mourned for all !
A man was starving in Capri ;
He moved his eyes and looked at me ;
I felt his gaze, I heard his moan,
And knew his hunger as my own.
I saw at sea a great fog bank
Between two ships that struck and sank ;
A thousand screams the heavens smote ;
And every scream tore through my throat.
No hurt I did not feel, no death
That was not mine ; mine each last breath
That, crying, met an answering cry

G

From the compassion that was I.
All suffering mine, and mine its rod ;
Mine, pity like the pity of God.
Ah, awful weight !   Infinity
Pressed down upon the finite Me !
My anguished spirit, like a bird,
Beating against my lips I heard ;
Yet lay the weight so close about
There was no room for it without.
And so beneath the weight lay I
And suffered death, but could not die.

Long had I lain thus, craving death,
When quietly the earth beneath
Gave way, and inch by inch, so great
At last had grown the crushing weight,
Into the earth I sank till I
Full six feet under ground did lie,
And sank no more,—there is no weight
Can follow here, however great.
From off my breast I felt it roll,
And as it went my tortured soul
Burst forth and fled in such a gust
That all about me swirled the dust.
Deep in the earth I rested now ;
Cool is its hand upon the brow
And soft its breast beneath the head
Of one who is so gladly dead.
And all at once, and over all
The pitying rain began to fall ;
I lay and heard each pattering hoof
Upon my lowly, thatchèd roof,
And seemed to love the sound far more
Than ever I had done before.
For rain it hath a friendly sound
To one who's six feet under ground ;
And scarce the friendly voice or face :
A grave is such a quiet place.

The rain, I said, is kind to come
And speak to me in my new home.

I would I were alive again
To kiss the fingers of the rain,
To drink into my eyes the shine
Of every slanting silver line,
To catch the freshened, fragrant breeze
From drenched and dripping apple-trees.
For soon the shower will be done,
And then the broad face of the sun
Will laugh above the rain-soaked earth
Until the world with answering mirth
Shakes joyously, and each round drop
Rolls, twinkling, from its grass-blade top
How can I bear it, buried here,
While overhead the sky grows clear
And blue again after the storm?
O, multi-coloured, multiform,
Beloved beauty over me,
That I shall never, never see
Again! Spring-silver, autumn-gold,
That I shall never more behold!
Sleeping your myriad magics through,
Close-sepulchred away from you!
O God, I cried, give me new birth,
And put me back upon the earth!
Upset each cloud's gigantic gourd
And let the heavy rain, downpoured
In one big torrent, set me free,
Washing my grave away from me!

I ceased: and through the breathless hush
That answered me, the far-off rush
Of herald wings came whispering
Like music down the vibrant string
Of my ascending prayer, and—crash!
Before the wild wind's whistling lash
The startled storm-clouds reared on high
And plunged in terror down the sky,
And the big rain in one black wave
Fell from the sky and struck my grave.
I know not how such things can be;
I only know there came to me

A fragrance such as never clings
To aught save happy living things
A sound as of some joyous elf
Singing sweet songs to please himself,
And, through and over everything,
A sense of glad awakening.
The grass, a-tiptoe at my ear,
Whispering to me I could hear ;
I felt the rain's cool finger-tips
Brushed tenderly across my lips,
Laid gently on my sealèd sight,
And all at once the heavy night
Fell from my eyes and I could see,—
A drenched and dripping apple-tree,
A last long line of silver rain,
A sky grown clear and blue again.
And as I looked a quickening gust
Of wind blew up to me and thrust
Into my face a miracle
Of orchard-breath, and with the smell,—
I know not how such things can be !—
I breathed my soul back into me.

Ah ! Up then from the ground sprang I
And hailed the earth with such a cry
As is not heard save from a man
Who has been dead, and lives again.
About the trees my arms I wound ;
Like one gone mad I hugged the ground ;
I raised my quivering arms on high ;
I laughed and laughed into the sky,
Till at my throat a strangling sob
Caught fiercely, and a great heart-throb
Sent instant tears into my eyes ;
O God, I cried, no dark disguise
Can e'er hereafter hide from me
Thy radiant identity !
Thou canst not move across the grass
But my quick eyes will see Thee pass,
Nor speak, however silently,
But my hushed voice will answer Thee

I know the path that tells Thy way
Through the cool eve of every day ;
God, I can push the grass apart
And lay my finger on Thy heart !

The world stands out on either side
No wider than the heart is wide ;
Above the world is stretched the sky,—
No higher than the soul is high.
The heart can push the sea and land
Farther away on either hand ;
The soul can split the sky in two,
And let the face of God shine through.
But East and West will pinch the heart
That cannot keep them pushed apart ;
And he whose soul is flat—the sky
Will cave in on him by and by.

Edna St. Vincent Millay.

HATE POEMS

UP, LORD, DISAPPOINT HIM AND CAST

HIM DOWN

PS. XVII

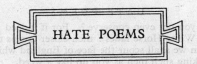

HATE POEMS

TO A FAT LADY SEEN FROM THE TRAIN

O W H Y do you walk through the fields in gloves,
    Missing so much and so much ?
O fat white woman whom nobody loves,
Why do you walk through the fields in gloves,
When the grass is soft as the breast of doves
    And shivering-sweet to the touch ?
O why do you walk through the fields in gloves,
    Missing so much and so much ?

Frances Cornford.

WISHES OF AN ELDERLY MAN

(WISHED AT A GARDEN-PARTY, JUNE, 1914)

I W I S H I loved the Human Race ;
I wish I loved its silly face ;
I wish I liked the way it walks ;
I wish I liked the way it talks ;
And when I'm introduced to one
I wish I thought *What Jolly Fun !*

Walter Raleigh.

TO A LANDLORD

*Accused of neglecting one of the White Horses connected
with Alfred the Great.*

I F you have picked your lawn of leaves and snails,
If you have told your valet, even with oaths,
Once a week or so, to brush your clothes,
If you have dared to clean your teeth, or nails,
While the Horse upon the holy mountain fails—
Then God that Alfred to his earth betrothes
Send on you screaming all that honour loathes,
Horsewhipping, Hounsditch, debts, and *Daily Mails.*

G *

169

Can you not even conserve ?   For if indeed
The White Horse fades : then closer creeps the fight
When we shall scour the face of England white,
Plucking such men as you up like a weed,
And fling them far beyond a shaft shot right
When Wessex went to battle for the creed.

G. K. Chesterton.

ON ROBERT DUDLEY, EARL OF LEICESTER

HERE lieth the worthy warrior
Who never blooded sword ;
Here lieth the noble councillor,
Who never held his word ;
Here lieth his excellency,
Who ruled all the state ;
Here lieth the Earl of Leicester
Whom all the world did hate.

Anon., 1588.

ON GEORGE III

IN the first year of freedom's second dawn
    Died George the Third ; although no tyrant, one
Who shielded tyrants, till each sense withdrawn
    Left him nor mental nor external sun :
A better farmer ne'er brush'd dew from lawn,
    A worse King never left a realm undone !
He died—but left his subjects still behind,
One half as mad—and t'other no less blind.

    .   .   .   .   .   .

" God save the King ! "   It is a large economy
    In God to save the like ; but if He will
Be saving, all the better ; for not one am I
    Of those who think damnation better still.

    .   .   .   .   .   .

He ever warred with freedom and the free :
    Nations as men, home subjects, foreign foes,
So that they uttered the word " Liberty ! ",
    Found George the Third their first opponent. Whose

History was ever stain'd as his will be
  With national and individual woes ?
I grant his household abstinence, I grant
His neutral virtues, which most monarchs want ;
I know he was a constant consort ; own
  He was a decent sire and middling lord,
All this is much, and most upon a throne ;
  His temperance, if at Apicius' board,
Is more than at an anchorite's supper shown.
  I grant him all the kindest can accord :
And this was well for him, but not for those
Millions who found him what oppression chose.

Byron (A Vision of Judgement).

TO SIDMOUTH AND CASTLEREAGH

  A S from an ancestral oak
  Two empty ravens sound their clarion,
  Yell by yell, and croak by croak,
  When they scent the noonday smoke
  Of fresh human carrion :

  As two gibbering night-birds flit
  From their bowers of deadly yew
  Through the night to frighten it,
  When the moon is in a fit,
  And the stars are none or few :

  As a shark and dog-fish wait
  Under an Atlantic isle,
  For the negro-ship, whose freight
  Is the theme of their debate,
  Wrinkling their red gills the while—

  Are ye, two vultures sick for battle,
  Two scorpions under one wet stone,
  Two bloodless wolves, whose dry throats rattle,
  Two crows perched on the murrained cattle,
  Two vipers tangled into one.

P. B. Shelley.

ODE

To a Pig while His Nose was being bored.

HARK! hark! that Pig—that Pig! the hideous note,
　More loud, more dissonant, each moment grows—
Would one not think the knife was in his throat?
　And yet they are only boring through his nose.

Pig! 'tis your master's pleasure—then be still,
　And hold your nose to let the iron through!
Dare you resist your lawful Sovereign's will?
　Rebellious Swine! you know not what you do

To man o'er beast the power was given;
　Pig, hear the truth, and never murmur more!
Would you rebel against the will of Heaven?
　You impious beast, be still, and let them bore!

The social Pig resigns his natural rights
　When first with man he covenants to live;
He barters them for safer stye delights,
　For grains and wash, which man alone can give.

Sure is provision on the social plan,
　Secure the comforts that to each belong!
Oh, happy Swine! the impartial sway of man
　Alike protects the weak Pig and the strong.

And you resist! you struggle now because
　Your master has thought fit to bore your nose!
You grunt in flat rebellion to the laws
　Society finds needful to impose!

Go to the forest, Piggy, and deplore
　The miserable lot of savage Swine!
See how young Pigs fly from the great Boar,
　And see how coarse and scantily they dine!

Behold their hourly danger, when who will
　May hunt or snare or seize them for his food!
Oh, happy Pig! whom none presumes to kill
　Till your protecting master thinks it good!

And when, at last, the closing hour of life
   Arrives (for Pigs must die as well as Man),
When in your throat you feel the long sharp knife,
   And the blood trickles to the pudding-pan ;

And when, at last, the death wound yawning wide,
   Fainter and fainter grows the expiring cry,
Is there no grateful joy, no loyal pride,
   To think that for your master's good you die ?
                         Robert Southey.

BALLADE D'UNE GRANDE DAME

HEAVEN shall forgive you Bridge at dawn,
The clothes you wear—or do not wear—
And Ladies' Leap-frog on the lawn
And dyes and drugs, and *petits verres*.
Your vicious things shall melt in air . . .
. . . But for the Virtuous Things you do,
The Righteous Work, the Public Care,
It shall not be forgiven you.

Because you could not even yawn
When your Committees would prepare
To have the teeth of paupers drawn,
Or strip the slums of Human Hair ;
Because a Doctor Otto Maehr
Spoke of " a segregated few "—
And you sat smiling in your chair—
It shall not be forgiven you.

Though your sins cried to—Father Vaughan,
These desperate you could not spare
Who steal, with nothing left to pawn ;
You caged a man up like a bear
For ever in a jailor's care
Because his sins were more than *two* . . .
. . . I know a house in Hoxton where
It shall not be forgiven you.

HATE POEMS

Princess, you trapped a guileless Mayor
To meet some people that you knew. . . .
When the Last Trumpet rends the air
It shall not be forgiven you.

G. K. Chesterton.

AT THE HOUSE OF MRS. KINFOOT

A T the house of Mrs. Kinfoot
Are collected
Men and women
Of all ages.
They are supposed
To sing, paint, or to play the piano.
In the drawing-room
The fireplace is set
With green tiles
Of an acanthus pattern.
The black curls of Mrs. Kinfoot
Are symmetrical.
—Descended, it is said,
From the Kings of Ethiopia—
But the British bourgeoisie has triumphed.

Mr. Kinfoot is bald
And talks
In front of the fireplace
With his head on one side,
And his right hand
In his pocket.
The joy of catching tame elephants,
And finding them to be white ones,
Still gleams from the jungle-eyes
Of Mrs. Kinfoot,
But her mind is no jungle
Of Ethiopia,
But a sound British meadow.

174

HATE POEMS

Listen then to the gospel of Mrs. Kinfoot :

The world was made for the British bourgeoisie,
They are its Swiss Family Robinson ;
The world is not what it was.
We cannot understand all this unrest !

Adam and Eve were born to evening dress
In the southern confines
Of Belgravia.
Eve was very artistic, and all that,
And felt the fall
Quite dreadfully.
Cain was such a man of the world
And belonged to every club in London ;
His father simply adored him,
—But had never really liked Abel,
Who was rather a milk-sop.
Nothing exists which the British bourgeoisie
Does not understand ;
Therefore there is no death
—And, of course, no life.

The British bourgeoisie
Is not born,
And does not die,
But, if it is ill,
It has a frightened look in its eyes.

The War was splendid, wasn't it ?
Oh yes, splendid, splendid.

Mrs. Kinfoot is a dear,
And so artistic.

Osbert Sitwell.

" BLIGHTERS "

THE House is crammed : tier beyond tier they grin
And cackle at the Show, while prancing ranks
Of harlots shrill the chorus, drunk with din ;
" We're sure the Kaiser loves the dear old Tanks ! "

175

I'd like to see a Tank come down the Stalls,
Lurching to rag-time tunes, or " Home, sweet Home,"—
And there'd be no more jokes in Music-Halls
To mock the riddled corpses round Bapaume.

Siegfried Sassoon.

BASE DETAILS

IF I were fierce, and bald, and short of breath,
    I'd live with scarlet Majors at the Base,
And speed glum heroes up the line to death.
    You'd see me with my puffy petulant face,
Guzzling and gulping in the best hotel,
    Reading the Roll of Honour. " Poor young chap,"
I'd say—" I used to know his father well ;
    Yes, we've lost heavily in this last scrap."
And when the war is done and youth stone dead,
I'd toddle safely home and die—in bed.

Siegfried Sassoon.

ON A POET LAUREATE

HE had written praises of a regicide ;
    He had written praises of all kings whatever ;
He had written for republics far and wide,
    And then against them bitterer than ever ;
For pantisocracy he once had cried
    Aloud—a scheme less moral than 'twas clever ;
Then grew a hearty anti-Jacobin—
Had turn'd his coat—and would have turn'd his skin.

He had sung against all battles, and again
    In their high praise and glory : he had call'd
Reviewing " the ungentle craft," and then
    Become as base a critic as e'er crawl'd—
Fed, paid and pamper'd by the very men
    By whom his muse and morals had been maul'd :
He had written much blank verse, and blanker prose,
And more of both than anybody knows.

Byron (The Vision of Judgement).

ON THE DUKE OF BUCKINGHAM

A MAN so various that he seemed to be
Not one, but all mankind's epitome.
Stiff in opinions, always in the wrong ;
Was everything by starts, and nothing long ;
But, in the course of one revolving moon,
Was chemist, fiddler, statesman and buffoon :
Then all for women, painting, rhyming, drinking :
Besides ten thousand freaks that died in thinking.
Blest madman, who could every hour employ,
With something new to wish, or to enjoy !
Railing and praising were his usual themes ;
And both (to show his judgement) in extremes :
So over violent, or over civil,
That every man, with him, was god or devil.
In squanderibg wealth was his peculiar art :
Nothing went unrewarded, but desert.
Beggared by fools, whom still he found too late :
He had his jest, and they had his estate.

John Dryden (*Absalom and Ahitophel*).

LINES TO A DON

REMOTE and ineffectual Don
That dared attack my Chesterton,
With that poor weapon, half-impelled,
Unlearnt, unsteady, hardly held,
Unworthy for a tilt with men—
Your quavering and corroded pen ;
Don poor at Bed and worse at Table,
Don pinched, Don starved, Don miserable
Don stuttering, Don with roving eyes,
Don nervous, Don of crudities ;
Don clerical, Don ordinary,
Don self-absorbed and solitary ;
Don here-and-there, Don epileptic ;
Don puffed and empty, Don dyspeptic ;
Don middle-class, Don sycophantic,
Don dull, Don brutish, Don pedantic ;

177

Don hypocritical, Don bad,
Don furtive, Don three-quarters mad ;
Don (since a man must make an end)
Don that shall never be my friend.

* * *

Don different from those regal Dons !
With hearts of gold and lungs of bronze,
Who shout and bang and roar and bawl
The Absolute across the hall,
Or sail in amply bellowing gown
Enormous through the Sacred Town,
Bearing from College to their homes
Deep cargoes of gigantic tomes ;
Dons admirable !   Dons of Might !
Uprising on my inward sight
Compact of ancient tales, and port
And sleep—and learning of a sort.
Dons English, worthy of the land ;
Dons rooted ; Dons that understand.
Good Dons perpetual that remain
A landmark, walling in the plain—
The horizon of my memories—
Like large and comfortable trees.

* * *

Don very much apart from these,
Thou scapegoat Don, thou Don devoted,
Don to thine own damnation quoted
Perplexed to find thy trivial name
Reared in my verse to lasting shame.
Don dreadful, rasping Don and wearing,
Repulsive Don—Don past all bearing.
Don of the cold and doubtful breath,
Don despicable, Don of death ;
Don nasty, skimpy, silent, level ;
Don evil ; Don that serves the devil.
Don ugly—that makes fifty lines.
There is a Canon which confines
A Rhymed Octosyllabic Curse
If written in Iambic Verse

178

To fifty lines. I never cut;
I far prefer to end it—but
Believe me I shall soon return.
My fires are banked, but still they burn
To write some more about the Don
That dared attack my Chesterton.

Hilaire Belloc.

THE TRAVELLER'S CURSE AFTER MISDIRECTION

(FROM THE WELSH)

MAY they wander stage by stage
Of the same vain pilgrimage,
Stumbling on, age after age,
Night and day, mile after mile,
At each and every step, a stile;
At each and every stile, withal,
May they catch their feet and fall;
At each and every fall they take,
May a bone within them break,
And may the bones that break within
Not be, for variation's sake,
Now rib, now thigh, now arm, now shin,
But always, without fail, THE NECK.

Robert Graves.

THE MOTOR BUS

WHAT is this that roareth thus?
Can it be a Motor Bus?
Yes, the smell and hideous hum
Indicat Motorem Bum!
Implet in the Corn and High
Terror me Motoris Bi:
Bo Motori clamitabo
Ne Motore caedar a Bo—
Dative be or Ablative
So thou only let us live—
Whither shall thy victims flee?

Spare us, spare us, Motor Be !
Thus I sang ; and still anigh
Came in hordes Motores Bi,
Et complebat omne forum
Copia Motorum Borum.
How shall wretches live like us
Cincti Bis Motoribus ?
Domine, defende nos
Contra hos Motores Bos !

A. Godley.

THE NUN'S LAMENT FOR PHILIP SPARROW

WHEN I remember'd again
How my Philip was slain,
I wept and I wailed,
The tears down hailed ;
But nothing it avail'd
To call Philip again
Whom Gib our cat hath slain.
Heu, heu, me,
That I am woe for thee !
Levavi oculos meos in montis ;
Would that I had Xenophontis
Or Socrates the Wise,
To show me their device
Moderately to take
This sorrow that I make
For Philip Sparrow's sake !
    It had a velvet cap,
And would sit on my lap,
And seek after small worms,
And sometimes white bread crumbs
And many times and oft
Within my breast soft
It would lie and rest.
    Sometimes he would gasp
When he saw a wasp ;
A fly or a gnat,
He would fly at that ;
And prettily he would pant
When he saw an ant ;

Lord, how he would pry
After the butterfly !
Lord, how he would hop
After the grasshop !
And when I said, Phip, Phip,
Then he would leap and skip,
And take me by the lip.
        De profundis clamavi
When I saw my sparrow die.
    Vengeance I ask and cry,
By way of exclamation,
On all the whole nation
Of cats wild and tame ;
That cat especially
    That slew so cruelly
My little pretty sparrow
That I brought up at Carow.
    O cat of churlish kind,
The fiend was in thy mind.
I would thou hadst been blind !
The leopards savage,
The lions in their rage,
May they catch thee in their paws,
And gnaw thee in their jaws ;
The dragons with their tongues
May they poison thy liver and lungs.
Of India the greedy gripes
May they tear out all thy tripes ;
Of Arcady the bears
May they pluck away thine ears ;
The wild wolf Lycaon
Bite asunder thy back-bone ;
Of Ætna the burning hill,
That night and day burneth still,
Set thy tail in a blaze,
That all the world may gaze
And wonder upon thee,
From Ocean, the great sea,
Unto the Isles of Orchadye ;
From Tilbury Ferry
To the plain of Salisbury.   *J. Skelton.*

A PORTRAIT

I AM a kind of farthing dip,
  Unfriendly to the nose and eyes ;
A blue-behinded ape, I skip
  Upon the trees of Paradise.

At mankind's feast I take my place
  In solemn sanctimonious state,
And have the air of saying grace
  While I defile the dinner plate.

I am " the smiler with the knife,"
  The battener upon garbage, I—
Dear Heaven, with such a rancid life,
  Were it not better far to die ?

Yet still, about the human pale,
  I love to scamper, love to race,
To swing by my irreverent tail
  All over the most holy place ;

And when at length, some golden day,
  The unfailing sportsman, aiming at,
Shall bag me—all the world shall say :
  Thank God, and there's an end of that !
                              R. L. Stevenson.

TO EDWARD FITZGERALD

I CHANCED upon a new book yesterday :
I opened it, and, where my finger lay
  'Twixt page and uncut page, these words I read
  —Some six or seven at most—and learned thereby
That you, Fitzgerald, whom by ear and eye
She never knew, " thanked God my wife was dead."
Ay, dead ! and were yourself alive, good Fitz,
How to return you thanks would task my wits :
  Kicking you seems the common lot of curs—
  While more appropriate greeting lends you grace :
Surely to spit there glorifies your face—
  Spitting from lips once sanctified by Hers.
                              Robert Browning.

CROMEK

A PETTY sneaking knave I knew—
O! Mr. Cromek, how do ye do?

William Blake.

NORA CRIONA

I HAVE looked him round and looked him through
Know everything that he will do
In such a case, and such a case,
And when a frown comes on his face
I dream of it, and when a smile
I trace its sources in a while.

He cannot do a thing but I
Peep to find the reason why,
For I love him, and I seek,
Every evening in the week,
To peep behind his frowning eye
With little query, little pry,
And make him if a woman can
Happier than any man.

Yesterday he gripped her tight
And cut her throat—and serve her right!

James Stephens.

EPISODE OF DECAY

BEING very religious, she devoted most of her time to fear.
Under her calm visage, terror held her,
Terror of water, of air, of earth, of thought,
Terror lest she be disturbed in her routine of eating her
husband.
She fattened on his decay, but she let him decay without
pain.
And still she would ask, while she consumed him particle
by particle,

183

" Do you wish me to take it, dear ?   Will it make you
    happier ? "
And down the plump throat he went day after day in tid-
    bits ;
And he mistook the drain for happiness,
Could hardly live without the deadly nibbling . . .
She had eaten away the core of him under the shell,
Eaten his heart and drunk away his breath ;
Till on Saturday, the seventeenth of April,
She made her breakfast on an edge of his mind.
He was very quiet that day, without knowing why.
A last valiant cell of his mind may have been insisting that
    the fault was not hers but his ;
But soon he resumed a numbness of content ;
The little cell may have been thinking that one dies sooner
    or later
And that one's death may as well be useful. . . .
For supper, he offered her tea and cake from behind his
    left ear ;
And after supper they took together the walk they always
    took together after supper.

Witter Bynner.

A PSALM OF MONTREAL

T H E *City of Montreal is one of the most rising and, in many
respects, most agreeable on the American continent, but its
inhabitants are as yet too busy with commerce to care greatly
about the masterpieces of old Greek Art.   In the Montreal
Museum of Natural History I came upon two plaster casts, one
of the Antinous and the other of the Discobolus—not the good
one, but in my poem, of course, I intend the good one—
banished from public view to a room where were all manner of
skins, plants, snakes, insects, etc., and, in the middle of these,
an old man stuffing an owl.
" Ah," said I, " so you have some antiques here ; why don't
you put them where people can see them ? "
" Well, sir," answered the custodian, " you see they are rather
vulgar."
He then talked a great deal and said his brother did all Mr.
Spurgeon's printing.*

184

The dialogue—perhaps true, perhaps imaginary, perhaps a little of the one and a little of the other—between the writer and this old man gave rise to the lines that follow :

Stowed away in a Montreal lumber room
The Discobolus standeth and turneth his face to the wall ;
Dusty, cobweb-covered, maimed and set at naught,
Beauty crieth in an attic and no man regardeth :
O God ! O Montreal !

Beautiful by night and day, beautiful in summer and in winter,
Whole or maimed, always and alike beautiful—
He preacheth gospel of grace to the skin of owls
And to one who seasoneth the skins of Canadian owls :
O God ! O Montreal !

When I saw him I was wroth and I said, " O Discobolus !
Beautiful Discobolus, a Prince both among gods and men !
What doest thou here, how camest thou hither, Discobolus,
Preaching thy gospel in vain to the skins of owls ? "
O God ! O Montreal !

And I turned to the man of skins and said unto him, " O thou man of skins,
Wherefore hast thou done thus to shame the beauty of the Discobolus ? "
But the Lord had hardened the heart of the man of skins
And he answered, " My brother-in-law is haberdasher to Mr. Spurgeon."
O God ! O Montreal !

" The Discobolus is put here because he is vulgar—
He has neither vest nor pants with which to cover his limbs ;
I, Sir, am a person of most respectable connections—
My brother-in-law is haberdasher to Mr. Spurgeon."
O God ! O Montreal !

Then I said, " O brother-in-law to Mr. Spurgeon's haberdasher,
Who seasonest also the skins of Canadian owls,
Thou callest trousers ' pants,' whereas I call them ' trousers,'
Therefore thou art in hell-fire and may the Lord pity thee ! "
O God ! O Montreal !

185

" Preferrest thou the gospel of Montreal to the gospel of
  Hellas,
The gospel of thy connection with Mr. Spurgeon's haber-
  dashery to the gospel of the Discobolus ? "
Yet none the less blasphemed he beauty saying, " The
  Discobolus hath no gospel,
But my brother-in-law is haberdasher to Mr. Spurgeon."
          O God ! O Montreal !
                              Samuel Butler.

SOLILOQUY OF THE SPANISH CLOISTER

G R - R - R - there go, my heart's abhorrence !
    Water your damned flower-pots, do !
If hate killed men, Brother Lawrence,
    God's blood, would not mine kill you !
What ? your myrtle-bush wants trimming ?
    Oh, that rose has prior claims—
Needs its leaden vase filled brimming ?
    Hell dry you up with its flames !

At the meal we sit together ;
    Salve tibi ! I must hear
Wise talk of the kind of weather,
    Sort of season, time of year :
*Not a plenteous cork-crop : scarcely
    Dare we hope oak-galls, I doubt ;*
What's the Latin name for " parsley " ?
    What's the Greek name for Swine's Snout ?

Whew ! We'll have our platter burnished,
    Laid with care on our own shelf !
With a fire-new spoon we're furnished,
    And a goblet for ourself,
Rinsed like something sacrificial
    Ere 'tis fit to touch our chaps—
Marked with L. for our initial !
    (He-he ! There his lily snaps !)

Saint, forsooth ! While brown Dolores
    Squats outside the Convent bank
With Sanchicha, telling stories,
    Steeping tresses in the tank,

Blue-black, lustrous, thick like horsehairs,
  —Can't I see his dead eye glow,
Bright as 'twere a Barbary corsair's ?
  (That is, if he'd let it show !)

When he finishes refection,
  Knife and fork he never lays
Cross-wise, to my recollection,
  As do I, in Jesu's praise.
I, the Trinity illustrate,
  Drinking watered orange-pulp—
In three sips the Arian frustrate ;
  While he drains his at one gulp !

Oh, those melons ! If he's able
  We're to have a feast ; so nice !
One goes to the Abbot's table,
  All of us get each a slice.
How go on your flowers ? None double ?
  Not one fruit-sort can you spy ?
Strange !—And I, too, at such trouble,
  Keep them close-nipped on the sly !

There's a great text in Galatians,
  Once you trip on it, entails
Twenty-nine distinct damnations,
  One sure, if another fails ;
If I trip him just a-dying,
  Sure of heaven as sure can be,
Spin him round and send him flying
  Off to hell, a Manichee ?

Or, my scrofulous French novel
  On grey paper with blunt type !
Simply glance at it, you grovel
  Hand and foot in Belial's gripe ;
If I double down its pages
  At the woeful sixteenth print,
When he gathers his greengages,
  Ope a sieve and slip it in't ?

Or, there's Satan !—one might venture
    Pledge one's soul to him, yet leave
Such a flaw in the indenture
    As he'd miss till, past retrieve,
Blasted lay that rose-acacia
    We're so proud of ! *Hy, Zy, Hine.* . . .
'St, there's Vespers ! *Plena gratia*
    Ave, Virgo ! Gr-r-r—you swine !

Robert Browning.

THE REBEL

O H, I'm a good old Rebel,
    Now that's just what I am ;
For this " fair Land of Freedom "
    I do not care a dam.
I'm glad I fit against it—
    I only wish we'd won,
And I don't want no pardon
    For anything I've done.

I hates the Constitution,
    This great Republic, too ;
I hates the Freedmen's Buro,
    In uniforms of blue.
I hates the nasty eagle,
    With all his brag and fuss ;
The lyin', thievin' Yankees,
    I hates 'em wuss and wuss.

I hate the Yankee Nation
    And everything they do ;
I hate the Declaration
    Of Independence, too.
I hates the glorious Union,
    'Tis dripping with our blood ;
I hates the striped banner—
    I fit it all I could.

I followed old Mars' Robert
    For four year, near about,
Got wounded in three places,
    And starved at Pint Lookout.
I cotch the roomatism
    A-campin' in the snow,
But I killed a chance of Yankees
    I'd like to kill some mo'.

Three hundred thousand Yankees
    Is stiff in Southern dust ;
We got three hundred thousand
    Before they conquered us.
They died of Southern fever
    And Southern steel and shot ;
I wish it was three millions
    Instead of what we got.

I can't take up my musket
    And fight 'em now no more,
But I ain't agoin' to love 'em,
    Now that is sartin sure.
And I don't want no pardon
    For what I was and am ;
I won't be reconstructed,
    And I don't care a dam.

                                        Innes Randolph.

THE CURSE

WHOEVER guesses, thinks, or dreams he knows
Who is my mistress, wither by this curse ;
        Him, only for his purse,
        May some dull whore to love dispose,
And she yield then to all that are his foes ;
    May he be scorned by one, whom all else scorn,
    Forswear to others, what to her he hath sworn,
    With fear of missing, shame of getting, torn.

Madness his sorrow, gout his cramp, may he
Make, by but thinking, who hath made him such ;
    And may he feel no touch
    Of conscience, but of fame, and be
Anguished, not that 'twas sin, but that 'twas she ;
  In early and long scarceness may he rot,
  For land which had been his, if he had not
  Himself incestuously an heir begot.

May he dream treason, and believe that he
Meant to perform it, and confess, and die,
    And no record tell why ;
    His sons, which none of his may be,
Inherit nothing but his infamy ;
  Or may he so long parasites have fed,
  That he would fain be theirs whom he hath bred,
  And at the last be circumcised for bread.

The venom of all stepdames, gamesters' gall,
What tyrants and their subjects interwish,
    What plants, mines, beasts, fowl, fish,
    Can contribute, all ill which all
Prophets or poets spake, and all which shall
  Be annexed in schedules unto this by me,
  Fall on that man ; for if it be a she
  Nature beforehand hath out-cursed me.

                    John Donne.

STATE POEMS

PERMIT THE TRANSPORTS OF A BRITISH MUSE

AND PARDON RAPTURES THAT YOURSELVES INFUSE

NAHUM TATE, POET LAUREATE, TO THE

NEW PARLIAMENT (1701).

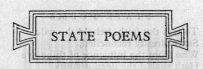

STATE POEMS

TO THE KING (CHARLES I) AND QUEEN UPON THEIR UNHAPPY DISTANCES

W O E, woe to them, who (by a ball of strife)
Doe, and have parted here a Man and Wife :
CHARLS the best Husband, while MARIA strives
To be, and is, the very best of Wives :
Like Streams, you are divorc'd ; but 'twill come when
These eyes of mine shall see you mix agen.
Thus speaks the Oke, here ; C. and M. shall meet,
Treading on Amber, with their silver-feet :
Nor wil't be long, ere this accomplish'd be ;
The words found true, C.M. remember me.

Robert Herrick.

TO THE QUEEN

[OF CHARLES I]

T H O U great commandress, that dost move
Thy sceptre o'er the crown of Love,
And through his empire, with the awe
Of thy chaste beams, dost give the law ;
From his profaner altars we
Turn to adore thy deity :
He only can wild lust provoke,
Thou those impurer flames canst choke ;
And where he scatters looser fires,
Thou turn'st them into chaste desires ;
His kingdom knows no rule but this,
Whatever pleaseth, lawful is ;
Thy sacred lore shows us the path
Of modesty and constant faith,
Which makes the rude male satisfied
With one fair female by his side ;
Doth either sex to each unite,
And form Love's pure hermaphrodite,

H 193

To this thy faith, behold the wild
Satyr already reconciled,
Who from the influence of thine eye
Hath suck'd the deep divinity.
O free them then, that they may teach
The Centaur and the horse-man, preach
To beasts and birds, sweetly to rest
Each in his proper lair and nest;
They shall convey it to the flood,
Till there thy law be understood:
    So shalt thou with thy pregnant fire
    The water, earth, and air inspire.

Thomas Carew.

GREAT BRITAIN'S GLORY
A Poem

ASPIRING Muse, commence a Noble Flight,
And strike thy joyful Wings in open Light;
New string thy Harp, and Tune thy chearful Lays,
To sacred GEORGE, and great AUGUSTUS Praise;
In sounds to move the Ravisht *Hermon's* Hill,
And faster make the *Gilead-Balm* distil.

Come BRITAINS, you whom needless Fears possess
See how kind Heav'n confirms your Happiness:
Behold Great GEORGE, the Sacred Promis'd Prince,
Whom Wond'rous Prophets many Ages since Foretold:
" That when the Mystick Figures of the Year
" To such a certain Number should Amount
" (As fill this present Lucky Year's Account,)
" O'er *England* there should Reign a shining Star,
" Of that Divine, and Gracious Influence,
" Should make Proud Neighb'ring Nations Fear;
" And mightier *Britain's* Happy Genius prove,
" Blessing the Land with Plenty, Peace, and Love.
'Tis You, O *Sacred Sir*, for Empire Born,
That makes this Strange and Great Prediction true;
And yet another Miracle perform,
'Tis *You* shall make us Blest, and make us own it too!

All Hail, Great K I N G ! Whom ev'ry Miracle,
Has still Preserv'd for *Universal Rule !*
Thou Mighty *Fabius* of a Mournful State,
Whom Heav'n hath sent i'th' Crisis of our Fate !
We bless the Winds, and Waves, and Flowing Tide,
That did Espouse and Battle on thy Side,
And ev'ry Smiling and Conspiring Gale,
That did impregnate the Extended Sail :
We bless th' *Almighty's* Steady Pow'rful Hand,
That held the Rudder, till the *Bark* did Land ;
The Happy *Bark*, that all our Blessings brought,
Charg'd with thy Self and Son, a doubly Royal
    Fraught.

  But see, the Mighty *Hero* now draws near,
Loud *Io Pæons* glad the Ecchoing Air,
And Troops of Vig'rous Youth his joyful Way prepare.
See, how beneath his large extensive Shade,
Th' oppress'd and Languid at Repose are laid !
Whilst Aged Parents his just Praise Proclaim,
And untaught Stam'ring Infants Bless his Name !
A Gen'ral Joy springs up in ev'ry Face,
And all Mankind meets with Distinguisht Grace.
O may each Rising Sun his *Age* Renew,
And each Revolving Morn fresh *Triumphs* View !
May Blooming *Honours*, as His Years Increase ;
Our Sacred *Guide* in *War*, and *Guard* in *Peace !*
And oh, Thou ever *Blest !* Now to my Pray'rs
    incline
For *Him*, whose *Fame* and *Glory* best resembles Thine !

But now I draw the Veil. . . . The Dazzling Light
Of Glory, Shines too Heavenly Fierce and Bright !
Yet never shall my *Muse*, my K I N G forget,
The Pension of a Prince's Praise is great !
'Tis the Bright Bullion of the Shining Mind :
'Tis like the Work of G O D, in *Man* Refin'd !
What Heav'n to Saints, the same do K I N G S below,
Alike these Blessings, and their Gifts bestow :
Mercy in both's the Type of Sacred Grace,
And shows the *Monarch's* Born of Heav'nly Race !

Long may *He* Shine, and spread his Beams as far,
As from the Morning to the Evening Star ;
Till His convincing Rays His Foes o'ercome,
And for his *Glorious Magnitude,* the Scanted Globe want
    room !

                                   Joseph Harris.

BIRTHDAY ODE, 1732

L E T there be light !
Such was at once the word and work of heav'n,
   When from the void of universal night
   Free nature sprung to the Creator's sight,
And day to glad the new-born world was giv'n.

Succeeding days to ages roll'd,
And ev'ry age some wonder told :
At length arose this glorious morn !
   When, to extend his bounteous pow'r,
   High heav'n announc'd this instant hour
The best of monarchs shall be born !

   Born to protect and bless the land !
And while the laws his people form,
His scepter glories to confirm
   Their wishes are his sole command.

The word that form'd the world
   In vain did make mankind ;
Unless, his passions to restrain,
   Almighty wisdom had design'd
Sometimes a W I L L I A M or a G E O R G E should reign.
Yet farther, *Britons,* cast your eyes,
Behold a long succession rise
Of future fair felicities.

   Around the royal table spread,
See how the beauteous branches shine !
   Sprung from the fertile genial bed
Of glorious G E O R G E and C A R O L I N E.

             Colley Cibber (Poet Laureate).

ON THE LATE QUEEN'S SICKNESS AND
DEATH

S A Y, Muse, if Sighs will give thee leave,
For thou hast ample Cause to grieve,
Th' Alarm united Kingdoms took,
Th' Emotions which each Bosom shook,
The wild Distress, unceasing Moan,
The weeping Eye, heart-breaking Groan,
In every Corner heard and seen,
When late our darling *Caroline*,
Britannia's, and her King's Delight,
The Joy of every Subject's Sight,
Oppress'd with mortal Sickness lay :

What Pen th' Amazement can display,
Or Tongue describe the piercing Grief,
When Physick's Aid brought no Relief,
And *George* with all his blooming Race,
Tears trickling down each Royal Face,
Regardless of their Health and Rest,
Contended which should nurse her best,
Eager with pious Zeal to save
The Wife, the Mother, from the Grave ?

. . . .

Deep-piercing was the rude Alarm,
When she, who wont our Eyes to charm,
Our Ears with Musick to rejoice
When e'er she deigned to lift her Voice,
Who with a Smile each Heart could win,
Tho' Disappointment rag'd within,
Who with a Word could Passion chain,
And render all its Fury vain,
Withdrawn, and languishing in Bed,
Was more than once reported dead.

The News attended with less Woe
Had been of an invading Foe.
But if, while this Event we fear'd,
Some glimpse of flattering Hope appear'd,

How soon to Rapture turn'd Despair,
As when o'ercast the dusky Air
At once grows brighter than a Ray,
Shot from th' effulgent Source of Day !
New Life in every Face was seen,
And more erect each alter'd Mein.

But, ah ! how false is *Syren*-Joy,
That flatters only to destroy,
And, as when Fevers intermit,
Holds but till next returning Fit.
Then Hope with all its chearful Train,
Like Tides at Ebb, flows back again.

Yet, e're her native Skies the Queen
Rejoin'd, how moving was the Scene !
How tender was the last Adieu,
When round her Bed a Glance she threw,
And saw her Lord, the Kingdom's Chief,
Dissolv'd in Tears, and dumb with Grief,
Attended with his numerous Line,
In whom a Thousand Graces shine,
But then so chang'd with haggard Woe,
Scarce could she her own off-spring know.

Like *Niobe*, one Speechless stood,
Insensible as Stone or Woods.
Her Anguish took a Root so deep,
She look'd amaz'd, but could not weep,
As if Affliction's wonted Train
Were inexpressive of her Pain.
Another, seiz'd with mortal Fright,
Sunk Lifeless at the killing Sight.
The Rest, in various Shapes, impart
The Symptoms of a wounded Heart.

Hast thou not equal Cause to mourn
O'er *Carolina's* sacred Urn,
Thou self-tormented Isle, for she
A nursing Mother was to Thee ?

Say then, what monumental Praise,
What Trophy do'st Thou mean to raise
For her, who with a Parent's View
Was once thy Queen and Guardian too ?
If Honour, Safety, Truth you prize,
The following Scheme will best advise.

Henceforth let Party-Fury cease,
The Worm that prays upon your Peace.

Anonymous, 1738.

TO THE INFANT PRINCESS ROYAL

WELCOME, bud beside the rose,
On whose stem our safety grows ;
Welcome, little Saxon Guelph ;
Welcome for thine own small self ;
Welcome for thy father, mother,
Proud the one and safe the other ;
Welcome to three kingdoms ; nay,
Such is thy potential day,
Welcome, little mighty birth,
To our human star the earth.

Some have wish'd thee boy ; and some
Gladly wait till boy shall come,
Counting it a genial sign
When a lady leads the line.
What imports it, girl or boy ?
England's old historic joy
Well might be content to see
Queens alone come after thee,—
Twenty visions of thy mother
Following sceptred, each the other,
Linking with their roses white
Ages of unborn delight.
What imports it who shall lead,
So that the good line succeed ?
So that love and peace feel sure
Of old hate's discomfiture ?

199

Thee appearing by the rose
Safety comes, and peril goes ;
Thee appearing, earth's new spring ;
Fears no winter's " grisly king "
Hope anew leaps up, and dances
In the hearts of human chances :
France, the brave, but too quick-blooded,
Wisely has her threat re-studied ;
England now, as safe as she
From the strifes that need not be,
And the realms thus hush'd and still,
Earth with fragrant thought may fill,
Growing harvests of all good,
Day by day, as planet should,
Till it clap its hands and cry,
Hail, matur'd humanity !
Earth has outgrown want and war ;
Earth is now no childish star.

But behold, where thou dost lie,
Heeding nought, remote or nigh !
Nought of all the news we sing
Dost thou know, sweet ignorant thing ;
Nought of planet's love, nor people's :
Nor dost hear the giddy steeples
Carolling of thee and thine,
As if heav'n had rain'd them wine :

* * * * *

Nor dost know thy very mother's
Balmy bosom from another's,
Though thy small blind lips pursue it,
Nor the arms that draw thee to it,
Nor the eyes, that, while they fold thee,
Never can enough behold thee.
Mother true and good has she,
Little strong one, been to thee,
Nor with listless indoor ways
Weaken'd thee for future days ;
But has done her strenuous duty
To thy brain and to thy beauty,

Till thou cam'st, a blossom bright,
Worth the kiss of air and light;
To thy healthy self a pleasure;
To the world a balm and treasure.

Leigh Hunt.

ODE SUNG AT THE EXHIBITION, 1862

UPLIFT a thousand voices full and sweet,
　　In this wide hall with earth's invention stor'd,
　　And praise th' invisible universal Lord,
Who lets once more in peace the nations meet,
　　Where, Science, Art, and Labour have outpour'd
Their myriad horns of plenty at our feet.
O silent father of our Kings to be,
Mourn'd in this golden hour of jubilee,
For this, for all, we weep our thanks to thee!

The world-compelling plan was thine,
And, lo! the long laborious miles
Of Palace; lo! the giant aisles,
　　Rich in model and design;
Harvest-tool and husbandry,
Loom, and wheel, and engin'ry,
　　Secrets of the sullen mine,
　　Steel and gold, and corn and wine,
　　Fabric rough, or fairy fine,
　　Sunny tokens of the Line,
Polar marvels, and a feast
Of wonder, out of West and East,
　　And shapes and hues of Art divine!
All of beauty, all of use
That one fair planet can produce,
　　Brought from under every star,
Blown from over every main,
And mixt, as life is mixt with pain,
　　The works of peace with works of war.
War himself must make alliance
With rough Labour and fine Science,
Else he would but strike in vain.

H *

201

And is the goal so far away?
Far, how far, no tongue can say:
Let us have our dream to-day.

O ye, the wise who think, the wise who reign,
From growing Commerce loose her latest chain,
And let the fair, white-winged peacemaker fly
To happy havens under all the sky,
And mix the seasons and the golden hours,
Till each man find his own in all men's good,
And all men work in noble brotherhood,
Breaking their mailed fleets and armed towers,
And ruling by obeying nature's powers,
And gathering all the fruits of Peace and crown'd
    with all her flowers.

Alfred, Lord Tennyson (*Poet Laureate*).

MAFEKING

OCTOBER 15, 1899 TO MAY 16, 1900

ONCE again, banners, fly!
Clang again, bells, on high,
Sounding to sea and sky,
    Longer and louder,
Mafeking's glory with
Kimberley, Ladysmith,
Of our unconquered kith
    Prouder and prouder.

Hemmed in for half a year,
Still with no succour near,
Nor word of hope to cheer
    Wounded and dying,
Famished, and foiled of sleep
By the fierce cannon's leap,
They vowed still, still to keep
    England's Flag flying.

Nor was their mettle shown
By male and strong alone,
But, as intrepid grown,
    Fragile and tender,

202

Without or tear or sigh,
Echoed the brave old cry,
" We, too, would rather die,
    Die than surrender."

As pressed the foe more near,
Only with naked spear,
Ne'er knowing what to fear,
    Parley, or blench meant,
Forward through shot and shell,
While still the foremost fell,
They with resistless yell
    Stormed his intrenchment.

Then, when hope dawned at last,
And fled the foe, aghast
At the relieving blast
    Heard in the melley,—
O our stout, stubborn kith !
Kimberley, Ladysmith,
Mafeking, wedded with
    Lucknow and Delhi !

Sound for them martial lay !
Crown them with battle-bay,
Both those who died, and they
    'Gainst death could wrestle.
Powell of endless fame,
All, all with equal claim,
And, of the storied name,
    Gallant young Cecil !

Long as the waves shall roll,
Long as Fame guards her scroll,
And men through heart and soul
    Thrill to true glory,
Their deed, from age to age,
Shall voice and verse engage,
Swelling the splendid page
    Of England's Story.

        Alfred Austin (*Poet Laureate*).

THE DIAMOND JUBILEE 1897

QUEEN VICTORIA sixty years the Monarch of our
   Realm
Shows the grand old lady has kept a steady helm.
She often tacked, she never backed, she always heaved
   her lead,
And never turned into her bunk when breakers were
   ahead.

Roy Dalziel.

ON THE DEATH OF KING EDWARD VII

THE will of God we must obey.
Dreadful—our King taken away !
The greatest friend of the nation,
Mighty monarch and protection !

Heavenly Father, help in sorrow
Queen-Mother, and them to follow,
What to do without him who has gone !
Pray help ! help ! and do lead us on.

Greatest sorrow England ever had
When death took away our dear Dad ;
A king was he from head to sole,
Loved by his people one and all.

His mighty work for the Nation,
Making peace and strengthening Union—
Always at it since on the throne :
Saved the country more than one billion.

Broadsheet sold in London streets
at Edward VII's funeral.

EPIGRAMS

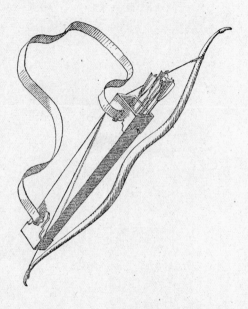

GEORGE HERBERT :

A BOX WHERE SWEETS COMPACTED LIE

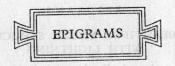

EPIGRAMS

CHLOE

BRIGHT as the day, and like the morning fair,
Such Chloe is—and common as the air.

Lansdowne.

A CURE FOR POETRY

SEVEN wealthy towns contend for Homer dead
Thro' which the living Homer beg'd his bread.

Thomas Seward (from *John Heywood*).

THE MODERN POET (1925)

WITH what small pains procures the poet now
A wreath of bays with which to deck his brow ;
For two things only can obscure his fame—
A love of beauty or a sense of shame.

Sylvis.

¶

DAPHNE, eluding Phœbus' flame,
Remained the laurel she became,
For Poets, observation proves,
Prefer their laurels to their loves.

Richard Garnett.

OF TREASON

TREASON doth never prosper ; what's the reason ?
For if it prosper, none dare call it treason.

John Harington.

¶

FORTUNE advanced thee that all might aver
That nothing is impossible to her.

Richard Garnett.

EPIGRAMS

ON A BEAUTIFUL YOUTH STRUCK BLIND WITH LIGHTNING

SURE, 'twas by Providence design'd
Rather in pity than in hate,
That he should be, like Cupid, blind,
To save him from Narcissus' fate.

O. Goldsmith.

DON'S HOLIDAY

PROFESSOR ROBINSON each summer beats
The fishing record of the world—such feats
As one would hardly credit from a lesser
Person than a history professor.

G. R. Hamilton.

THE FIVE REASONS FOR DRINKING

IF all be true that I do think,
There are five reasons we should drink;
Good wine—a friend—or being dry—
Or lest we should be by and by—
Or any other reason why.

Henry Aldrich.

BURLESQUE

IF the man who turnips cries,
Cry not when his father dies,
'Tis a proof that he had rather
Have a turnip than his father.

Samuel Johnson.

THE KISS

" I SAW you take his kiss ! " " 'Tis true."
" O, modesty ! " " 'Twas strictly kept :
He thought me asleep : at least, I knew
He thought I thought he thought I slept."

Coventry Patmore.

EPIGRAMS

ON A CERTAIN LADY AT COURT

I KNOW the thing that's most uncommon;
(Envy be silent, and attend!)
I know a reasonable woman,
Handsome and witty, yet a friend.
Not warp'd by passion, awed by rumour,
Not grave thro' pride, or gay thro' folly,
An equal mixture of good humour,
And sensible soft melancholy.
" Has she no faults then (Envy says), Sir?"
Yes, she has one, I must aver:
When all the world conspire to praise her,
The woman's deaf, and does not hear.

Alexander Pope.

ON LADY POLTAGRUE, A PUBLIC PERIL

THE Devil, having nothing else to do,
Went off to tempt My Lady Poltagrue.
My Lady, tempted by a private whim,
To his extreme annoyance, tempted him.

Hilaire Belloc.

A PORTRAIT PAINTER

GOOD Mr. Fortune, A.R.A.,
Rejoiced in twenty sons,
But even there he failed, they say,
To get a likeness once.

G. R. Hamilton (from Lucillus).

ON A DISTANT PROSPECT OF AN ABSCONDING BOOKMAKER

ALAS! what boots it that my noble steed,
Chosen so carefully, the field outran?
I did not reckon, bookie, on *your* speed:
The proper study of mankind is man.

G. R. Hamilton.

209

EPIGRAMS

ON AN UPRIGHT JUDGE

IN church your grandsire cut his throat;
To do the job too long he tarried:
He should have had my hearty vote
To cut his throat before he married.

Jonathan Swift.

ON CHARLES II

HERE lies our sovereign Lord the King,
  Whose word no man relies on,
Who never said a foolish thing
  Nor ever did a wise one.

Rochester.

ON PETER ROBINSON

HERE lies the preacher, judge and poet, Peter,
Who broke the laws of God, and man, and metre.

Francis Jeffrey.

EPIGRAM

YOU beat your pate, and fancy wit will come:
Knock as you please, there's nobody at home.

Alexander Pope.

ON A CERTAIN LORD'S GIVING SOME THOUSAND POUNDS FOR A HOUSE

SO many thousands for a house
For you, of all the world, Lord Mouse!
A little house would best accord
With you, my very little lord!
And then exactly match'd would be
Your house and hospitality.

David Garrick.

EPIGRAM

MY Lord complains that Pope, stark mad with gardens,
Has cut three trees, the value of three farthings.
" But he's my neighbour," cries the peer polite :
" And if he visit me, I'll waive the right."
What ! on compulsion, and against my will,
A lord's acquaintance ?   Let him file his bill !

Alexander Pope.

DOCTOR FELL

I DO not love thee, Doctor Fell ;
The reason why I cannot tell.
But this I'm sure I know full well,
I do not love thee, Doctor Fell.

T. Brown (from *Martial*).

THE CHOSEN PEOPLE

HOW odd
Of God
To choose
The Jews.

W. N. Ewer.

FOOLS—AND FOOLS

ANSWER not a fool according to his folly,
Lest thou also be like unto him.

Answer a fool according to his folly,
Lest he be wise in his own conceit.

The Book of Proverbs.

EPIGRAM

SIR, I admit your general rule,
That every poet is a fool :
But you yourself may serve to show it,
That every fool is not a poet.

Matthew Prior.

THE MAIDEN'S CHOICE

A FOOL and knave with different views,
    For Julia's hand apply :
The knave, to mend his fortune sues,
    The fool, to please his eye.

Ask you, how Julia will behave ?
    Depend on't for a rule,
If she's a fool, she'll wed the knave—
    If she's a knave, the fool.

S. Bishop.

¶

"I HARDLY ever ope my lips," one cries,
"Simonides, what think you of my rule ? "
"If you're a fool I think you're very wise ;
If you are wise I think you are a fool."

Richard Garnett.

A RIDDLE SOLVED

KIND souls, you wonder why, love you,
When you, you wonder why, love none.
We love, Fool, for the good we do,
Not that which unto us is done !

Coventry Patmore.

ETERNITY

HE who bends to himself a Joy
Doth the wingèd life destroy ;
But he who kisses the Joy as it flies
Lives in Eternity's sunrise.

William Blake.

212

THE LADY AND HER LOOKING-GLASS

VENUS, take my votive glass;
Since I am not what I was,
What from this day I shall be,
Venus, let me never see.
Matthew Prior (from *Ausonius*).

TO SILENCE

WHY the warning finger-tip
Pressed for ever on thy lip?
To remind the pilgrim Sound
That it moves on holy ground,
In a breathing-space to be
Hushed for all eternity.
J. B. Tabb.

RESPICE FINEM

MY soul, sit thou a patient looker-on;
Judge not the play before the play is done:
Her plot hath many changes; every day
Speaks a new scene; the last act crowns the play
Francis Quarles.

DUSTING

THE dust comes secretly day after day,
Lies on my ledge and dulls my shining things.
But O this dust that I shall drive away
    Is flowers and kings,
Is Solomon's temple, poets, Nineveh.
Viola Meynell.

ON HIS SEVENTY-FIFTH BIRTHDAY

I STROVE with none; for none was worth my strife.
Nature I loved and, next to Nature, Art;
I warmed both hands before the fire of life;
It sinks, and I am ready to depart.
W. S. Landor.

DIRCE

STAND close around, ye Stygian set,
    With Dirce in one boat conveyed,
Or Charon, seeing, may forget
    That he is old and she a shade.

W. S. Landor.

ON THE PHRASE, "TO KILL TIME"

THERE'S scarce a point whereon mankind agree
So well, as in their boast of killing me :
I boast of nothing, but, when I've a mind,
I think I can be even with mankind.

From *Voltaire : Dodd's* Select Epigrams.

MY OWN EPITAPH

LIFE is jest, and all things show it ;
I thought so once, but now I know it.

John Gay.

EPITAPH

HERE lie I, Martin Elginbrodde :
Ha'e mercy o' my soul, Lord God,
As I wad do, were I Lord God
And ye were Martin Elginbrodde.

From an *Aberdeen tombstone.*

UPON A CHILD

HERE a pretty baby lies
Sung asleep with lullabies ;
Pray be silent, and not stir
Th' easy earth that covers her.

R. Herrick.

ON DRAKE

ENGLAND his heart ; his corpse the waters have :
And that which raised his fame, became his grave.

Richard Barnfield.

EPIGRAMS

ON THE DEATH OF SIR ALBERTUS AND LADY MORTON

HE first deceas'd—she, for a little, try'd
To live without him, lik'd it not and dy'd.

Henry Wotton.

THE BETTER WAY

IF you desire to paralyse
Your enemy, don't " damn his eyes ";
From futile blasphemy desist ;
Send him to Blank the oculist.

Walter Leaf (from *Nicarchus*).

THE BALANCE OF EUROPE

NOW Europe balanced, neither side prevails ;
For nothing's left in either of the scales.

Alexander Pope.

LINES WRITTEN BY WARREN HASTINGS

OFT have I wonder'd that, on Irish Ground
No poisonous reptiles ever yet were found :
Reveal'd the secret stands, of Nature's Work !
She saved her venom, to create a Burke.

THE MODERN WORLD

STRANGER, here lies that one time " modern " world,
That noble and courageous age which hurled
Its gauntlet in the very teeth of fate
And dared and died—What are you laughing at ?

E. S.

EPITAPH BY A SON

BENEATH this stone, in hopes of Zion,
Doth lie the landlord of the Lion ;
His son keeps on the business still,
Resigned unto the heavenly will.

From *Fairley's Epitaphiana*.

EPIGRAMS

BYWAYS IN BIOGRAPHY

ALFRED de Musset
Used to call his cat Pusset.
His accent was affected.
That was to be expected.

Maurice Hare.

EMINENT PHYSICISTS

I

NATURE, and Nature's laws, lay hid in night :
God said, *Let Newton be !* and all was light.

Alexander Pope.

II

IT did not last : the Devil, howling *Ho !*
Let Einstein be ! restored the status quo.

J. C. Squire.

RELATIVITY

THERE was a young lady named Bright
Who would travel much faster than light.
   She started one day
   In the relative way,
And came back the previous night.

Anonymous.

THE MENDELIAN THEORY

THERE was a young fellow called Starky
Who had an affair with a darky.
   The result of his sins
   Was quadruplets, not twins :
One black, and one white, and two khaki.

Anonymous.

216

EPIGRAMS

THE JUNG IDEA

THE young things who frequent picture-palaces
Have no use for this psycho-analysis;
   And although Doctor Freud
   Is distinctly annoyed
They cling to their long-standing fallacies.

P. H.

ON MONSIEUR COUÉ

THIS very remarkable man
Commends a most practical plan;
   You can do what you want
   If you don't think you can't
So don't think you can't think you can.

Charles Inge.

MIND OVER MATTER

THERE was a faith-healer of Deal
Who said, "Although pain isn't real,
   If I sit on a pin
   And it punctures my skin
I dislike what I fancy I feel."

Anonymous.

MATERIALISM

THERE was a professor of Beaulieu
Who said mind was matter or ὕλη,
   This contempt for the εἶδος;
   Though common at Cnidos
Distressed the New Forest unduly.

C. E. M. Joad.

IDEALISM

THERE once was a man who said " God
Must think it exceedingly odd
   If he finds that this tree
   Continues to be
When there's no one about in the Quad."

Ronald Knox.

EPIGRAMS

A REPLY

DEAR SIR,
              Your astonishment's odd :
I am always about in the Quad.
          And that's why the tree
          Will continue to be,
Since observed by
                  Yours faithfully,
                       God.

FREE-WILL AND PREDESTINATION

THERE was a young man who said " Damn !
It appears to me now that I am
    Just a being that moves
    In predestinate grooves—
Not a bus, not a bus, but a tram."

Maurice Hare.

ON SOME SOUTH AFRICAN NOVELISTS

They praise the firm restraint with which you write.
    I'm with you there, of course.
You use the snaffle and the curb all right,
    But where's the bloody horse ?

Roy Campbell.

GROWN-UP

WAS it for this I uttered prayers,
And sobbed and cursed and kicked the stairs,
That now, domestic as a plate,
I should retire at half-past eight ?

Edna St. Vincent Millay.

¶

MY candle burns at both ends ;
It will not last the night ;
But ah, my foes, and oh, my friends—
It gives a lovely light !

Edna St. Vincent Millay.

218

THE ZOO

THE LIVING CREATURE AFTER HIS KIND

GENESIS

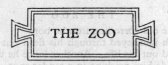

THE ZOO

THE BEASTS

I T H I N K I could turn and live with animals, they are so
    placid and self-contain'd ;
I stand and look at them long and long.
They do not sweat and whine about their condition ;
They do not lie awake in the dark and weep for their sins ;
They do not make me sick discussing their duty to God ;
Not one is dissatisfied—not one is demented with the
    mania of owning things ;
Not one kneels to another, nor to his kind that lived
    thousands of years ago ;
Not one is respectable or industrious over the whole earth.

Walt Whitman.

FOUR BEASTS

T H E R E be four things which are little upon the earth
But they are exceeding wise ;
The ants are a people not strong,
Yet they prepare their meat in the summer ;
The conies are but a feeble folk,
Yet they make their houses in the rocks ;
The locusts have no king,
Yet they go forth all of them by bands ;
The spider taketh hold with her hands,
And is in kings' palaces.

The Authorized Version.

JONAH AND THE WHALE

H E sported round the watery world.
His rich oil was a gloomy waveless lake
Within the waves.   Affrighted seamen hurled
    Their weapons in his foaming wake.

221

THE ZOO

One old corroding iron he bore
Which journeyed through his flesh but yet had not
Found out his life.   Another lance he wore
Outside him pricking in a tender spot.

So distant were his parts that they
Sent but a dull faint message to his brain.
He knew not his own flesh, as great kings may
Not know the farther places where they reign.

His play made storm in a calm sea ;
His very kindness slew what he might touch ;
And wrecks lay scattered on his anger's lee.
The Moon rocked to and fro his watery couch.

His hunger cleared the sea.   And where
He passed, the ocean's edge lifted its brim.
He skimmed the dim sea-floor to find if there
Some garden had its harvest ripe for him.

But in his sluggish brain no thought
Ever arose.   His law was instinct blind.
No thought or gleam or vision ever brought
Light to the dark of his old dreamless mind.

Until one day sudden and strange
Half-hints of knowledge burst upon his sight.
Glimpses he had of Time, and Space, and Change,
And something greater than his might ;

And terror's leap to imagine sin ;
And blinding Truth half-bare unto his seeing.
It was the living man who had come in . . .
Jonah's thoughts flying through his being.

Viola Meynell.

Fish

HEAVEN

FISH (fly-replete, in depth of June
Dawdling away their wat'ry noon)
Ponder deep wisdom, dark or clear,
Each secret fishy hope or fear.

Fish say, they have their Stream and Pond
But is there anything Beyond ?
This life cannot be All, they swear,
For how unpleasant, if it were !
One may not doubt that, somehow, good
Shall come of Water and of Mud ;
And, sure, the reverent eye must see
A Purpose in Liquidity.
We darkly know, by Faith we cry,
The future is not Wholly Dry.
Mud unto Mud !—Death eddies near—
Not here the appointed End, not here !
But somewhere, beyond Space and Time,
Is wetter water, slimier slime !
And there (they trust) there swimmeth One
Who swam ere rivers were begun,
Immense, of fishy form and mind,
Squamous, omnipotent, and kind ;
And under that Almighty Fin
The littlest fish may enter in.
Oh ! never fly conceals a hook,
Fish say, in the Eternal Brook,
But more than mundane weeds are there,
And mud, celestially fair ;
Fat caterpillars drift around,
And Paradisal grubs are found ;
Unfading moths, immortal flies,
And the worm that never dies.
And in that Heaven of all their wish,
There shall be no more land, say fish.

Rupert Brooke.

THE TYGER

(*First version.*)

TYGER, Tyger, burning bright
In the forests of the night,
What immortal hand or eye
Dare frame thy fearful symmetry ?

223

Burnt in distant deeps or skies
The cruel fire of thine eyes?
On what wings dare he aspire?
What the hand dare seize the fire?

And what shoulder and what art
Could twist the sinews of thy heart?
And when thy heart began to beat
What dread hand and what dread feet

Could fetch it from the furnace deep
And in thy horrid ribs dare steep?
In what clay and in what mould
Were thy eyes of fury roll'd?

Where the hammer?   Where the chain?
In what furnace was thy brain?
What the anvil?   What dread grasp
Dare its deadly terrors clasp?

When the stars threw down their spears
And water'd heaven with their tears
Dare he laugh his work to see?
Dare he who made the lamb make thee?

Tyger, tyger, burning bright
In the forests of the night,
What immortal hand and eye
Dare frame thy fearful symmetry?

William Blake.

MILK FOR THE CAT

WHEN the tea is brought at five o'clock,
And all the neat curtains are drawn with care,
The little black cat with bright green eyes
Is suddenly purring there.

At first she pretends, having nothing to do,
She has come in merely to blink by the grate,
But, though tea may be late or the milk may be sour,
She is never late.

224

And presently her agate eyes
Take a soft large, milky haze
And her independent casual glance
Becomes a stiff, hard gaze.

Then she stamps her claws or lifts her ears,
Or twists her tail and begins to stir,
Till suddenly all her lithe body becomes
One breathing, trembling purr.

The children eat and wriggle and laugh,
The two old ladies stroke their silk :
But the cat is grown small and thin with desire,
Transformed to a creeping lust for milk.

The white saucer like some full moon descends
At last from the clouds of the table above ;
She sighs and dreams and thrills and glows,
Transfigured with love.

She nestles over the shining rim,
Buries her chin in the creamy sea ;
Her tail hangs loose ; each drowsy paw
Is doubled under each bending knee.

A long, dim ecstasy holds her life ;
Her world is an infinite shapeless white,
Till her tongue has curled the last holy drop,
Then she sinks back into the night,

Draws and dips her body to heap
Her sleepy nerves in the great arm-chair,
Lies defeated and buried deep
Three or four hours unconscious there.

Harold Monro.

Dog

THE SONG OF QUOODLE

THEY haven't got no noses,
The fallen sons of Eve ;
Even the smell of roses
Is not what they supposes ;
But more than mind discloses
And more than men believe.

THE ZOO

They haven't got no noses,
They cannot even tell
When door and darkness closes
The park a Jew encloses,
Where even the Law of Moses
Will let you steal a smell.

The brilliant smell of water,
The brave smell of a stone,
The smell of dew and thunder,
The old bones buried under,
Are things in which they blunder
And err, if left alone.

The wind from winter forests,
The scent of scentless flowers,
The breath of brides' adorning,
The smell of snare and warning,
The smell of Sunday morning,
God gave to us for ours.

.   .   .   .   .   .

And Quoodle here discloses
All things that Quoodle can,
They haven't got no noses,
They haven't got no noses,
And goodness only knowses
The Noselessness of Man.

G. K. Chesterton.

THE COW

THE friendly cow all red and white,
  I love with all my heart :
She gives me cream with all her might,
  To eat with apple-tart.

She wanders lowing here and there,
  And yet she cannot stray,
All in the pleasant open air,
  The pleasant light of day ;

And blown by all the winds that pass
   And wet with all the showers,
She walks among the meadow grass
   And eats the meadow flowers.

R. L. Stevenson.

Cow

THE LILY-POOL

WHAT sees our mailie in the lily-pool,
   What sees she with that large surprise?
What sees our mailie in the lily-pool
   With all the violet of her big eyes—
     Our mailie in the lily-pool?

She sees herself within the lily-pool,
   Herself in flakes of brown and white—
Herself beneath the slab that is the lily-pool,
   The green and liquid slab of light
     With cups of silver dight,
   Stem-rooted in the depths of amber night
That hold the hollows of the lily-pool—
     Our own dear lily-pool!

And does she gaze into the lily-pool
   As one that is enchanted?
Or does she try the cause to find
   How the reflection's slanted,
That sleeps within the lily-pool?
   Or does she take it all for granted
With the sweet natural logic of her kind?
   The lazy logic of the lily-pool,
     Our own bright, innocent, stupid lily-pool!

She knows that it is nice—our lily-pool:
   She likes the water-rings around her knees;
   She likes the shadow of the trees,
That droop above the lily-pool;
   She likes to scatter with a silly sneeze
The long-legged flies that skim the lily-pool—
The peaceful-sleeping, baby lily-pool.

227

So may I look upon the lily-pool,
    Nor ever in the slightest care
    Why I am there ;
Why upon land and sea
Is ever stamped the inevitable me ;
But rather say with that most gentle fool—
" How pleasant is this lily-pool !
How nice and cool !
Be off, you long-legged flies !   O what a spree !
To drive the flies from off the lily-pool !
From off this most sufficient, absolute lily-pool ! "

                                        T. E. Brown.

EPITAPH ON A HARE

HERE lies, whom hound did ne'er pursue,
    Nor swifter greyhound follow,
Whose foot ne'er tainted morning dew,
    Nor ear heard huntsman's hollo ;

Old Tiney, surliest of his kind,
    Who, nursed with tender care,
And to domestic bounds confined,
    Was still a wild Jack-hare.

Though duly from my hand he took
    His pittance every night,
He did it with a jealous look,
    And when he could, would bite.

His diet was of wheaten bread,
    And milk, and oats, and straw,
Thistles, or lettuces instead,
    With sand to scour his maw.

On twigs of hawthorn he regaled,
    On pippins' russet peel ;
And, when his juicy salads fail'd,
    Sliced carrot pleased him well.

A Turkey carpet was his lawn,
    Whereon he loved to bound,
To skip and gambol like a fawn,
    And swing his rump around.

His frisking was at evening hours,
    For then he lost his fear;
But most before approaching showers,
    Or when a storm drew near.

Eight years and five round-rolling moons
    He thus saw steal away,
Dozing out all his idle noons,
    And every night at play.

I kept him for his humour's sake,
    For he would oft beguile
My heart of thoughts that made it ache,
    And force me to a smile.

But now, beneath this walnut-shade
    He finds his long last home,
And waits, in snug concealment laid,
    Till gentler Puss shall come.

He, still more aged, feels the shocks
    From which no care can save,
And, partner once of Tiney's box,
    Must soon partake his grave.

William Cowper.

TO A MOUSE, ON TURNING HER UP IN HER NEST WITH THE PLOUGH, NOVEMBER, 1785

WEE, sleekit, cow'rin', tim'rous beastie,
O what a panic's in thy breastie!
Thou need na start awa sae hasty,
        Wi' bickering brattle!
I wad be laith to rin an' chase thee
        Wi' murd'ring pattle!

I'm truly sorry man's dominion
Has broken Nature's social union,
An' justifies that ill opinion
        Which makes thee startle
At me, thy poor earth-born companion,
        An' fellow-mortal!

229

I doubt na, whiles, but thou may thieve ;
What then ? poor beastie, thou maun live !
A daimen-icker in a thrave
            'S a sma' request :
I'll get a blessin' wi' the lave,
            And never miss 't !

Thy wee bit housie, too, in ruin !
Its silly wa's the win's are strewin' !
An' naething, now, to big a new ane,
            O' foggage green !
An' bleak December's winds ensuin',
            Baith snell an' keen !

Thou saw the fields laid bare and waste,
An' weary winter comin' fast,
An' cozie here, beneath the blast,
            Thou thought to dwell,
Till crash ! the cruel coulter past
            Out-thro' thy cell.

That wee bit heap o' leaves an' stibble
Has cost thee mony a weary nibble !
Now thou's turn'd out, for a' thy trouble,
            But house or hald,
To thole the winter's sleety dribble,
            An' cranreuch cauld !

But, Mousie, thou art no thy lane,
In proving foresight may be vain :
The best laid schemes o' mice an' men
            Gang aft a-gley,
An' lea'e us nought but grief an' pain
            For promis'd joy.

Still thou art blest compar'd wi' me !
The present only toucheth thee :
But oh ! I backward cast my e'e
            On prospects drear !
An' forward tho' I canna see,
            I guess an' fear !

                              Robert Burns.

THE RABBIT

THE rabbit has a charming face :
Its private life is a disgrace.
I really dare not name to you
The awful things that rabbits do ;
Things that your paper never prints—
You only mention them in hints.
They have such lost, degraded souls
No wonder they inhabit holes ;
When such depravity is found
It only can live underground.

Anon. : 20th Cent.

THE HORSE

I KNOW two things about the horse
And one of them is rather coarse.

Anon. : 20th Cent.

THE KINGFISHER

IT was the Rainbow gave thee birth,
    And left thee all her lovely hues ;
And, as her mother's name was Tears,
    So runs it in thy blood to choose
For haunts the lonely pools, and keep
In company with trees that weep.

Go you and, with such glorious hues,
    Live with proud Peacocks in green parks ;
On lawns as smooth as shining glass,
    Let every feather show its marks ;
Get thee on boughs and clap thy wings
Before the windows of proud kings.

Nay, lovely Bird, thou art not vain ;
    Thou hast no proud ambitious mind ;
I also love a quiet place
    That's green, away from all mankind ;
A lonely pool, and let a tree
Sigh with her bosom over me.

W. H. Davies.

231

JENNY WREN

HER sight is short, she comes quite near;
A foot to me's a mile to her;
And she is known as Jenny Wren,
The smallest bird in England. When
I heard that little bird at first,
Methought her frame would surely burst
With earnest song. Oft had I seen
Her running under leaves so green,
Or in the grass when fresh and wet,
As though her wings she would forget.
And, seeing this, I said to her—
" My pretty runner, you prefer
To be a thing to run unheard
Through leaves and grass, and not a bird ! "
'Twas then she burst, to prove me wrong,
Into a sudden storm of song ;
So very loud and earnest, I
Feared she would break her heart and die.
" Nay, nay," I laughed, " be you no thing
To run unheard, sweet scold, but sing !
O I could hear your voice near me,
Above the din in that oak tree,
When almost all the twigs on top
Had starlings chattering without stop."

W. H. Davies.

Blackbird

VESPERS

O BLACKBIRD, what a boy you are !
How you do go it !
Blowing your bugle to that one sweet star—
How you do blow it !
And does she hear you, blackbird boy, so far ?
Or is it wasted breath ?
" Good Lord ! she is so bright
To-night ! "
The blackbird saith.

T. E. Brown.

232

THE OCTOBER REDBREAST

AUTUMN is weary, halt, and old ;
   Ah, but she owns the song of joy !
Her colours fade, her woods are cold.
   Her singing-bird's a boy, a boy.

In lovely Spring the birds were bent
   On nests, on use, on love, forsooth !
Grown-up were they.   This boy's content,
   For his is liberty, his is youth.

The musical stripling sings for play
   Taking no thought, and virgin-glad.
For duty sang those mates in May.
   This singing-bird's a lad, a lad.

Alice Meynell.

THE EAGLE

HE clasps the crag with crooked hands ;
Close to the sun in lonely lands,
Ringed with the azure world, he stands.

The wrinkled sea beneath him crawls ;
He watches from his mountain walls,
And like a thunderbolt he falls.

Alfred Tennyson.

THE GRASSHOPPER

O THOU that swing'st upon the waving hair
   Of some well-fillèd oaten beard,
Drunk every night with a delicious tear
   Dropt thee from Heaven, where thou wert rear'd !

The joys of earth and air are thine entire,
   That with thy feet and wings dost hop and fly ;
And when thy poppy works, thou dost retire
   To thy carved acorn-bed to lie.

I *

Up with the day, the Sun thou welcom'st then,
   Sport'st in the gilt plaits of his beams.
And all these merry days mak'st merry men,
   Thyself, and melancholy streams.

Richard Lovelace.

THE ANT

FORBEAR, thou great good husband, little ant ;
   A little respite from thy flood of sweat !
Thou, thine own horse and cart under this plant,
   Thy spacious tent, fan thy prodigious heat ;
Down with thy double load of that one grain !
It is a granarie for all thy train.

Cease, large example of wise thrift, awhile
   (For thy example is become our law),
And teach thy frowns a seasonable smile :
   So Cato sometimes the nak'd Florals saw.
And thou, almighty foe, lay by thy sting,
Whilst thy unpay'd musicians, crickets, sing.

Lucasta, she that holy makes the day,
   And 'stills new life in fields of feuillemort,
Hath back restor'd their verdure with one ray,
   And with her eye bid all to play and sport,
Ant, to work still ! age will thee truant call ;
And to save now, th'art worse than prodigal.

Austere and cynick ! not one hour t'allow,
   To lose with pleasure, what thou got'st with pain ;
But drive on sacred festivals thy plow,
   Tearing high-ways with thy o'er-chargèd wain ;
Not all thy life-time one poor minute live,
And thy o'er-labour'd bulk with mirth relieve ?

Look up then, miserable ant, and spie
   Thy fatal foes, for breaking of their law,
Hov'ring above thee : Madam *Margaret Pie* :
   And her fierce servant, meagre Sir *John Daw* :
Thy self and storehouse now they do store up,
And thy whole harvest too within their crop.

234

THE ZOO

Thus we unthrifty thrive within earth's tomb
   For some more rav'nous and ambitious jaw :
The grain in th' ant's, the ant in the pie's womb,
   The pie in th' hawk's, the hawk i' th' eagle's maw.
So scattering to hoard 'gainst a long day,
Thinking to save all, we cast all away.

Richard Lovelace.

ODE TO THE MOSQUITO

VOCIFEROUS Culicids ! From what vast
   Ancestral arthropod were you derived
That hovered through a dim Silurian past
   Or in some dank primeval forest thrived ?
Perhaps you pestered some huge dinosaur
   And purged his Mesozoic dreams of joy ;
   Or made a flapping pterodactyl screech
And hastily flap more,
   In swift remonstrance at your kisses coy
   Impressed in some soft spot he could not reach.

Æons have passed. We meet you once again !
   Though shrunk in size, your sins are still as great—
Reduplicated punctures fraught with pain ;
   Your hideous hum—a haunting hymn of hate.
O hedonists, whose hectic lives but wake
   For aliment and love, you little know
   That fever-germs within you laugh and leap
Until their nuclei shake !
   And yet you think to mock us ! Have it so!
   Your young are at our mercy : Oil is cheap.

Gilbert Brooke.

THE FLY

HOW large unto the tiny fly
Must little things appear !—
A rosebud like a feather-bed,
Its prickle like a spear ;

A dewdrop like a looking-glass ;
A hair like golden wire ;
The smallest grain of mustard-seed
As fierce as coals of fire ;

235

A loaf of bread, a lofty hill;
A wasp, a cruel leopard;
And specks of salt as bright to see
As lambkins to a shepherd.

Walter de la Mare.

SONNET TO A MONKEY

O LIVELY, O most charming pug,
Thy graceful air, and heavenly mug;
The beauties of his mind do shine,
And every bit is shaped and fine.
Your teeth are whiter than the snow,
You're a great buck, you're a great beau;
Your eyes are of so nice a shape,
More like a Christian's than an ape;
Your cheek is like the rose's blume,
Your hair is like the raven's plume;
His nose's cast is of the Roman,
He is a very pretty woman.
I could not get a rhyme for Roman,
So was obliged to call him woman.

Marjorie Fleming (obit 1811, ætat : 8).

Man

HYMN TO MOLOCH

O THOU who didst furnish
The fowls of the air
With loverly feathers
For leydies to wear,
Receive this Petition
For blessin an aid,
From the principal Ouses
Engaged in the Trade.

The trouble's as follows :
A white livered Scum,
What if they was choked
T'would be better for some,

236

THE ZOO

S'been pokin about an
Creatin a fuss
An talkin too loud to be
Ealthy for us.

Thou'lt ardly believe
Ow damn friendly they are,
They say there's a time
In the future not far
When birds worth good money'll
Waste by the ton
An the Trade can look perishin
Pleased to look on.

With best lines in Paradies
Equal to what
Is fetchin a pony
A time in the at,
An ospreys an ummins
An other choice goods
Wastefully oppin
About in the woods.

They're kiddin the papers,
An callin us names,
Not Yorkshire ones neither,
That's one of their games,
They've others as pleasin
An soakin with spite,
An it don't make us appy,
Ow can it do, quite!

We thank thee most earty
For mercies to date,
The Olesales is pickin
Nice profits per crate,
Reports from the Retails
Is pleasin to read
We certainly thank thee
Most earty indeed.

237

Vouchsafe, then, to muzzle
These meddlesome swine,
An learn em to andle goods
More in their line,
Be faithful, be foxy
Till peril is past,
An plant thy strong sword
In their livers at last.

Ralph Hodgson.

MAN AND BEAST

I AM less patient than this horse
And it is fleeter far than I.
Its hair is silky, mine is coarse ;
Grasses have shaped that larger eye,
While to feed me live things must die.

The birds make little darts in air,
And fishes little darts in water,
Old sheep a silver glory share,
Peacocks are peacocks everywhere . . .
Man lies awake, planning the slaughter.

What woman has this old cat's graces ?
What boy can sing as the thrush sings ?
For me, I'd rather not run races
With dragon-flies, nor thread the mazes
Of a smooth lawn with ants and things.

Yet horse and sheep tread leaf and stem
And bud and flower beneath their feet ;
They sniff at Stars-of-Bethlehem
And buttercups are food to them,
No more than bitter food or sweet.

I, to whom air and waves are sealed,
I yet possess the human part.
O better beasts, you now must yield !
I name the cool stars of the field,
I have the flowers of heaven by heart.

Francis Meynell.

238

S O N G S

EVERYONE SUDDENLY BURST OUT SINGING

SIEGFRIED SASSOON

GREEN GROW THE RASHES, O

With point and not too quickly.

There's naught but care on ev'-ry hand, In
ev'ry hour that pass-es, O! What
signifies the life o' man, An' 'twere na for the lasses, O?
Green grow the rashes, O! Green grow the rashes, O! The
sweetest hours that e'er I spent, were
spent among the lasses, O! *Repeat from the double bar for chorus.*

Gie me a cannie hour at e'en,
My arms about my dearie, O !
An warldly cares and warldly men,
May a' gae tapsalteerie, O !

For you sae douce wha sneer at this,
Ye're nought but senseless asses, O !
The wisest man the warld 'ere saw,
He dearly lo'ed the lasses, O !

Auld nature swears the lovely dears,
Her noblest work she classes, O !
Her 'prentice han' she tried on man,
An' then she made the lasses, O !

Robert Burns.

241

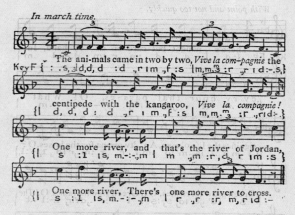

In march time.

The ani-mals came in two by two, *Vive la com-pagnie* the
centipede with the kangaroo, *Vive la compagnie!*
One more river, and that's the river of Jordan,
One more river, There's one more river to cross.

The animals came in three by three,
    Vive la compagnie.
The elephant on the back of the flea,
    Vive la compagnie.
      One more river, etc.

The animals came in four by four, etc.

The camel, he got stuck in the door.

Some were dead and some were alive.

The monkey he was up to his tricks.

Some went to Hell, and some went to Heaven.

The worm was early, the bird was late.

Some had water and some had wine.

If you want any more you must sing it again.

BILLY BOY

Loud and with good rhythm.

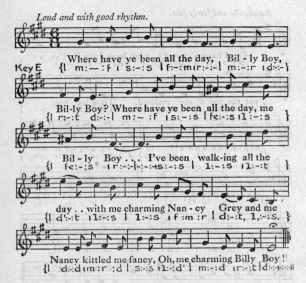

Where have ye been all the day, Bil-ly Boy,

Key E {|m:—:f|s:—:s |f:—:m|r:—:—| m:—:r|d:—:}

Bil-ly Boy? Where have ye been all the day, me

{|r:—:t d:—:|m:—:f |s:—:s |fe:—:s|l:—:s }

Bil-ly Boy... I've been walk-ing all the

{|fe:—:s |r:—:l:—:|—s:—:s | l:—:s |l:—:t }

day..with me charming Nan-cy Grey and me

{|d:—:t |l:—:s | l:—:s |f:m:r|d:—:t, 1,:—:s. }

Nancy kittled me fancy, Oh, me charming Billy Boy!

{|l d:d:d|m:r:d|l s:—:s|l:—:d' |m:—:d|r:—:t|d:—:—||}

Can she cook a bit o' steak, Billy Boy, Billy Boy?
Can she cook a bit o' steak, me Billy Boy?
    She can cook a bit o' steak,
    Aye, and make a girdle cake.
       And me Nancy, etc.

Is she fit to be your wife, Billy Boy, Billy Boy?
Is she fit to be your wife, me Billy Boy?
    She's as fit to be my wife
    As the fork is to the knife.
       And me Nancy, etc.

Did she lie close unto thee, Billy Boy, Billy Boy?
Did she lie close unto thee, Billy Boy?
    Yes, she lay close unto me
    As the bark is to the tree.
       And me Nancy, etc.

243

THE MALLARD

Bucolically and fairly fast.

* Repeat this half bar so as to take in a fresh addition with every verse, for instance "a thigh-thigh, a leg-leg,1 voot-voot, a toe-toe, nippens and all," etc. The order is: (1) Toe; (2) Voot; (3) Leg; (4) Thigh; (5) Hip; (6) Rump; (7) Zide; (8) Wing; (9) Back, etc.

BUNYAN'S HYMN

(*From the English Hymnal*)

Fairly quickly and with fervour.

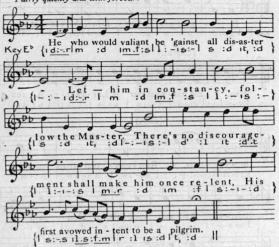

He who would valiant be 'gainst all dis-as-ter

Key E♭ { :d :- r|m :d |m .f:s|l :- :s :- | s :d |t₁ :d }

Let him in con-stan-cy, fol-

{ l :- :- |d :- r |l m :d |m .f :s |l |l :- :s :- }

low the Mas-ter. There's no discourage-

{ l s :d |t₁ :d|- :- :s :- | d' :l |t :d .t }

ment shall make him once re-lent, His

{ l|l :- :- s |m .r :d |m |m :f|l s :- :- :d }

first avowed in - tent to be a pilgrim.

{ l s :- s|l s :f .m|r :l :s |d|t₁ :d ‖ }

Who so beset him round
    With dismal stories,
Do but themselves confound—
    His strength the more is.
No foes shall stay his might,
    Though he with giant's fight :
He will make good his right
    To be a pilgrim.

Since, Lord, thou dost defend
    Us with Thy Spirit,
We know we at the end
    Shall life inherit.
Then fancies flee away !
    I'll fear not what men say,
I'll labour night and day
    To be a pilgrim.

245

EN PASSANT PAR LA LORRAINE

At a good swinging pace.

En pas - sant par la Lor - raine, A - vec mes sa

Key F |d:-:d |s:-:s |s:-:s |l:-:f:-:s|l:-:l

(Chorus.)

bots, En pas - sant par la Lor - rain - e A - vec

|s:-:-|:|:d:-:d |s:-:s |s:-:s |l:-:f |s:-:s

(Solo.)

mes sa - bots, Ren - con - trai trois cap - i -

|l:-:l |s:-:-|: : |s:-:s |d':-:s |s:-:f

tain - es, Av - vec mes sabots, Don - dain - e

|m:-:r |m:-:m |m:s|s:-:f | m :- :r

Oh! Oh! Oh! A - vec mes sa - bots.

|d:-:m |s:-:-|: :|l:-:f |r:-:t, |d:-:-|- : :

(Chorus.)

Ren - con - trai trois ca - pi - tai - nes, Av - vec

|s:-:s |d:-:s |s:-:f |m:-:r | m:-:m

mes sa - bots, Don - dai - ne, Oh! Oh! Oh!

|m:-:s |s:-:f |m:-:r |d:-:m |s:l:- :

A - vec mes sa - bots.

|l:-:f |r:-:t |d:-:-|-:||

Rencontrai trois capitaines, Avec mes sabots,
(*Repeat chorus.*)

Ils m'ont appelé vilaine, Avec mes sabots,
Dondaine, Oh ! Oh ! Oh ! Avec mes sabots.
(*Repeat chorus.*)

Ils m'ont appelé vilaine, Avec mes sabots,
Je ne suis pas si vilaine, Avec, etc.

Je ne suis pas si vilaine, etc.
Puisque le fils du roi m'aime, etc.

Puisque le fils du roi m'aime,
Il m'a donné pour étrenne.

Il m'a donné pour étrenne,
Un bouquet de marjolaine.

Un bouquet de marjolaine,
S'il fleurit, je serai reine.

S'il fleurit, je serai reine,
S'il y meurt je perds ma peine.

MR. REILLY

Fairly fast.

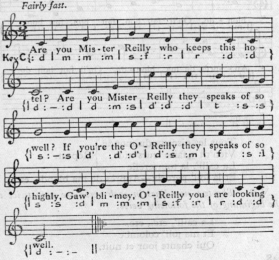

247

AUPRÈS DE MA BLONDE

In march time.

Tous les oiseaux du monde   }
Vien'nt y faire leurs nids   } Repeat.
La caill', la tourterelle   }
Et la joli' perdrix—Auprès de ma blonde, etc.

N.B.—The two new lines in each verse are sung twice at the beginning of the following verse.

La caill', etc., etc.
Et ma joli' colombe
Qui chante jour et nuit.

Qui chante pour les filles
Qui n'ont pas de mari.

Pour moi ne chante guère
Car j'en ai un joli.

Dites-nous donc la belle,
Ou donc est votr' mari.

Il est dans la Hollande
Les Hollandais l'ont pris.

Que donneriez-vous belle,
Pour avoir votre ami ?

Je donnerais Versailles,
Paris et Saint Denis.

Les tours de Notre Dame,
Et l'clocher d'mon pays.

Et ma joli' colombe,
Pour avoir mon mari.

THEY WERE ONLY PLAYING LEAP-FROG

Quick march time.

They were on-ly play-ing leap-frog.

They were on-ly play-ing leap-frog.

They were on-ly play-ing leap-frog, When
one grass-hop-per jumped up-on the
other grass-hop-per's back.

BOBBY SHAFTOE

Fairly quickly.

(Chorus.)

Key A

1. Bobby Shaftoe's gone to sea, Silver buckles
{ :d :d :d :d .f | :m .s :m .d | :s, .s, :s, .d }

on his knee; He'll come back and marry me,—
{ :t, .r :t, .s, | :d .t, :d .f | :m .s :m .d }

(Verse.)

Bonny Bobby Shaf-toe. Bobby Shaftoe's
{ :r .f :r .t, | :d :d || :m .s :m .d }

bright and fair, Combing down his yellow hair;
{ :m .s :m | :r .f :r .t, | :r .f :r }

(Repeat Chorus.)

He's my ain for ever mair, Bonny Bobby Shaf-toe.
{ :m .s :m .d | :m .s :m | :r .f :r .t, | :d :d || }

Bobby Shaftoe's tall and slim,
He's always dressed so neat and trim,
The lassies they all keek at him,
Bonny Bobby Shaftoe.
    Chorus.

Bobby Shaftoe's gett'n a bairn,
For to dangle on his airm,
On his airm and on his knee,
Bonny Bobby Shaftoe.

Final Chorus :
    Bobby Shaftoe's been to sea,
    Silver buckles on his knee,
    He's come back and married me,
    Bonny Bobby Shaftoe.
    (And so on, *ad infinitum*, getting faster and faster.)

THE BARLEY MOW

With inebriation.

Here's a health to the Bar - ley Mow, my boys, A
Key D {: s   s | d':r':d|t :-:t | l:-:t | l :s:-:m

health to the Bar - ley   Mow {(1) We'll
{| f :-.m | f :r :-:t | d':-:-|(2) :-:s

drink   it out of a   nut - - brown bowl, A
{|d':-:r | d':t :t :t | l:-:t : l | s :-:m

health to the Bar-ley Mow. The nip-perkin, pipperkin
{| f:-.m:f |r:-:t |d':-:-:s|m :f :s |m:f:s

and the brown bowl, A health to the Bar - ley
{|m :r :d | d':-:m| f :-.m:f |r:-:t

Repeat to the double bar.

Mow, my boys, A health to the Barley Mow.
{|d':-:s |m:-:-m | f :-.m:f |r:-:t |d':-:-:|| D.S.

We'll drink it out of the pint, my boys,

We'll drink it out of the gallon, my boys,

We'll drink it out of the river, my boys,

We'll drink it out of the ocean, my boys.

MASSA'S IN DE COLD, COLD GROUND

Slowly and sadly.

When de Autumn leaves are falling,
When de days were cold,
'Twas hard to hear old Massa calling,
Cayse he was so weak and old.

Now de orange tree am blooming
  On de sandy shore,
Now de summer days are coming
  Massa nebber calls no more.
    Down, etc.

Massa makes de darkeys love him,
  Cayse he was so kind,
Now dey sadly weep above him,
  Mourning cayse he leave dem behind.
I cannot work before to-morrow,
  Cayse de tear-drop flow,
I try to drive away my sorrow,
  Picking on de old banjo.
    Down, etc.

GOLDEN SLUMBERS KISS YOUR EYES

Quietly and rather slowly.

Gold-en slum-bers kiss your eyes, Smiles a-
wake you when you rise, Sleep, pretty wan-tons,
do-not cry, And I will sing a lul-la-by, lul-la-
by, lu - - - la - by.

Care is heavy, therefore sleep,
You are care, and care must keep,
Sleep, pretty wantons, etc.

253

AND WHEN I DIE

Slowly and with much pathos.

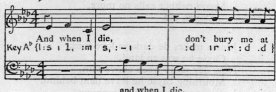

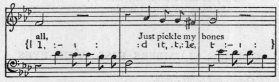

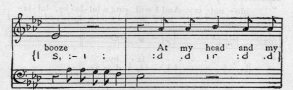

254

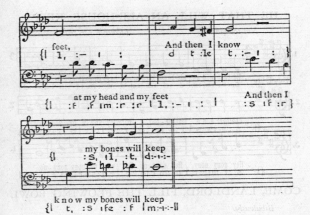

FRÈRE JACQUES

HE THAT WILL AN ALE-HOUSE KEEP

Not too quickly. (Round for three voices.)

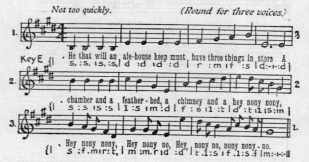

He that will an ale-house keep must have three things in store

chamber and a feather-bed, a chimney and a hey nony nony,

Hey nony nony, Hey nony no, Hey, nony no, nony nony - no.

COME, LANDLORD, FILL THE FLOWING BOWL

Bibulously.

Come, land-lord, fill the flowing bowl, Un-

til it doth run ov - er. Come, land-lord, fill the

flowing bowl un - til it doth run ov - er.

For to-night we'll merry, merry be, For to-night we'll

merry, merry be, For-to-night we'll

merry, merry be, to - mor - row we'll be so - ber.

The man who drinketh small beer,
　　And goes to bed quite sober,
Fades as the leaves do fade,
　　That drop off in October.
　　　　For to-night, etc.

The man who drinketh strong beer,
　　And goes to bed quite mellow,
Lives as he aught to live,
　　And dies a jolly good fellow.
　　　　For to-night, etc.

But he who drinks just what he likes
　　And getteth half-seas over,
Will live until he dies perhaps,
　　And then lie down in clover.
　　　　For to-night, etc.

The man who kisses a pretty girl,
　　And goes and tells his mother,
Ought to have his lips cut off,
　　And never kiss another.
　　　　For to-night, etc.

ROUND THE CORNER

Roisterously and in march time.

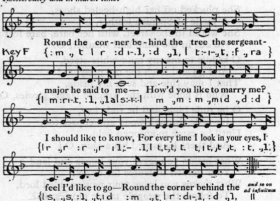

Round the cor-ner be-hind the tree the sergeant-

Key F {:m ., t | r :d--.,1, | d .,1, | t:-1,.,t, :f, ra }

major he said to me— How'd you like to marry me?

{| m :r-.t, :1, .,1a|s-:-:-| m .,m : m .,m|d .,d :d }

I should like to know, For every time I look in your eyes, I'

{|r .,r : r .,r |1 ;- .1,| t,t,t, t, | t,t,t, t, : t, .,1, }

feel I'd like to go—Round the corner behind the *and so on*
ad infinitum

{|s, .,s, :1, .,t,|d :m .,t, | r :d--.,1, | d .,1, ‖ }

K
257

THE WRAGGLE TAGGLE GIPSIES, O!

Not slowly.

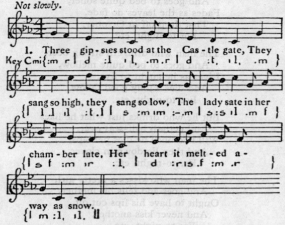

1. Three gip-sies stood at the Cas-tle gate, They
sang so high, they sang so low, The lady sate in her
cham-ber late, Her heart it melt-ed a-
way as snow.

They sang so sweet, they sang so shrill,
    That fast her tears began to flow.
And she laid down her silken gown,
    Her golden rings and all her show.

She plucked off her high-heeled shoes,
    A-made of Spanish leather, O
She would in the street, with her bare, bare feet;
    All out in the wind and weather, O.

O saddle to me my milk-white steed,
    And go and fetch me my pony, O!
That I may ride and seek my bride,
    Who is gone with the wraggle taggle gipsies, O!

O he rode high, and he rode low,
    He rode through wood and copses too,
Until he came to an open field,
    And there he espied his a-lady, O!

What makes you leave your house and land?
    Your golden treasures for to go?
What makes you leave your new-wedded lord,
    To follow the wraggle taggle gipsies, O?

What care I for my house and my land?
  What care I for my treasure, O?
What care I for my new-wedded lord,
  I'm off with the wraggle taggle gipsies, O!

Last night you slept on a goose-feather bed,
  With the sheet turned down so bravely, O!
And to-night you'll sleep in a cold open field,
  Along with the wraggle taggle gipsies, O!

What care I for a goose-feather bed,
  With the sheet turned down so bravely, O!
For to-night I shall sleep in a cold open field,
  Along with the wraggle taggle gipsies, O!

MR. McKINLEY

Not slowly.

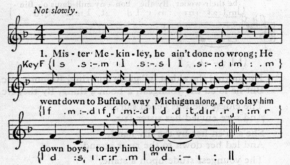

1. Mis-ter Mc-kin-ley, he ain't done no wrong; He
went down to Buffalo, way Michigan along, For to lay him
down boys, to lay him down.

Mr. McKinley, he went there for fun,
But Sholgosh he shot him with an Ivor-Johnson gun,
For to lay him down boys, to lay him down.

Mrs. McKinley, she hollered and she swore
When they told her her good man wasn't coming home
      no more,
For to lay him down boys, to lay him down.

Sholgosh, they took him and put him in the electric chair,
And shocked him so hard that they shocked off all his
      hair,
For to lay him down boys, to lay him down.

259

BINNORIE, OR THE CRUEL SISTER

Sadly, but with strength.

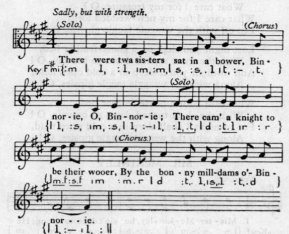

(Solo) (Chorus)

There were twa sis-ters sat in a bower, Bin-

Key F# mi :m | l, :l, | m,:m, | s, :s, | l, | t, :- .t,

(Solo)

nor-ie, O, Bin-nor-ie; There cam' a knight to

| l, :s, | m,:s, | l, :-l, | :l .t, | d :t,.l, | r : r

(Chorus)

be their wooer, By the bon-ny mill-dams o'- Bin-

| m.f:s.f | m :m.r | d :t, | l,.s,.l, | t,.d

nor - - ie.

| l, :- .l, : ||

He courted the eldest wi' glove and ring, Binnorie, etc.
But he lo'ed the youngest, a-boon a thing, By the, etc.

The eldest she was vexed sair,
And sore envied her sister fair.

She's ta'en her by the lily hand,
And led her down to the river strand.

The youngest stude upon a stane,
The eldest cam' and pushed her in.

Sometimes she sank, sometimes she swam,
Until she cam' to the miller's dam.

The miller's daughter was baking bread,
And gaed for water as she had need.

Oh, father, father, draw your dam,
There's either a mermaid or a milk-white swan.

The miller hasted and drew his dam,
And there he found a drowned woman.

A famous harper passing by,
The sweet pale face he chanced to spy.

He made a harp o' her breast bone,
Whose sounds would melt a heart of stone.

The strings he framed of her yellow hair,
Their notes made sad the listener.

He brought it to her father's ha'
There was the court assembled a'.

He laid the harp upon a stane,
And straight it began to play alane.

" O' yonder sits my father, the king,
And yonder sits my mother, the queen."

" And yonder sits my brother Hugh,
And by him my William, sweet and true."

But the last time that the harp did play,
Was, " woe to my sister, false Helen."

ADAM BUCKHAM, O !

March time.

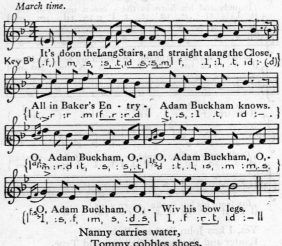

It's doon the Lang Stairs, and straight alang the Close,
All in Baker's En - try. Adam Buckham knows.
O, Adam Buckham, O, - O, Adam Buckham, O, -
O, Adam Buckham, O, - Wiv his bow legs.

Nanny carries water,
  Tommy cobbles shoes,
And Adam gans about,
  Geth'ring in the news.
    O Adam Buckham, etc.

JOHN PEEL

With vigour.

1. D'ye ken John Peel with his coat so gay, D'ye ken John Peel at the break of the day, D'ye ken John Peel when he's far, far away, With his hounds and his horn in the morn ing? For the sound of his horn brought me from my bed, And the cry of his hounds which he oft-times led Peel's view hall'oo would a – waken the dead, or the fox from his lair in the morn – ing.

Yes, I ken John Peel and Ruby too !
Ranter and Ringwood, Bellman and True,
From a find to a check, from a check to a view,
From a view to a death in the morning.
    For the sound, etc.

Then here's to John Peel from my heart and soul,
Let's drink to his health, let's finish the bowl,
We'll follow John Peel thro' fair and thro' foul,
If we want a good hunt in the morning.
   For the sound, etc.

D'ye ken John Peel with his coat so gay?
He lived at Troutbeck once on a day;
Now he has gone far, far away;
We shall ne'er hear his voice in the morning.
   For the sound, etc.

SWING LOW, SWEET CHARIOT

Intensely and rather slowly.

Swing low, sweet cha-ri ot, Coming for to carry me home. Swing low, sweet cha-ri-ot, Coming for to carry me home. 1. I look'd over Jordan, What did I see, coming for to carry me home—? A band of angels coming after me—— Coming for to carry me home.

Repeat chorus after second verse.

263

GO DOWN, MOSES

Boldly. Not too fast.

When Is-rael was in E-gypt's lan',
Let my people go, Opp-press'd so hard they
could not stand, Let my people go! Go down,
Moses, 'Way down in E-gypt's lan'
Tell - ole - - Pha - raoh Let my people go!

Thus saith the Lord, bold Moses said,
    Let my people go !
If not I'll smite your first-born dead,
    Let my people go !
        Go down, Moses, etc.

This world's a wilderness of woe,
    Let my people go !
Oh, let us on to Canaan go,
    Let my people go !
        Go down, Moses, etc.

MADEMOISELLE FROM ARMENTIÈRES

In rousing march time.

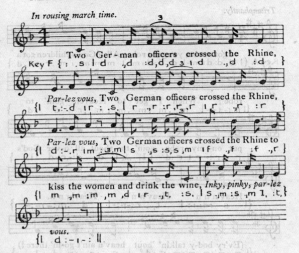

Key F

Two Ger-man officers crossed the Rhine,

{ :s |s |d :d, |d :d,d,d :d |s |d., |d :d }

Par-lez vous, Two German officers crossed the Rhine,

{ l t, :d |r :r, :s, |r :r, :r, r |r :r, :r }

Par-lez vous, Two German officers crossed the Rhine to

{ l d :-,r |m :,m |s :,s, :s,s,m |f :,f :f ,r }

kiss the women and drink the wine, Inky, pinky, par-lez

{ l m ,m :m ,m ,d :r ,t, :s, |s ,m :s, ,m 1, :t, }

vous.

{ l d :-1-: ‖

They came to an inn at the top of the rise,
Parlez vous,
A famous French inn of enormous size,
Parlez vous,
They saw a maiden all dimples and sighs,
Then both together said, " Damn her eyes."
Inky, pinky, parlez vous.

Oh, landlord, have you a daughter fair,
Parlez vous,
Oh, landlord, have you a daughter fair,
Parlez vous,
Oh, landlord, have you a daughter fair,
With lily-white arm, and golden hair ?
Inky, pinky, parlez vous.

N.B.—Other verses may be written on the blank pages at the end of this book.

K *

265

Triumphantly.

I got a robe, you got a robe; All of God's children got a
robe; When I get to Heaven goin' to
put on my robe, goin' to shout all o-ver God's
Heav'n n n   Heav'n n n   Heav'n n n.
(Ev'ry bod-y talkin' 'bout heav'n ain't goin' there!)
Heav'n,   Heav'n—— Goin' to shout all o-ver God's
Heav'n.

I got a shoes, you got a shoes,
All of God's children got a shoes;
When I get to Heav'n goin' to put on my shoes,
Goin' to walk all over God's Heav'n,
   Heav'n, Heav'n . . . etc.

I got a harp, you got a harp,
All of God's children got a harp;
When I get to Heav'n goin' to play on my harp,
Goin' to play all over God's Heav'n,
   Heav'n, Heav'n . . . etc.

266

I got a song, you got a song,
All of God's children got a song;
When I get to Heav'n goin' to sing a new song,
Going to sing all over God's Heav'n,
  Heav'n, Heav'n . . . etc.

ETON BOYS

With feeling and a nasal Cockney intonation.

E-ton boys, Eton boys, boys of the good old
school, Eton boys, Eton boys, what
cheers for the red, white and blue.
Some makes for fame, others for shame, while
others with life plays the fool; But bring
life what it may, We're all proud to say, We're
boys of the old E-ton Sch-ool.

SINNER, PLEASE, DOAN LET DIS HARVES' PASS

With ecstasy and not too slowly.

Sin - ner, please, doan let dis har - ves' pass;

Sin - ner, please, doan let dis har - ves' pass, an'
die an' lose yo' soul at las'. —— I. I know that
my Re - deem - er lives, (Yes, He lives) I know that
my Re - deem - er lives, (Yes, He lives) I know that
my Re - deem - er lives, Sin - ner, please, doan
let dis har - ves' pass (har - ves' pass).

268

My God is a mighty man of war (man of war),
My God is a mighty man of war (man of war),
My God is a mighty man of war,
Sinner, please, doan let dis harves' pass (harves' pass).

I'M A MAN THAT'S DONE WRONG TO MY PARENTS

Sentimentally and with a Cockney accent.

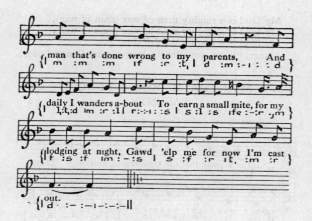

{man that's done wrong to my parents, And

{daily I wanders a-bout To earn a small mite, for my

{lodging at night, Gawd 'elp me for now I'm cast

{out.

Then my father will say when 'e meets me,
    " You beggar, you still are at large,
And mind, sir, that you don't come near me,
    Or by 'eaven I'll give you in charge."
My mother, poor thing's broken-'earted,
    To meet me she oft-times will try,
For to give me a crown with 'er 'ead 'anging down,
    And a tear rolling out of 'er eye.
            I'm a man, etc.

I've a sister that's married a squire,
    She'll ne'er look, nor speak unto me :
Because in this world she's much 'igher,
    And rides in 'er carriage so free.
And I try to be honest and upright
    And do all the good that I can,
And I try all I know to get on in this world,
    And prove to my friends I'm a man.
            I'm a man, etc.

THE SHAN WAN WOCHT

Quick march time. Very rhythmically.

Key D

{ :s₁.,f₁ | m₁.,d :r .,l₁ |d .,l₁ :s₁ .,d }

Oh—— Boney's on the sea, says the

{ :r | r :r |r :s₁.,f | m₁.,d :r .,l₁ |d .,l₁ :s₁ .,l₁ }

Shan wan wocht, Oh—— Boney's on the sea, says the

{ |d :d |d :d .,r |m .,m :f .,s |t :d' .,l }

Shan wan wocht, Oh—— Boney's on the sea, He'll be

{ :s .,m :r .,d |r :s .,f }

here the first o' May, And the

{ |m .,d :r .,l₁ |d .,l₁ :s |d .,r :r :r |r :s .,f }

Orange will decay, says the Shan wan wocht, And the

{ |m .,d :r .,l₁ |d .,l₁ :s .,l₁ |d :d |d : }

Orange will decay, says the Shan wan wocht

Oh, Boney's on the shore,
   Says the Shan wan wocht, [*twice*
Boney's on the shore,
Don't you hear his cannon's roar?
We'll be Orangemen no more,
   Says the Shan wan wocht.

Oh, Boney's on dry land,
   Says the Shan wan wocht, [*twice*
Oh, Boney's on dry land,
He's a sword in ev'ry hand,
He's a loyal Ribbon man,
   Says the Shan wan wocht.

271

O, ME TATERS

As you like it.

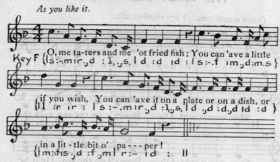

Key F {s :- m| r ,d : l ,s| l ,d : d| d :l :s:- f| m ,d:m .s }
O, me ta-ters and me 'ot fried fish; You can 'ave a little

{l :r| r : l :s :- .m| r ,d : l ,s| l ,d :d ,d| d| :d }
if you wish, You can 'ave it on a plate or on a dish, or

{l m:fis ,d :f,m| r :- d| : ll }
in a lit - tle bit o' pa - - - per!

THE LAST LONG MILE

Quick march time. With a good swing.
(Solo.)

Key Eb {:s, | d ,d :d ,d| d| :t ,,t, :s, | ,s, }
They put us in the Army and they

{| d ,d :d ,d| t, :- .s | d ,t, :d ,t,| d :r| m ,r :r| :d ,m }
handed us a pack, They took away our nice new clothes and

{| r ,d :r ,m| d :- .s, | d ,t, :d ,r| d| :t, :l| ,s, }
dress'd us up in kak, They marched us twenty miles and more to

{| d ,r:m .f| s :- .m| f ,m :f| | :r| m :f| :s ,m }
(Chorus.)
fit us for the war, We did'nt mind the nineteen but the

{| m ,d :r| r ,t, | d| :s ,s| d :- .d| t, | :s ,s, }
last one made us sore. Oh, it's not the pack, that you

{| l ,d:d ,d| d| :t :s ,s| d :r :m .f| s :- .m| :l| s }
carry on your back, nor the gun upon your shoulder, Nor the

Key Eb

five-inch crust of France's dirty dust That makes you feel your limbs are growing old-er. It's not the load on the hard straight road that drives a-way your smile; If the sox of sister raise a blis-ter, Blame it on the last long mile.

One day we had manœuvres on dear old Salisbury
    Plain,
We marched and marched and marched and marched
    and marched and marched again.
I thought the Duke of York a fool, but he wasn't in
    the van
With us who marched and marched and marched and
    marched back home again.

Chorus.

Oh, it's not the pack, that you carry on your back,
Nor the gun upon your shoulder,
If there's never any ham, there's plum and apple jam
To make you feel your limbs are growing older.
Oh, it's not the camp, nor the echoes of the tramp
That drives away your smile,
It's the sergeant-major's little wager,
To beat you on the last long mile.

273

THE FIRE SHIP

Breezily.

As I strolled out one ev'-ning out for a night's ca-

{ :s, d :s, | m, :s, | d :s im :d | t, :-l, | s, :l }

reer, I spied a lof-ty fire--ship, and af--ter her I

{ s, :- :s, | d :s, m, :s, | d :s im :d | t, :-.l, | s, :l }

steered; I hoisted her my sig-a-nals which

{ s, :-l :s, | r :-.r ir :m | r :t, ls, | :s, }

she very quickly knew, And when she see'd my

{ m :r .r im :f | m :-l :m | f :r is :f }

bunting fly, she im- med-iate-ly hove to-o-o. She'd a

{ m :d if :m .m | r :d lt, :l | s, :l lt, :s, .s, }

dark and a rolling eye, And her hair hung down in

{ d :d d | d :rl d :-l :t, | d lr :r ir :d }

ring-a-lets, She was a nice girl, a decent girl, But

{ t, .l, :s, .s, | s, .s, | m, :s, :-.s | s :f if :r }

one of the rakish kind.

{ d :m .m im :r | d :-l :-ll }

O Sir you must excuse me for being out so late,
For if my parents knew of it, then sad would be my
fate,
My father he's a minister, a true and honest man,
My mother she's a Methodist, and I do the best I can.
    She'd a dark and a rolling eye, etc.

I took her to a tavern and I treated her to wine,
Little did I think she belonged to the rakish kind;
I handled her, I dandled her, and found to my
    surprise,
She was nothing but a fire-ship rigged up in a disguise.
        She'd a dark and a rolling eye, etc.

SHENANDOAH

Slowly, with great longing.

Oh Shenandoah, I love your daughter.
Oh Shenandoah, I love your daughter.

'Tis seven long years since last I see thee.
'Tis seven long years since last I see thee.

Oh Shenandoah, I took a notion
To sail across the stormy ocean.

Oh Shenandoah, I'm bound to leave you.
Oh Shenandoah, I'll not deceive you.

275

THE EASTER HYMN

("*Unser lieben Frauen Osterfreud*") 1623

With much elation.

Lasst uns er - freu - en herz - lich sehr! Ma - ri - a
Come, let our songs of glad - ness rise! Ma - ry no

seufzt und weint nicht mehr Al - le - lu - ja, Al - le -
lon - ger weeps and sighs, Hal - le - lu - ia, Hal - le -

lu - ja. Ver - schwun - den al - le Ne - bel
lu - ia. For gloom and cloud have passed a -

sein, Jetzt scheint der lie - be — Son - nen - schein, Al - le
way, Now shines the bless - ed light of day, Hal - le

-lu - ja, Al - le lu - ja, Al - le lu - ja, Al - le
-lu - ia, Hal - le lu - ia, Hal - le lu - ia, Hal - le

-lu - ja, Al - le - lu - ja.
-lu - ia, Hal - le - lu - ia.

Aus Seinen Wunden fliessen hier,
Fünf Freuden-See, fünf Freuden-Meer. Alleluja.
Und über dich die Freuden giess,
Dir in dein Herz der Freuden Fluss. Alleluja.

Dein Herz jetzund in Freuden schwimmt,
Je mehr und mehr die Freud' zunimmt. Alleluja.
Ach Frau, vergiss nur unser nicht,
Und teil' uns auch die Freuden mit. Alleluja.

276

See from the wounds of thy dear Son
Five healing streams of gladness run.   Halleluia.
The flowing tide thy grief shall still,
Thy heart with floods of gladness fill.   Halleluia.

Now thy glad heart with joy o'erflows,
Now more and more thy gladness grows.   Halleluia.
O, Mary, keep us in thy care,
And let us all thy gladness share.   Halleluia.

MY AUNT

March time.

My aunt she died a month a-go, and left me all her riches, A feather-bed and a wooden leg, And a pair of cali-co breech-es; A coffee-pot with-out a stroup, And a mug without a handle, a-bac-cy box with-out a lid, And half a farden candle, A —. *Repeat from the double bar.*

THE TREES THEY DO GROW HIGH

Very sadly and not too fast.

Key G

The trees they do grow high, and the leaves they do grow green, And many a cold winter's night my love and I have seen. Of a cold winter's night, my love, you and I a-lone have been, Whilst my bon-ny boy is young; he's a grow-ing.

(Chorus)

Grow-ing, grow-ing, whilst my bon-ny lad is young, he's a-grow-ing.

"Oh father, dearest father, you've done to me much harm.
You've tied me to a boy when you know he is too young."
"Oh daughter, dearest daughter, if you'll wait a little
A lady you shall be whilst he's growing." [while
     Growing, growing, a lady, etc.

"I'll send your love to college all for a year or two,
And then in the meantime he will do for you;

278

I'll buy him white ribbons, tie them round his bonny
To let the ladies know that he's married."   [waist,
     Married, married, to let, etc.

At the age of sixteen he was a married man,
At the age of seventeen he was father to a son,
At the age of eighteen the grass grew over him,
Cruel death soon put an end to his growing,
     Growing, growing, cruel death, etc.

" And now my love is dead, and in his grave doth lie,
The green grass grows over him so very very high,
I'll sit and mourn his fate until the day I die,
And I'll watch all over his child, whilst he's growing,"
     Growing, growing, and I'll, etc.

SONG OF THE HAULERS ON THE VOLGA

Slowly and heavily.

all together. *Repeat to the double bar getting gradually softer.*

279

MRS. DYER, THE BABY FARMER

Indignantly.

1. The old baby far-mer 'as been exe-cuted, It's quite time she was put out of the way. She was a bad wo-man, it is not dis-puted, Not a word in her fa-vour can an-y-one say.

Chorus.

The old baby farmer, the wretched Mrs. Dyer,
    At *the* Old Bailey her wages is paid.
In times long ago we'd ha' made a big fyer
    And roasted so nicely that wicked old jade.

It seems rather hard to run down a woman,
    But this one was hardly a woman at all ;
To get a fine livin' in a way so unhuman,
    Crossin' (carousing?) in luxury on poor girls' downfall.
                     Chorus.

Poor girls who fall from the straight path of virtue,
    What *could* they do with a child in their arms ?
The fault they committed they could not undo,
    So the baby was sent to the cruel baby farms —*Chorus.*

To all these sad crimes there must be an ending,
    Secrets like these for ever can't last.
Say as you like, there is no defending
    The 'orrible tales we have heard in the past.—*Chorus.*

What did she think as she stood on the gallows,
    Poor little victims in front of her eyes ?
Her heart if she 'ad one must have been callous,
    The rope round her neck—how quickly time flies !

Chorus.

Down through the trap-door quickly disappearing,
    The old baby farmer to eternity 'ome.
The sound of her own death bell she was 'earing.
    Maybe she was sent to the cruel baby farm.

Chorus.

I'M SEVENTEEN COME SUNDAY

Fairly fast.

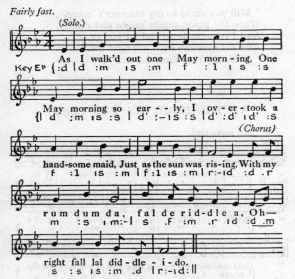

" Where are you going, my sweet pretty maid,
Where are you going, my honey ? "
She answered me right cheerfully,
" With an errand for my mammy."
    With my rum dum da, etc.

" Will you take a man, my sweet pretty maid,
Will you take a man, my honey ? "
She answered me right cheerfully,
" I dare not, for my mammy."
  With my rum dum da, etc.

" How old are you, my sweet pretty maid,
How old are you, my honey ? "
She answered me right cheerfully,
" I'm seventeen come Sunday."
  With my rum dum da, etc.

" Will you come to my mammy's house,
When the moon shines bright and clearly,
And I'll come down and let you in,
And my mammy shall not hear me."
  With my rum dum da, etc.

AT THE HALT, ON THE LEFT

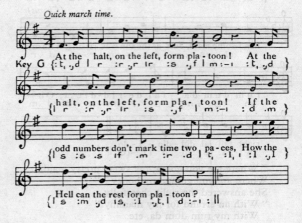

Quick march time.

Key G

At the halt, on the left, form pla - toon ! At the
halt, on the left, form pla - toon ! If the
odd numbers don't mark time two pa - ces, How the
Hell can the rest form pla - toon ?

282

WIDDECOMBE FAIR

With point.

Key G

(Solo.)
Tom Pearce, Tom Pearce, lend me your grey mare.
{ :s | d:—:d | m:—:r | t₁:—:l₁ | :s₁ | d:—:}

(Chorus.)   (Solo.)
(All along,   down along,   out along lee,)   For I
{ | d:—.d:d | m:—.r:d | t₁:—.t₁:d | r:—:s₁ }

want for to go—   to Wid - de - combe Fair, Wi' Bill
{ | d:—:d | m:r:d | t₁:—:l₁ | :s₁ | l₁:—:s₁ .s₁ }

Brewer, Jan Stewer, Peter Gurney, Peter Davy, Dan'l
{ | l₁:—:s₁ | l₁:—:s₁ | l₁:—:s₁ }

(Chorus.)
Whiddon, Harry Hawk, Old Uncle Tom Cobleigh and
{ | l₁:—:s₁ | l₁:—:s₁ | s₁:f:m | r:—.d:t₁ }

all—   Old   Uncle Tom Cobleigh and   all.
| s:—:—:—:f | m:—:f :m | r:—.d :t₁ | d:—:—:—:—:|| }

And when shall I see again my grey mare ?
By Friday soon or Saturday noon.
    Wi' Bill Brewer, etc.

Then Friday came and Saturday noon,
Tom Pearce's old mare hath not trotted home.
    Wi' Bill Brewer, etc.

So Tom Pearce he got up to the top of the hill,
And he see'd his old mare a-making her will—
    Wi' Bill Brewer, etc.

283

So Tom Pearce's old mare her took sick and died,
And Tom he sat down on a stone and he cried—
   Wi' Bill Brewer, etc.

But this isn't the end of this shocking affair,
For, tho' they be dead, of the horrid career,
Of Bill Brewer, etc.

Then the wind whistles cold on the moor of a night,
Tom Pearce's old mare doth appear ghastly white—
   Wi' Bill Brewer, etc.

And all the night long he heard skirling and groans
From Tom Pearce's old mare in her rattling bones—
   Wi' Bill Brewer, etc.

THE BELLS OF HELL

THE RIO GRANDE

With spirit.   At moderate speed.

Now you Bowery ladies, we'd have you to know,
    O, you Rio !
We're bound to the Southward, O Lord, let us go !
    For we're bound for the Rio Grande.
        Then away love, etc.

So it's pack up your donkey and get under way,
The girls we are leaving can take our half-pay.
    For we're bound, etc.

And good-bye, fare you well, all you ladies of town,
We've left you enough for to buy a silk gown.
    For we're bound, etc.

ALL THROUGH THE NIGHT

Slowly and religiously.

1. Deep the silence round us spreading,
All through the night; Dark the path that
we are treading All through the night.
Still the coming day discerning, By the hope with-
in us burning, To the dawn our footsteps turning,
All through the night.

Key F

{| d :- .t, |l, :d | r :- d |t, :s, }
{|l, :- |t, :- .t, | d :- 1 :- | d :- .t, |l, :d }
{| r :- d |t, :s, | l, :- |t, :- .t, | d :- 1 :- ||
{| f :m |f :s |l :- .s |f :m | f :m |r :d }
{| m :- .r |d :t, | d :- .t, |l :d | r :- d |t, :s, }
{| l, :- |t, :- .t, | d :- 1 :- ||

Star of Faith the dark adorning
All through the night,
Leads us fearless toward the morning
All through the night.
Though our hearts be wrapt in sorrow
From the hope of dawn we borrow
Promise of a glad to-morrow
All through the night.

O GOOD ALE, THOU ART MY DARLING

With hearty humour.

The Land-lord he looks very big With his

high cock'd hat and his powder'd wig; Me-

thinks he looks both fair and fat, But

he may thank you and me for that, For 'tis

O, good ale, thou art my darling, And my joy both

night and morning.

The brewer brew'd thee in his pan,
The tapster draws thee in his can;
Now I with thee will play my part,
And lodge thee next unto my heart.
    For 'tis O, etc.

Thou oft hast made my friends my foes,
And often made me pawn my clothes;
But since thou art so nigh my nose,
Come up, my friend—and down he goes.
    For 'tis O, etc.

287

CHICKA-HANKA

At a moderate pace.

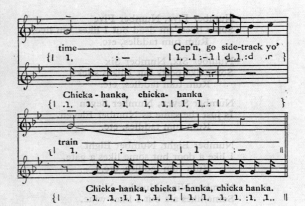

time———— Cap'n, go side-track yo'

{| l, : — | l, .l :-l | d .l :d .r }

Chicka-hanka, chicka-hanka

{| .l, .l, .l, .l, | l, l,| l, .l :l }

train

{| l, : — | l : — ||

Chicka-hanka, chicka-hanka, chicka hanka.

{| .l, .l, :l, .l, .l, .l, | l, l, .l, .l, .l, :l, l,.. ||

OWD JOE BRADDLES

Bucolically

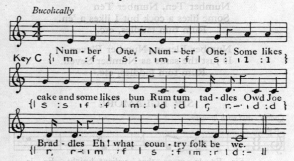

Key C {| m :f | s : | m :f | s : | l :l }

Num-ber One, Num-ber One, Some likes

{| s :s |f :f | m :d :d | r, r—:d :d }

cake and some likes bun Rum tum tad-dles Owd Joe

{| r, r—:m :f | s :f |m :r | d :- ||

Brad-dles Eh! what coun-try folk be we.

Number Two, Number Two
They all likes me and some likes you.
Rum tum taddles, etc.

Number Three, Number Three
Some likes you but they all like me.
Rum tum taddles, etc.

Number Four, Number Four
Some likes a gate but I like a door.
Rum tum taddles, etc.

L

Number Five, Number Five
Some likes 'em dead but I likes 'em live.
　　Rum tum taddles, etc.

Number Six, Number Six
Some like posts but I likes sticks.
　　Rum tum taddles, etc.

Number Seven, Number Seven
Is just the same as Number Eleven.
　　Rum tum taddles, etc.

Number Eight, Number Eight
I like a door but some likes a gate.
　　Rum tum taddles, etc.

Number Nine, Number Nine
Some likes ale but I likes wine.
　　Rum tum taddles, etc.

Number Ten, Number Ten
Some likes a cock but I likes a 'en.
　　Rum tum taddles, etc.

Number Eleven, Number Eleven
Is just the same as Number Seven.
　　Rum tum taddles, etc.

SIR EGLAMORE

Quickly and with humour.

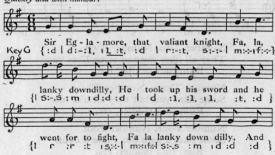

Sir Eg-la-more, that valiant knight, Fa, la,
lanky downdilly, He took up his sword and he
went for to fight, Fa la lanky down dilly, And

290

as he rode o'er hill and dale, All armed with a
{| m :=: f | s :−: m | l :−: s | f :−: m | r :=d | t, :−: l, }

coat of mail, Fa - lanky down, La - lanky down,
{| s, :=: s, | s, :=: | s :−: d :−. r | :m | f :−: t :r :−. m | :f }

Fa - la - lanky down dilly.
{| s :=: d | d :−. r | :t, | d :=d :−: − ||

There starts a huge dragon out of his den, fa, la, etc.
Which had killed I know not how many men, fa, la, etc.
But when he see Sir Eglamore,
If you'd but heard how that dragon did roar, fa, la, etc.

This dragon had a plaguey hard hide,
Which could the strongest steel abide ;
But as the dragon yawning did fall,
He thrust his sword down hilt and all.

The dragon laid him down and roared,
The knight was sorry for his sword ;
The sword it was a right good blade,
As ever Turk or Spaniard made.

When all was done to the ale-house he went,
And presently his tuppence was spent ;
He was so hot with fighting the dragon,
And nought could quench his thirst but a flagon.

Well now let us pray for the King and the Queen,
And eke in London that may be seen,
As many knights and as many more,
And all as good as Sir Eglamore.

With fervour.

On this day, Earth shall ring With the song children sing To the Son, Christ our King, Born on earth to save us; Him the Father gave us. I-de-o - o - o, I-de-o - o - o, I-de-o glo-ri-a in ex-cel-sis De-o!

His the doom, ours the mirth,
When He came down to earth
Bethlehem saw His birth ;
Ox and ass beside Him
From the cold would hide Him.—*I-de-o, etc.*

God's bright star, o'er His head,
Wise men three to Him led
Kneel they low by His bed,
Lay their gifts before Him,
Praise Him and adore Him.—*I-de-o, etc.*

On this day angels sing ;
With their song earth shall ring
Praising Christ, Heaven's King,
Born on earth to save us ;
Peace and love He gave us.—*I-de-o, etc.*

ALLELUIA, I'M A BUM

Very noisily.

1. A la-dy came out when I knocked at the door: "You'll get no-thing here, for I've seen you be-fore," Al-le-lu-ia, I'm a bum, bum, Al-le-lu-ia, bum a-gain, Al-le-lu-ia give us a hand-out to re-vive us a-gain.

" Oh why don't you work as the other fellows do ? "
" How the hell can I work when there's no work to do ? "
      Alleluia, etc.

" Oh why don't you pray for your daily bread ? "
" If that's all I did I would damn soon be dead."
      Alleluia, etc.

" Oh I love my boss, he's a good friend of mine,
And that's why I am starving out on the bread line."
      Alleluia, etc.

*N.B.—A " bum " is a migratory worker. This is a
popular I.W.W. or " wobbly " song.*

CAN'T YOU DANCE THE POLKA?

Lively.

[Solo].

As I walk'd down the Broadway, one
ev'ning in Ju-ly I met a maid who
axed my trade, "A sailor John," says

[Chorus].

I, And a-way you Santee, my dear Annie.
O you New York girls, can't you dance the Polka?

To Tiffany's I took her,
I did not mind expense;
I bought her two gold earrings,
They cost me fifty cents.
    And away, etc.

Says she, "You lime-juice sailor,
Now see me home my way."
But when we reached her cottage door
She unto me did say—
    And away, etc.

"My flash man—he's a Yankee,
With his hair cut short behind;
He wears a tarry jumper
And he sails on the Black-Ball line."
    And away, etc.

294

SÆTERJENTENS SÖNDAG

Slowly and sadly.   (Ole Bull)

O, sweet fa's the eve on Craig-ie-burn, And blythe a-wakes the morrow, But a' the pride o' spring's return Can yield me nocht but sorrow. I see the flowers and spread-ing trees, I hear the wild birds singing; But what a weary wight can please, And care his bo-som wringing.

Fain, fain would I my griefs impart,
    Yet dare na for your anger ;
But secret love will break my heart,
    If I conceal it langer.
If thou refuse to pity me,
    If thou shalt love anither,
When yon green leaves fa' frae the tree,
    Around my grave they'll wither.

Robert Burns.

QUELLE EST CETTE ODEUR AGRÉABLE

Fairly quickly.

Quelle est cette o-deur agré-a--ble Bergers qui
ra-vit tous nos sens? S'ex-ha-le-t il rien
de sem-bla-ble, Au mi-lieu des fleurs
du prin-temps? Quelle est cette o-deur
a-gré-a-ble. Bergers qui ra-vit tous nos
sens?

A Bethléem, dans une crêche
Il vient de vous naître un sauveur ;
Allons, que rien ne vous empêche
D'adorer votre Redempteur.
A Bethléem, dans une crêche
Il vient de vous naître un sauveur.

(*Note.*—If the smaller alternative notes are sung, this
becomes the melody to which the following words are sung
in " The Beggar's Opera.")

> Fill every glass, for wine inspires us
> And fires us with courage, love and joy !
> Women and wine should life employ ;
> Is there ought else on earth desirous ?
> Fill every glass, for wine inspires us
> And fires us with courage, love and joy !

Fairly fast.   *Round for three voices.*
(Purcell.)

"Fie, nay, prithee John, Do not quarrel, man,

Key A♭ {|d :—.m |r :t, :s, | l, :—.d |t, :s, :m, }

Let's be merry and drink a - - bout."

{|f, :—.l |s, .m, :d | f, :s, | d, :— }

"You're a rogue, you cheated me, I'll

{|d .s :s |d .t, :s, :s, | t, }

prove before this company, I

{|l, |f, :f | l, |s, .m, :m, .s, }

caren't a farthing, Sir, for all you are so stout."

{|f, .r :r |r .f, :m, .d :d .m, |r, :t, :d, :— }

"Sir, you lie; I scorn your word or

{|s, .m :d |.l :f |.r :t, .s }

any man that wears a sword, For

{|m .d :l, |.f :r .t, :s, |.m }

all your huff, who cares a damn, and,

{|d .l :f, |.r :t .s, :m, |.m }

who cares for you?"

{|l :s ,f |m :— || }

HEY, HO, TO THE GREENWOOD

WILLIAM BYRD

--ty roe, sing heave and ho. Hey ho to the
heart and hind and the little pret-ty roe, sing heave and ho. Hey
and ho, The hart and hind, and the little pret-ty roe, sing heave and
greenwood now *(Repeat from double bar.)*
ho

FRAGMENT

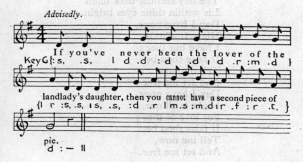

Advisedly.

If you've never been the lover of the
landlady's daughter, then you cannot have a second piece of
pie.

Rather slowly and passionately.

I. Ma-rish-ka, Ma-rish-ka, Look not at me,
Ma-ry. Thy glan-ces are lan-ces, With their darts be
wa-ry. All my joy they've chas'd a way, And
my peace has flown; My heart pines with
one de-sire, To be thine own. *Repeat from double bar.*

The sunlight, the moonlight,
I know not in thy sight ;
The day and the dark night
Lie within thine eyes bright.
Day I have none,
Night is all one,
I have but thee ;
If false thou be
Tell me now,
And set me free ;
Day I have none,
Night is all one,
For love of thee ;
If false thou be,
Tell me now,
And set me free.

THE OLD MAN THAT LIVED NEAR HELL

Loud and lively.

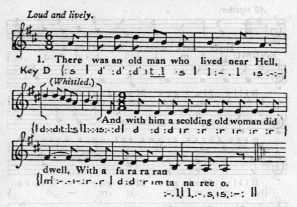

1. There was an old man who lived near Hell,
And with him a scolding old woman did
dwell, With a fa ra ra ran

The *devil* came to him one *day* at the plough,
" It's *one* of your family I do want now."

" It *isn't* your son that I do crave,
But it *is* your oul' wife, it's her I maun ha'e."

" *Tak*' her awa' wi *all* ma guid hert,
Hoping that you and her never will part."

He *hoisted* her up on the *oul'* de'ils back,
And like a bold pedlar he carried his pack.

It's *when* they came unto Hell's door,
He then threw her down with a clash on the floor.

There were *seven* de'ils there tied *up* wi' chains,
She lifted her crutch and she knocked out their brains.

There were *three* de'ils more holdin' *up* the wall,
" *Tak*' her awa' she will kill us all.

" She's *not* fit for heaven an' *nay*ther for Hell,
We must *build* her house, she maun live by her sel'."

" And *on* her dresser, she maun *have* some delf ;
If you *want* any more, you maun sing it yourself ! "

301

Said one old crow unto his mate,
" What shall we do for our grub to ate ? "

" There lies a horse on yonder plain,
Whose by some cruel butcher slain."

" We'll perch ourselves on his backbone,
And pick his eyes out one by one."

" The meat we'll eat before it's stale,
Till nought remain but bones and tail."

FRANKIE AND JOHNNIE

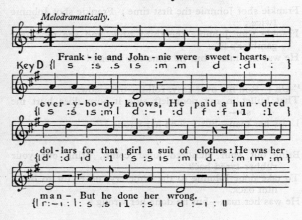

Melodramatically.

Frank-ie and John-nie were sweet-hearts,
every-bo-dy knows, He paid a hun-dred
dol-lars for that girl a suit of clothes : He was her
man – But he done her wrong.

Frankie went to the beer-shop, she ordered a bottle of beer,
She said, " Now, Mr. Bar-tender-man, have you seen my
    Johnnie here ?
He was my man—but he done me wrong ! "

303

The Bar-tender said, " Frankie, I can't tell you no lie ;
Your Johnnie was here an hour ago, with a girl called Alice
    Fly :
She's pinched your man—who done you wrong ! "

Frankie went to the pawn-shop—she didn't go there for
    fun—
When she came out of that pawn-shop, she had a great, big,
    wonderful gun
To shoot that man—who done her wrong !

Frankie went to the Dance-hall, she rang the Dance-hall
    bell,
She said, " Clear out, you people, I'm going to blow this
    man to hell
For he was my man—and he done me wrong ! "

Frankie shot Johnnie the first time ; Frankie shot Johnnie
    twice ;
Frankie shot Johnnie the third time, and she took that
    gambler's life.
He was her man—but he done her wrong !

" Oh ! Roll me over easy, roll me over slow,
That bullet in my poor left side it sure does hurt me
    so—
I was her man—but I done her wrong ! "

Bring out your hundred-dollar coffin, bring out your
    rubber-tyred hack
To take poor Johnnie to the cemetery, never for to bring
    him back.
He was her man—but he done her wrong !

Now, the moral of this story is very plain to all—
Be careful you young ladies or you sure will have a
    fall :
Just watch these men—or they'll do you wrong ! ! !

304

MISS BAILEY

Fast but sad.
(Solo.)

Key G

A captain bold in Hali-fax that dwelt in country quar-ters, De-ceived a maid who hanged herself one morning in her gar-ters, His wicked conscience smited him, he lost his stomach dai-ly, He took to drinking turpentine, and thought upon Miss

(Chorus.)

Bai-ley, O, Miss Bailey, un-fortunate Miss Bai-ley, O Miss Bailey, un-fortunate Miss Bailey.

SPANISH LADIES

Raucously.

Fare - well and a - dieu to you, Fair Spanish
Key G { :s, | d .d :r | d .r :m | f .r :d }

La - dies, Fare - well and a - dieu to you,
{ |t,.1, :s, :s, | r .r :r :m | r : - :r :m }

Ladies of Spain, For we've re - ceived or - ders to
{ |f :m :r | s :s :m .f | s :s :s | m .r :d .r :m }

sail for old Eng - land, But we hope in a
{ |f :r :d | t,.1, :s, :s, .f | m :m :m }

(Chorus.)

short time to see you a - gain. We'll rant and we'll
{ |f :r :d | t :1, | t, .t, :d :- :s, | d :d :r }

roar, all o'er the wild o - cean, We'll rant and we'll
{ |d :- :r .m | f .r :d | t,.1, :s, :s, | r :r :m }

roar, all o'er the wild seas, Un -
{ |r :- :r .m | f .m :m :r | s :- : .m .f }

til we strike sound - ings in the Channel of Old
{ |s :s :s | m .r :d :r .m | f .f :r :d }

Eng - land, From Ushant to Scil - ly is thir - ty five
{ |t,.1, :s, :s, .f | m :m :m | f :r :d | t, :1, :t, }

leagues.
{ | d :- : - || }

306

We hove our ship to, with the wind at sou'west, boys,
    We hove our ship for to strike soundings clear;
Then filled the main topsail and bore right away, boys,
    And straight up the Channel our course we did steer.
            We'll rant and we'll roar, etc.

The first land we made was a point called the Dodman,
    Next Rame Head off Plymouth, Start, Portland and
        Wight,
We sailed then by Beachy, by Fairlee and Dung'ness,
    Then bore straight away for the South Foreland Light.

The signal was made for the Grand Fleet to anchor,
    We clewed up our topsails, stuck out tacks and sheets,
We stood by our stoppers, we brailed in our spanker,
    And anchored ahead of the noblest of fleets.

Then let every man here toss off a full bumper,
    Then let every man here toss off his full bowl,
For we will be jolly and drown melancholy,
    With a health to each jovial and true-hearted soul.

THE JONES BOYS

307

A-ROVING

Rollicking.
(Solo.)

Key F {: s, | d :d | r :f | m :r | d :- }

In Plymouth Town there lived a maid,

(Chorus.) (Solo.)

{| s :-|r :f |m :r| d :s,| d :d | r :-}

(Bless you young wo-men) In Plymouth Town there

(Chorus.) (Solo.)

{| m :r | d :-.d | s :-.s | l ,s :fe| s :-|-:s}

lived a maid, (O, mind what I - a - do say) In

{| l| :l |f :l |l :| s :s |m :s }

Plymouth Town there lived a maid, and

{| f :m| r :d.r | m :d| l, :s | d :-.r | m :f}

she was mis - tress of her trade, I'll go no more a-

{| s :d| l| :f | s :-.r :-| d :-|-:s | l :-.s| f.s :l }

ro - - ving with you fair maid. A- ro - ving, a-

(Chorus.)

{| s :-.f| m :f :s | f :m| r :d :r| m :d| l, :s. }

ro - - ving, Since rov - ing's been my ru - i - in, I'll

{| d :-.r | m :f | s :d| l| :f | m :-|r :-| d :-|-||}

go no more a- ro - - ving with you fair maid.

I took this fair maid for a walk
(Bless you young women)
I took this fair maid for a walk
(O, mind what I do say)

308

I took this fair maid for a walk
And we had such a loving talk,
I'll go no more a-roving with you, fair maid.

Chorus.

And didn't I tell her stories too, etc.
Of the gold we found in Timbuctoo, etc.

But when we'd spend my blooming screw, etc.
She cut her stick and vanished too, etc.

LILLIBURLERO

In rousing march time.

(Solo.)   (Chorus.)

Ho! bro - ther Teague dost hear de de-cree, Lilli-bur-ler-o.
Key D {|d :r |d' :m r :-|m r :m :r |f :-| m :s :d |f :-m}

(Solo.)

bullen a la. Dat we shall have a new de-pu-tie.
{|r :d :t,d:|d :r :d |m :-|m r :m :r |f :-:}

(Chorus.)   (Chorus.)

Lilli-bur-ler-o bullen a la. Le-ro, le-ro,
{|m :s :d |f :-m|r :d :t,d:|d' :-t :d :-s }

lilli-bur-le-ro, lilli-bur-le-ro bullen a la--
{|s :l :ta|l :-:s | s :l :t :d:s|l s :f :m|r :-:s}

le-ro, le-ro, le-ro, -le-ro lilli-bur-le-ro
{|l:s :f :m|m:f :s |l:s :t :m:f|s l:d' :d |f :-:m}

bullen a la.
{|r :d :t,|d:-:-||}

309

Joyously.

Here is joy for ev'-ry age Ev'-ry gen-er-

Key C {| s :s |l :t | d :t |l:- | t :s |l :f }

a-tion: Prince and pea-sant, Chief and sage,

{|s:-|s:- | s :s |l :t | d' :t |l:- }

Ev'-ry tongue and na-tion; Ev'-ry tongue and

{|t :s |l :f |s:-|s:- | t :t |d' :d' }

na-tion, Ev'-ry rank and sta-tion, Hath to-day sal-

{|r:- |r':- |r :m'|r':d' |r:- |t:- | t :t |d':t' }

va-tion Al-le-lu - ya.

{|l:- |t:- |t :s |l |f |s:- |-:- || }

When the world drew near its close
   Came our Lord and Leader:
From the lily sprang the rose,
   From the bush the cedar;
From the bush the cedar,
From the judg'd the pleader,
From the faint the feeder;
   Alleluya.

God, that came on earth this morn,
   In a manger lying,
Hallow'd birth by being born,
   Vanquish'd death by dying;
Vanquish'd death by dying,
Rallied back the flying,
Ended sin and sighing;
   Alleluya.

310

AYE WAUKIN' O!

Slowly and sadly.
(Solo.)

O I am wat, wat, O, I'm wat and weary, Yet
fain wad I rise and rin, If I thocht I wad meet my
dearie, Aye waukin' O! Waukin' aye an'
eerie, Sleep I can get nane. For thinking o' my
dearie, Aye waukin' O!

Spring's a pleasant time,
Flowers of ev'ry colour,
The water rins o'er the heugh,
And I long for my lover.
    Aye waukin' O! etc.

When I sleep I dream,
When I wauk I'm eerie;
Sleep I can get nane
For thinking on my dearie,

Lanely night comes on,
A' the lave are sleepin',
I think on my true love
And I bleer my een wi' greetin'.
                                        Robert Burns.

SUMER IS ICUMEN IN

(Cheerfully.) Round for three or four mixed voices and two basses.

Sum - er is i - cu - men in—— Lhu - de sing cuc -
Key Eb {|d:-:t |1:-:t |d:-:d it:-:1:s || m:=:m |f:-:r }

cu Grow - eth sed, And blow - eth med, And
{|m:-:-:1 d:=:m |r:-:f | m:=:m |r:-:d }

spring - 'th the wd - e nu. Sing cuc - - cu.
{| m:-: s |1:-:1 |s:-:-d:-:-1:-1 | d:-:-1: :}

Aw - e blet - eth af - ter lomb, Lhouth af - ter cal - ve
{|s:=:m |f:-:r |m:=:s |f:- :m | d:=:m |r:-:t.}

cu, Bul - luc ster - teth, Buck - e vert - eth,
{|d:-:-1::|m:=:m |r:-:f | s:-:s |1:-:t }

Mu - rie sing cu - cu, cu - cu,— cuc—cu, Wel
{|d:-:t |1:-:t |d':=:s |1:-:|s:-:-:f:-:m }

sing - es thu cuc - cu. Ne—— swik thu na - ver
|d:=:m |f:-:r | m:-:-:f:-:s |m:-:s |r:-:t }

Back to the beginning.

nu;
|d:-:-1: :||

312

These four bars are repeated ad infinitum by two male voices.

cuc - cu, cuc - cu cuc - cu cuc - cu —

| s:.f:-:.| s:-:.| :| d:-:r:.| d:-:r:-:m |
| d:-:r:-:.| d:-:r:-.m| s:-:f:.| s:-:.| :‖ |

★ *The 2nd, 3rd and 4th voices enter in turn, when the previous part has reached the beginning of the third bar.*

I WISH I WERE

As if you really were.

I wish I were a-- El-e-phan-

Key F {., d :d ,r | m :d ., d :r ,m -

ti-a-phus - And could pick off the co-co-nuts with my

{| s'.,f : r :-:s' .,f | m ., d :d .,m :s' .,f :r ,m |

nose-- But oh! I am not- (a-las I

{| d:-:- .,d : t .,d | r :s :-_,f :m ., r |

can - not be--) an El-e-phan-ti-El-e-phan-

{| d .,r : m :-.,d : t.,d | r :s' :-_,f :m ., r |

ti-a-phus - But I'm a cock-roach - And I'm a

{| m .,r :d :- .,d :d .,r | m :d :- .,d :r ,m |

wa-ter-bug-I can crawl a-round and hide be-hind the

-{| s' .,f : r :-:s' .,f | m .,d :d .,m :s' .,f :r ,m |

sink.

{| _.d:-:r : ‖

313

I wish I were a
Rhinosceréeacus
And could wear an ivory toothpick in my nose.
But, oh ! I am not,
(Alas ! I cannot be)
A Rhinoscōri-
Rhinosceréeacus.
But I'm a beetle
And I'm a pumpkin-bug,
I can buzz and bang my head against the wall.

I wish I were a
Hippopōpotamus
And could swim the Tigris and the broad Gangés.
But, oh ! I am not,
(Alas ! I cannot be)
A hippopōpo-
Hippopōpotamus.
But I'm a grasshopper
And I'm a katydid,
I can play the fiddle with my left hind-leg.

I wish I were a
Levileviāthan
And had seven hundred knuckles in my spine.
But, oh ! I am not,
(Alas ! I cannot be)
A Levi-ikey-
A Levi-ikey-mo.
But I'm a firefly
And I'm a lightning-bug,
I can light cheroots and gaspers with my tail.

(*And so ad infinitum.*)

" OH, DON'T TAKE MY PRAYER-BOOK "

Appealingly

Oh, don't take my prayer-book, Mister
Bur - gu - lar,—— But o - pen it and look in -
side—, You'll find in there a lock of mother's hair,
And a for-get-me-not be - side my ev'ning prayer. Oh,
don't take my prayer-book, Mis - ter Bur - gu - lar—— The
child in an - guish cried, 'Twas give' to me by
mother—— The night be - fore she died.

MICHAEL FINNIGIN

With great reserve

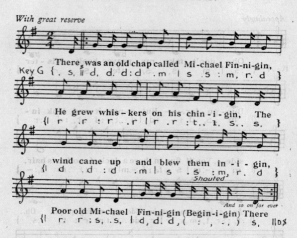

There was an old chap called Mi-chael Fin-ni-gin,

Key G { |: s, || d, d, d:d .m | s s :m, r d }

He grew whis–kers on his chin-i-gin, The

{ |r r r: r .r|r r :t, .t, s, s, }

wind came up and blew them in-i-gin,

{ |d, d d:d .m|s s :m, r d }

Shouted

Poor old Mi-chael Fin-ni-gin (Begin-i-gin) There

And so on for ever

{ |r r r:s, .s, |d, d, d, (: , –,) s, ||D$ }

Other verses, with lines ending sin-igin and in-igin, are believed to exist.

THE CHINESE BUMBOAT MAN

Dramatically

Solo

I'll sing you a sto-ry of trou-ble and woe that will

cause you to shud-der and shiv-er-Con-cern-ing a Chi-nee

Bum-boat man that sail'd on the Shang-hai

ri-ver. He was a hea-then of a high degree, As the

Joss-house re-cords show, His fam-i-ly name was

Wing Chang Loo, But the sail-ors all call'd him Jim

Chorus

Crow - i - o - i. Hit-chy-cum, kit-chy-cum, Yah, yah, yah,

Sailor-man no lik-ee me,— No sav-vy the sto-ry of

Wing Chang Loo, Too much-ee the bob-ber-i-

Shouted

ee, Ki - Yi!

Now Wing Chang Loo he fell in love
With a girl called Ah Chu Fong,
She 'ad two eyes like pumpkin seeds,
And 'er slipper was two inches long.
But Ah Chu Fong loved a pirate bold
With all 'er 'eart and liver,
He was captain of a double-deck junk
Up the Yangtsee Kiang River-i-iver-i.

Chorus.

When Wing Chang Loo 'e 'ear of this
He swore an 'orrible oath,
" If Ah Chu marries that pirate bold
I'll make sausage-meat of them both."
So he 'oisted his blood-red battle flag,
Put into the Yangtsee river,
He steered nor'-east and south by west
Till that pirate he did disciver-i-iver-i.

The drums they beat to quarters,
And the cannons did loudly roar,
The red-'ot dumperlins flew like lead,
And the scuppers they ran with gore.
The pirate paced the quarter-deck,
With never a shake or shiver,
He was shot in the neck with an 'ard-boiled egg,
That penitriated 'is liver-i-iver-i.

The dyin' pierate feebly cried,
" We'll give the foe more shot,
If I can't marry Ah Chu Fong,
Then Wing Chang Loo shall not."
When a pease-puddin' 'ot 'it the bumboat's side
It caused an 'orrible scene,
It upset a pot of 'ot bow-wow soup,
And exploded the magazieen-i-een-i.

318

GREENSLEEVES

With a gentle swing

If you intend thus to disdain,
It does the more enrapture me,
And even so I still remain
A lover in captivity.

Chorus.

Alas, my love, that you should own
A heart of wanton vanity,
So must I meditate alone
Upon your insincerity.

Chorus.

Greensleeves, now farewell . . . adieu . . .
And God I pray to prosper thee !
For I am still thy lover true,
Come once again and love me.

Chorus.

I'M NOT STRONG, SIR

Round for three voices

Key B♭

1. I'm not strong, Sir, Sure 'tis wrong, Sir,
   {| m :m | r :r | d :d | t, :t, |}

2. I'm quite hoarse, Sir, So of course, Sir,
   {| d :d | d :t, | t, :l, | l, :s, |}

3. I can't sing a note, Sir, Some-thing hurts my throat, Sir,
   {| d .r :m .f | s :s, | l, .t, :d .r | m :m |}

   Such high notes my voice to—— strain,
   {| l, :l, | s, :d | r :m .f | m :— ||}

   I can - not sing this Round a - gain,
   {| f :m .r | m :d | l d :t, | d :— ||}

   Tho' I try my best 'tis all in vain.
   {| f, .s, :l, .t, | d :d | d :t, | d :— ||}

I'LL STICK TO THE SHIP

In waltz time

I'll stick to the ship, boys, You save your
Key C {|s :-: l | m :r :d |s :-:- l | d :-:l s :-:- l |d :-: r }

lives; I've no one to love me, You've
{| t :-:-:-l :-l |-l :-: l | f : m : r |l :-:-|r :-:-|r :-:- }

sweet-hearts and wives– You take to the boats, boys
{| d : t : l |t :-:-l:-ld :-l d : t : l |t :-:-lt :-:- }

Trust - ing in Heav'n a - bove —— While I go
{| l : r : m l f :-: s lm :-:-l-:- r lm :-:m }

down in the an - gry deep with the ship I love.
{| m :r :d lt :-:- l l r : m : f ls :-:-lr :-:-ld :-:-ll }

It is probable that the hero of this tragical ballad had time to compose more verses before his ship went down. If they are known to the reader let them be added here.

DOWN AT THE WANGAN

Expressively

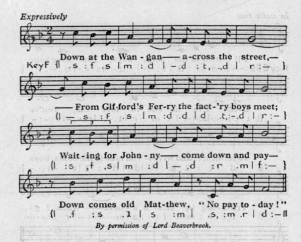

Down at the Wan - gan —— a-cross the street, —
Key F { l, :s :f, .s | m :d | – d | :t, .,d | r :– }

—— From Gif-ford's Fer-ry the fact-'ry boys meet;
{ l :– s₁ :f, .s | m :d .d | d | :t, .,d | r :– }

Wait - ing for John - ny —— come down and pay—
{ l, :s :f, .s | m :d | – d | :r | .m | f :– }

Down comes old Mat - thew, "No pay to - day!"
{ l, .f :s .,l | s :m | .s, :m | r | d :– || }

By permission of Lord Beaverbrook.

MY MOTHER'S AN APPLE-PIE BAKER

With unction

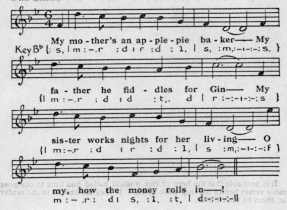

My mo - ther's an ap - ple - pie ba - ker —— My
Key B♭ { :s, | m :– .r :d | r :d | :l, | l, :s, :m,:–:–:s, }

fa - ther he fid - dles for Gin —— My
{ l m :– .r :d | d | :t, ., | d | r :–:–:–:s, }

sis - ter works nights for her liv - ing —— O
{ l m :– .r :d | r | :d | :l, | l, :s, :m,:–:–:f }

my, how the money rolls in ——!
m :– .,r: d | s, :l, | :t, | d :–:–:–:|| }

322

SHE WAS POOR

With moral significance

She was poor but she was honest, Victim of a
rich man's game, For she met the vil-lage
Squi-re, And she lost her mai-den name. It's the
same the whole world ov-er: It's the
poor as gets the blame, It's the rich as has the
plea-sure. Aint it all a bleeding shame?

So she hastened up to London
For to hide her grief and pain ;
There she met an army captain
And she lost her name again.

Chorus.

See him riding in his carriage
Past the gutter where she stands ;
He has made a stylish marriage
While she wrings her ringless hands.

See him in the House of Commons
Passing laws to put down crime ;
While the girl as he has ruined
Slinks away to hide her shame.

See him laugh at the theayter
In the front row with the best ;
While the girl as he has ruined
Entertains a sordid guest.

In the little country village
Where her aged parents live,
Though they drink champagne she sends them
Yet they never can forgive.

GAMES

"PLAY!"—Any Umpire.

GAMES

OUTDOOR ACTIVE GAMES

MAN-HUNT

THIS is strenuous and any number can join in. It is more exciting than a paper chase, and does not litter the country with paper.

First mark out an agreed area, say six miles by one, on the map, limited by recognizable natural features, outside which the men must not go, with your starting point on one end line and a suitable pub, as your objective, in the middle of the other end line. The hunters set off first and the two men a quarter of an hour later. The hunters may not block-ade the starting point nor the objective but should stretch a cordon across the area and ambush likely points in the attempt to stop the men from passing through.

You have lunch at your objective and man-hunt home. It is unsuitable for crowded suburban areas.

ROUNDERS

This *is* a good game, in spite of the quarrels which it engenders amongst those who do not study the observations following :

If a batsman's hit is caught, he only, and not the whole side, is out, unless a contrary convention has been made. (If you want to speed up the game, make such a convention.) Otherwise, a side is out only if, for any reason, there is none of the batting side home to bat. Further, a member of the batting side is out if he is touched by a ball, thrown or in the hand, when not on the base.

A player who is out may be redeemed by his side on payment of one rounder, if the side is in credit—otherwise as soon as a rounder is scored. This privilege cannot be

327

postponed until it is proved that there is a tactical necessity for the redemption (i.e. the emergency of the lack of batsmen to keep the side going, all others being on bases). A player on a base may feint to go to another base and retire to his former; but he must regain this before he is touched.

The Bowler may feint and, instead of bowling, throw to a fielder; but if the ball leaves his hand, it counts as one of the three throws out of which one must be a " good " ball to the Batsman.

A " good " ball is a slow ball between shoulder and knee of Batsman, outside his body to the offside, and within one yard of his body. If the Bowler delivers three " bad " balls, the penalty is a Rounder to the other side. There should, if possible, be a Referee who would decide on good and bad balls, and all other points. If a batsman fails to hit any of three good balls, he is out.

A hit behind the Batsman is not a " good " hit; it counts as a Good Ball not taken.

A Player on a base may run for a " bad " ball, or for a " good " ball not run for by the Batsman.

All running between bases is stopped by the bowler bouncing the ball. The runner must go unmolested to his nearest base.

Players on the batting side must *never* run inside the bases, whatever these may be—trees, walking-sticks, hats, or coats. In the latter cases, bases should not be stood upon. As anything may be used for bases, so also with the tools of the game; but a tennis-ball, and the handle of a walking-stick, are not only the best in themselves, but are generally available.

" SMALL " CRICKET

This is called " Small " Cricket, as opposed to the Greater Cricket as played at Lord's, because, though there must be rules which are adhered to, these rules in a house-party—especially where there are Women and Children—must be considerably modified if everybody is to enjoy the game. It is to be remembered that in games on which no Championship depend, it is far more important that they shall be good fun than that one side or t'other shall win—an automatic certainty, in any case. Nothing is more dull for a youthful or feminine member of the team than to be certain that it will be bowled first ball and spend the remainder of the day entirely by itself in a remote corner of the ground, waiting to field a ball that never comes. It is advocated, therefore, that

A. All bowlers should be given a chance in turn by the Captain, and Overs should consist of 9 balls instead of 6.

B. Good bowlers in bowling to the Small Fry should remember that Spofforth had his licence endorsed; " small " bowling should be the rule in Small Cricket.

C. Good Batsmen will *never* remember that very long hits, continually repeated, are a nuisance, and can ruin the game ; before the game starts, therefore, Captains should consult and firmly fix certain boundaries, according to the nature of the ground. Such boundaries would penalize long hits ; a hit into the cornfield or the pig-stye might count 6 ; but it should, at the same time, be " out."

D. Where the players are few and small, first-bounce catches should be " out." L.B.W. should also be strictly enforced ; this is essential, because our more womanly women still grossly exploit their skirts.

E. Where the players are small and few, and fielders scarce, both sides should field. Any players fielding against their own side should remember that it is far more necessary to field well than that their side should win.

F. A tennis-ball is the best sort of ball for this game. A cricket-stump is the best bat. But anything can be made to serve, as also for wickets.

G. Captains should be all-powerful, unless you have an Umpire ; but an Umpire is no use unless you trust him.

SMALL HOCKEY

Small Hockey is played as Ordinary Hockey ; with a solid rubber ball if possible, and walking-sticks ; but no freak sticks, cut specially for the purpose. Both sides of the stick may be used. Some " bunting " therefore will be unavoidable ; but it should be reduced to a minimum.

In Small Hockey there is no offside, and there is no

circle. A goal may be shot anywhere beyond the half-way line. For " Behind," instead of a Bully, there is a free hit for the goal from the " Go " line ; but after a goal is shot, there is always a new centre bully.

Captains, as in Small Cricket, should be all-powerful, and should see strict enforcement of Stick Rule ; sticks must *not* be raised above the shoulder, or the Hockey-Ground become a sacrificial altar to (and of Brains) and Beauty. Shoulder-height varies in all, however ; therefore, if our team happens to include Carnera or Charlie Chaplin, we must take our chances.

Any number of players on a side ; in proportioning his field afterwards, all the Captain has to remember is that there should be five times as many Forwards as there are Goal-Keepers.

HUMAN POLO

The biggest men are the ponies, and the girls or lighter weights mount them pick-a-back, hold on with one hand and use walking-sticks to drive a tennis-ball through goals at opposite ends of a lawn or tennis-court. Holding opponents with the hands is not allowed, nor kicking (of man or ball), but bumping, boring and hooking sticks are all part of the game. A player may remount ; but may not play from the ground.

FLAT-RACING

Ponies similarly mounted race thirty yards on hands and knees ; after which apply iodine to the kneecaps. Jockeys may not remount or touch the earth with their feet.

Wheelbarrow races and *Three-legged races* need no description ; we give them a passing recommendation.

Relay races are amusing, particularly if each team contains a very small child, who cannot be relied on to keep to the course.

TIERCE

Or Twos-and-Threes. One player is " He," the others stand in a fairly wide circle in pairs, one in front of the

330

other ; but in one group there are three. The Behind Man in this group begins to run, and " He " has to try to catch him before or touch him before he slips into the circle and stands in front of any other pair. The moment he does so the Behind Man of that pair has to run and take his chance of being caught, as there must never be more than two people in a group. If " He " touches his prey before it saves itself by joining a new group, " He " instantly places himself in safety before one of the pairs, and the player just caught becomes " He," and chases the Third Man on the outside of the circle.

THE ROOF GAME

is played by two persons with a discarded tennis ball and a sloping roof. The ideal roof is 60 feet long, slopes at an angle of 110°, ends 8 feet from the ground and has a perfectly clear space in front of it. Each player in turn serves one ball from any position in this run-way and at any speed. The ball must roll or bounce off the roof inside two imaginary walls projecting from the two ends of the roof at right angles to the front of the roof building. If the ball comes off the roof outside this imaginary space, it counts as a let, but the service passes. The receiver must catch the ball before it touches the ground. If he does so, neither scores ; if he fails, the server scores one point. In either event the service passes. The receiver scores one point if the server fails to reach the roof or throws the ball over the roof. In the latter event he must fetch it, as well as lose a point. A game is five points. All feints are legitimate, and there need be no delay between receiving and serving. Given the right roof, it is a great game, almost as sweaty as Squash.

A chimney is a hazard : a ball may be served against it with such force as frequently to elude the receiver ; but if the server misses it he risks the penalties for throwing over the roof. This game can be played as a foursome.

WATER GAMES

Les Joûtes, or *Tilting*, between champions in boats is played by French fishermen, and is dangerous to life and limb.

The lances should be long stout bamboos, and for safety well padded at the ends, with a mop-head sewn up in canvas. The champions stand upright in the extreme stern of the boats and should wear wooden or cork breast-plates from the chin to well below the fork. Rudders should be unshipped before beginning.

Water Polo need not be played according to elaborate rules, but there must be no tackling an opponent who has not got the ball, and care should be taken not to kick one's opponent in a vital spot. It can be played with a football or any other ball or with a tenni-quoit rubber ring, but if the ball is small players must pass when tackled and not fight their way through.

Racing on rubber animals is amusing, but there are few jockeys skilled enough to complete a course of twenty yards, even in still water.

Kissing at the bottom of the sea is a strange experience and not likely to be spotted by the guardians of our morals. The lovers should stand about ten yards apart up to their necks, empty their lungs, and crawl towards each other along the bottom with their eyes open.

INDOOR ACTIVE GAMES

BALL GAME

Y O U need a big barn, a football bladder and a badminton net. Two, three or four a side, according to the size of persons and barn. Scoring as in Squash, etc., i.e. only the serving side scores. The server punches the ball over the net, but he must not send it outside a prescribed area. (The area must vary according to your barn. In some cases the walls will fitly be included in the playing area, in others they will be " out.") The receiving side must punch back the ball, and a rally will, it is to be hoped, ensue. When the bladder is on your side of the net, any of your side may touch it once, and once only, before it is returned ; and there may be a bounce on the floor (or against the wall, if that is " in " for your barn) between each player on your side. Thus a back will tap the bladder to his half, his half to a forward, who should be in position to deliver a massive shot over the net. There is, of course, no obligation that all one side should have a touch of the ball before it is returned. Only one hand may be used (except in the act of serving) and the ball must not be allowed to touch the body. Invented and developed (highly) by H. G. Wells.

TISHY-TOSHY

An early version of the game is said to have taught Bosanquet the googly. You need a table (rectangular, the largest possible) and a tennis-ball. Two players stand at opposite ends, and throw the ball to each other in turn ; the Server may roll, bounce or full pitch the ball, but it must not drop off the sides of the table (only off the ends) and must only leave the table between imaginary parallel lines continuing the sides of the table. The Receiver may not put his hands over the table, or touch it with his hands or any part of his person. If he does so, or if he fails to catch the ball, the Server scores one point. If the Receiver catches the ball lawfully, neither scores. But the Receiver scores a point if the Server sends the ball off the sides of the table. Game is for any number of points agreed upon—say five. The very expert can make a rule to use one hand only, or to bar catches made against the body. Remember always that this is a game of skill, not of strength ; and the ball must never be thrown at all fast.

FLOUNCE-FLORIN

Put a Florin in the middle of a shiny table. Four people stand one on each side of the table with a tennis-ball for each opposite pair and bounce the tennis-balls on the table, trying to knock off the coin by a direct hit. Each catches the ball of his partner opposite and tries to knock the coin off in his turn. The table *must* be very shiny.

The man who wins pockets the coin and the others have to put up the new stake. Originating with war-profiteers (but which war?) the game is *now* usually played with pence or halfpence, but keeps its extravagant name.

333

UP-JENKYNS!

Orders can only be legally obeyed when given by one of the Captains; and if the team which is hiding the Sixpence obeys any other order, it loses. The "In" team, which is hiding the coin, must put up its hands the instant the opposing Captain calls "Up-Jenkyns!" but he ought to allow them at least five seconds before he calls. He can keep their hands in the air as long as he likes, for examination purposes; the "Down" calls are "Down-Jenkyns" (hands can be put down as players please); "Smashums!" (hands must be crashed down on the table); "Crawlers!" (hands placed quietly on the table, and fingers quietly undone till the hands lie flat); "Open Windows" (hands must lie on the table with all the fingers, but not the thumbs, apart); and "Lobster-Pots" (finger-tips only to rest on the table, and fingers to be held at an angle to the palm). In lifting the hands, only the Captain's order must be obeyed; but he should allow free and fair consultation to his own side first. Scores can be played for, by the number of separate "wins," or the show of hands on the table when the Sixpence is discovered. *Before* the game starts, all rings and spurs to be removed. *After* the game, let the provider of the sixpence see that he gets it back!

SLAP-PENNY

A racing game reminiscent of Up-Jenkyns. Two captains pick up sides which sit facing each other. Each side is armed with a shillingsworth of coppers, which are put on a table at the side of the two end men. At a signal the end men have to start sending off the pennies down the line to the other end, one after the other and as fast as possible. When all the pennies have got to the other end of the line they are sent back again. All hands have to be held perfectly flat and each penny slapped in turn from one palm to the next (never to the next but one). Dropped pennies must be replaced on the flat of the palm of the hand which did the slapping which caused the dropping, and the coins must ss in the sequence in which they are started. That side wins (did you guess it ?) which gets all its pennies to the end of its line (or, better, back to the starting-point) first.

BROCK

is an improved version of Hide and Seek in a dark house. The Brock (or Badger) is " He " and hides, and the rest have to venture out and draw him from his den, avoiding being captured while doing so, and get safe home again.

SARDINES

This may also be played in the dark ; *con amore*. Only one player hides, all the others seek ; the first to find him hides with him, the next to find *them* squashes in alongside. And so on till everybody but one solitary Seeker is hiding in the same spot.

FREE ASSOCIATION TEAM-RACE

Two Captains pick up sides, which line up face to face, and there's a Timekeeper-Scorer-Referee who says Go ! Then the Captain of the side in talks as fast as he can about anything or nothing, while the Referee counts the words : he can talk sentences, or any jumble of disconnected words he pleases (that's where the Free Association comes in, *and* the Psycho-Analysis, because you're always revealing your Inner Life by saying things like " post-prandial flower-pot puff ! "), but he mustn't take one word and stick to it, like " me-me-me-me-me ! " As soon as his flow stops (and it *will*, because of some Inhibition, as you know), the next in his team takes it up until *he* sticks ; and so on, down the line, and round again if necessary, until the Referee calls Time !—which is anything previously arranged from two to five minutes. Then the other side goes in ; you can have any number of innings you like ; and whichever side says most words wins.

335

THE ANIMAL AND STICK GAME

Two sides face to face, as before, but no Referee. Each Captain has a stick. A member of one side calls the name of any animal, bird, fish or insect, beginning with A, and his Captain instantly begins to count 10 aloud (not *too* fast), thumping the floor with his stick at each count. Before he reaches 10, some member of the opposing side must retaliate with another creature beginning with A, on which the second Captain begins to count and thump, while the first side thinks of a new beast. Captains are allowed to call like the rest ; but if two members of a side call out different names together, the opposing side may instantly bag the second name given. When one team wins, because the other has run out of A's, it may choose a member of the losing team and add him to their number. The second bout begins with B, and the game continues through the alphabet, until all of one side has been absorbed by the other. No penalty is incurred for Fake Names of animals, and if, when stumped for an N, you *can* bring off " Nicaragua " unchallenged, you may ; but on the whole these should not be indulged in too often, and, once disproved, the Opposing Captain takes up the count where the bluff interrupted it.

This game can also be played more quietly with pencils and paper.

QUIETER INDOOR GAMES

FAMOUS PEOPLE ON PAPER

You have two or three minutes for writing as many Famous People, or Flowers or Things in the Room, or whatever you like, beginning with a certain letter, and you read them out in turn and score marks ; if ten people are playing, nobody scores for a name everybody has thought of, but if nine people out of ten have it you each score one, and if eight people out of ten, they each score two, and so on. Bluffing with invented people is allowed, but only if the bluff is not challenged. A certain amount of feeling is generated if anyone persists in trying to put over St. Tradescantia for example.

HANGING

One member of the company is picked out and told that he is deemed guilty of murder and will be hanged at the end of five (or ten) minutes unless he can prove himself innocent. All the rest of the company are *omniscient* witnesses and have to answer any question he puts to them. He questions them in turn, and is acquitted if he can find any contradiction or flat inconsistency in their story. The wildest improbabilities are allowable, and are to be encouraged, in their answers, but witnesses cannot abrogate the laws of nature, though they may play tricks with artificial human ones. E.g. You may make the criminal travel by a non-existent train, but if you make him arrive at his destination before he started, he is acquitted.

SUGGESTIONS

One member of the company says a word (usually a noun) and the man sitting next him says any word suggested by the first. After a round or two you begin to unwind the chain of suggestions, backwards. Anyone who makes a slip or gets stuck loses a life, and anyone who loses two or three lives, as agreed on, is dead. At the end you see who's left alive.

CONSEQUENCES is well known to all, but

BOOK REVIEWS

is better for a round or two. It's played like Consequences, but first you invent the Title of a Book—say " Crimson Nights "—turn down, and pass on; on the paper you receive you write a sub-title, say, " Or 366 Ways of Cooking Lentils ".; round three is the Author's name, real or imaginary ; round four a brief extract from the book, poetry or prose ; round five another extract (for contrast) ; six, extract from a review of the book ; seven, name of Journal the review comes from ; eight, extract from another review (contrast again !) ; nine, and last, name of Journal.

337

REDUCED ANECDOTES

makes a variation. Each player writes some anecdote, or incident, in 80 words, and passes it on; he cuts down the anecdote he receives to 40 words, writing it out below the first one, leaving any sort of sense he can make without changing the order of the words or introducing any new ones; after the pass, this is reduced to 20, then to 10, finally to 5. The anecdotes are passed once more, and the result read aloud, from top to bottom; or vice versa. Papers should be folded so that the players see only the lines they are to reduce.

THE WORD AND QUESTION GAME

Each player takes two slips of paper and writes a question on one and a word on the other. The slips are pooled and everyone draws a word and a question. (Or all may be given the same problem.) The object then is to write a poem, answering or treating of the question and introducing the word. The time-limit is a quarter of an hour.

Here is an example by Sir Walter Raleigh:

Question: Who rang the bell?
Word: Life.

> Life rang the bell to call the people in;
> The play was played by Folly, Pride and Sin;
> Old Age, with fingers trembling and uncertain,
> Turned off the gas, and Death let down the curtain.

Maybe you won't write as good a morality as this, or any morality at all; but that doesn't invalidate the game.

BLINDFOLD COLLABORATION IN PROSE

Everyone writes down the beginning of a story occupying four lines and turns over the paper so that only the last line shows and passes it on. When the stories have come back to the writer of the first four lines, he writes the ending, and the stories are then read aloud.

Combination verses is played in the same way, but fixing a metre and rhyme scheme, and passing the papers round with the last line but one hidden.

GAMES

BOUTS-RIMÉS

Give the rhyme-endings of a poem, and let everyone fit a verse to them in a given time ; or else

LIMERICKS

on given places or people ; or

" CLERIHEWS "

(after Edward Clerihew Bentley, who wrote " Biography for Beginners ") on one's personal friends, with nice slack metres and sly points like

> Sir Christopher Wren
> Was going to dine with some men.
> He said, " If anybody calls,
> Say I'm designing Saint Paul's."

PERSONAL ANALOGIES

You write the names of those present perpendicularly down your paper, and each in turn chooses a subject—a Colour, Food, Drink, Street, Material, etc.—which are written horizontally across the top. Then everybody sets to and writes against each person's name the nearest analogy he can think of in the different subjects. They're read out afterwards, and no one need explain *why* he thinks you are Scarlet or Putty-Coloured, or like Suet-Pudding or Pêche Melba, or Bond Street or the City Road. It's a good way of paying compliments *and* old scores.

QUALITIES

You make a list of qualities, good, bad and indifferent. There's one at the end of the " Week-End Book " on page 524, ruled out ready to play on. The subject has to give himself marks for each quality and then pass the book on to the rest in turn to mark him. When all have finished with him, he would have to read out the verdicts and if you like, even work out his average for each quality. After all, he'll have his revenge later.

339

GAMES

RUSSIAN SLEDGES

We all write down the same list of a dozen of the dearest friends we have in common. Each of us then imagines himself crossing the steppes of Russia with all of them in a sledge pursued by packs of hungry wolves, and has to throw them out one by one. Whom do you throw out first, whom next? You have to decide this, and number the names on the list accordingly, in the order in which you would throw out your friends to be torn in pieces. Needless to say you may not throw yourself out. . . . The game provides valuable statistics, for all the marks we have given each person are added up afterwards. The man who gets the fewest is, of course, the least popular of our friends. When one list is exhausted you can start on another dozen, and after that make a composite list of the top six of each list. . . .

HUMAN SACRIFICES

is a variant impossible amongst normally sensitive persons. We propitiate a vengeful deity by sacrificing one after another of the company in turn. A slip of paper with all our names is silently handed round and each of us makes a cross against the name of the man or woman he would sacrifice first. Whoever has most crosses against his name after the first round is sent out of the room. Then the paper goes round again for the survivors to mark again. When only two people are left in the room they call out the one whom they regard as the less worthy to survive.

WHO AM I?

The Scorer first writes the names of lots of *very* Famous People, and Characters in Books, and Notorious Recent Criminals, and all that, on separate bits of paper, and has lots of pins, and a scoring-sheet with all the names of the other players. They line up before him, and he pins a name on each one's back and says Go! Your

340

object is to find out who you are. You may rush up to anybody, make him look at your back, and fire off three questions to which the only answers are " Yes " and " No " : Such as " Am I a Man ? " " Am I a Myth ? " " Am I a Foreigner ? " When your three questions are answered, you must answer three of his in return ; then you part, and grab somebody else, carrying on your investigation from the information gained. You mustn't ever ask more than three questions from a chap at one go. When you know who you are you tell the Scorer ; he replaces your old name with a new one, and scores a mark to you. The game stops when everybody's hoarse, or the Scorer runs out of names ; and the one who has guessed himself oftenest wins.

WHO ARE THEY ?

Two of us go outside and decide who we'll be, and return to hold a conversation in front of the others, always talking in character, but of course not mentioning our names. When you're guessed, two others go out. It's the best opportunity I know for bringing nice people together who would have liked to meet, but can't : Hobbs and Medusa, you know, or Dempsey and Little Nell.

SALTED ALMONDS

It's called that, because it takes place between two people who are supposed to meet at a dinner-table. Before they meet, A goes outside, and B is given three statements or remarks, invented by the audience, which he must engineer as naturally as possible into the dinner-table conversation : such as that he never *can* remember whether it's pronounced Bill Sykes or Bill Seeks ; and that the best cure for aeroplane-sickness is equal parts of Fuller's Earth and Petroleum ; and that the First Carpet-Slippers were worked by Lady Jane Grey for Roger Ascham. Then A comes in, the two sit side by side, and they begin to talk. A's job is to head off B's attempts to steer the conversation towards his statements, though A doesn't know what they are. The game ends when B makes his third statement.

341

GAMES

DRAMATIZED BALLADS

They make the most thrilling little plays and any one with
a dramatic sense can " produce " them. Look at the " Earl
of Moray " on page 9—what a marvellous love-and-hate
story could be done in dumb show to lead up to the critical
moment when it breaks into words !

THE TRAY-GAME

Someone fills a tray with twenty objects usual to any room
—a pencil, handkerchief, book, nib, and what not. The
tray is set down in the middle of the other players, who
stare at it for twenty or thirty seconds only, when it is
removed. The Tray-Filler (and Time-Keeper) then calls
Go ! and the players have two minutes in which to write
down all they can remember. The longest list wins.

LOOKING AT YOUR FEET THROUGH THE WRONG END OF THE OPERA-GLASSES

while you try to walk, step by step, one foot put straight in
front of the other, down a string laid on the floor.

RUMMY

which can be played by almost any number of players,
using two packs. The dealer gives each player seven cards,
and turns up one card, putting it beside the pack face
upwards. The next player has the option of taking this
exposed card, or the top card of the pack, before dis-
carding one of his own. He is allowed, if he likes, to
discard the one he has picked up. The discard is placed
face upwards on top of the exposed cards, and the next
player has the option of taking either that card or the next
card of the " blind " pack : and so on, each playing in
turn.

The object of the game is to reduce the " pippage " of
your seven cards. An Ace counts as one, a two as two, a
three as three, and so on up to ten ; all court cards count
as ten. When the sum of the values in your hand is down

342

to ten or under, you are allowed, though not forced, to
" rumble," which is usually done by tapping the underneath edge of the table. You may not rumble immediately
after taking a card, but you must wait your next turn. In
other words, when your turn comes, you may either rumble,
or draw a card, but not both in one turn. At the rumble,
each player's pippage is counted up, and the deal takes
place again.

The system of reducing pippage is as follows :

1. Three or more of a kind, or three or more in sequence
in the same suit count as 0. Thus three or four knaves,
or 5, 6, 7 in Clubs, do not count against you.

2. The same card can serve only one purpose in reducing
pippage, that is, either as part of a sequence, or as part
of a collection, but not both.

3. Jokers may serve as any card of any suit. Either one
or two may be included by agreement.

4. A flush (that is, a hand composed entirely of one suit)
counts 0.

5. If you reduce your score to 0 by holding a straight flush
(i.e. seven cards in sequence in the same suit) or seven of
a kind, the whole score standing against you from previous
rounds is wiped out.

When your debt account reaches 100 you are dead. The
later stages of the game usually become quicker and more
exciting, the ultimate survivor, who is winner, taking the
pool. The pool is sweetened after each hand by everyone
except the winner of the hand.

If the packs should be exhausted before a rumble the
discards are shuffled and re-dealt.

The skill in the game depends, obviously, on observing
the cards that are discarded ; thus, not preserving two
kings in your hand if six have already been thrown away.

DOUBLE-HANDED BRIDGE

Thirteen cards are dealt to both players, and the top card
of the twenty-six remaining in the pack is turned up. The
non-dealer leads, and thirteen tricks are played for which
no points are scored, the winner of the trick taking the
top exposed card of the pack and the loser taking the card

343

underneath, which remains unseen. The winner of the thirteenth trick has the call in the auction which follows, and thirteen tricks of serious bridge are played.

The game is an extremely good one except with people having prodigious memories. The tactics depend very largely on exhausting a suit by continually leading it when you suspect that your opponent is saving it up, and in disguising the fact that you are collecting a suit yourself.

GO

You play it with coffee and haricot beans, *ad lib.*, on a board, or piece of paper, ruled into squares, 19 by 21 ; the two players play one bean at a time, in turns, on any square they like ; you want to enclose your opponent's bean in a diagonal square of your own like this :

Which entitles you to remove the enclosed bean. The player who controls the greatest area of the board, so that it is useless for his opponent to put down more beans, as they will only be encircled, wins.

There's only one essential rule, called KO. In a situation like *this* :

Haricot could play in the empty square A, and remove

344

Coffee from B; but then, you see, Coffee could immediately play in B again, and remove Haricot from A; and so on, for ever. To prevent this, the Rule is that in this particular position the *first* encircler keeps his opponent's bean, and cannot have his own retaken in that grouping.

GO-BANG

Is played on a chessboard with 12 coloured beans, or counters or Halma-men each. You play in turns and the object is to get five of your own colour in a row, in any direction, straight or diagonal. It's a superior Noughts and Crosses. Four-handed *Six in a Row* played with 13 Halma men to each player, on a Halma board (16 by 16) is excellent. Four-handed *Four-in-a-row* is too tight and agonizing a game.

NINE MEN'S MORRIS

The players have nine men apiece—beans, or anything to show a difference—and if you look at the end-papers of the " Week-End Book " you'll see the sort of board it's played on. It has 24 bases which, read horizontally and perpendicularly, form 16 lines of three bases each. Players begin by placing their men alternately on any base that is vacant, and the great object (it's a sort of glorified Noughts and Crosses) is to get three of your men in a line, either up and down or across. As soon as you succeed, you can " Pound " any one of your opponent's men, and remove it from the board. When the placing of the men on the board is completed (during which one or more men may have been Pounded) you go on by moving in turns from base to base; a man can only move to a base adjacent to his own, and then only if it is unoccupied by another man. You can't take a man by moving on to his base, you can only take a man when you get a line of three. In this way, one of the players is presently reduced to three men, and when that happens he has the privilege of " hopping " from one base to another—that is, any of his men can " hop " to *any* base he likes, so long as it is vacant; but it need not be next the base he has just left. The player with more than three men must still go on moving in the old way, until he wins or is reduced to three. The game ends when one player has only two men left.

PROBLEM ONE

I will engage you, said the Managing Director, at a half-yearly salary of £50, with a half-yearly increase of £5 ; or, if you prefer it, at a yearly salary of £100, with an annual increase of £20. Which did the clerk choose and why ?

PROBLEM TWO

Two vessels, A and B, hold milk and water respectively. A spoonful of milk is taken from A and introduced into B, where it is mixed up. A spoonful of the B mixture is then put into A. What is the proportion of the amount of water in A to the amount of milk in B ?

PROBLEM THREE

You have two hollow steel balls, of the same size and weight, but made of steels of different specific gravity ; that is to say, the hollow in one is bigger than the hollow in the other. How do you tell them apart without damaging them in any way ?

PROBLEM FOUR

A ship's carpenter has to cover a square hole twelve feet by twelve. He is given a rectangular board sixteen feet by nine, and is told to cut the board into two pieces to cover the hole. How does he cut it ?

PROBLEM FIVE

In each of two differently furnished studios there are chairs and three-legged stools. If in each room all the legs had

346

been stools, all the stools had been chairs, and all the chairs had been removed, there would have been 100 too many legs in each room. How were the two rooms furnished ?

PROBLEM SIX

A penniless tramp picks up a dollar in the United States. (The value of a U.S. dollar in the U.S. for the purposes of this problem is 5s.) He decides to have a drink, which costs him 2d. He puts down his dollar and gets in return a Mexican dollar. (The value of a Mexican dollar in the U.S. is 4s. 10d.) He then crosses the border into Mexico and decides to have a drink, which costs him 2d. He puts down his Mexican dollar of which the value in Mexico is 5s. and gets in return an American dollar. (The value of an American dollar in Mexico is 4s. 10d.) He then crosses the border into America and decides to have a drink which costs him 2d. He puts down . . . And so on *ad infinitum*. Who pays for his drinks ?

PROBLEM SEVEN

With the help of a monkey, three men collected a large number of nuts. They counted them and found if they gave one to the monkey they could be equally divided. In the night each man got up, gave a nut to the monkey and took a third of what was then in the heap. In the morning they pretended nothing had happened and made the division according to plan, and there were no nuts over. What is the smallest number of nuts they must have collected ?

PROBLEM EIGHT

Two bowlers, A and B, have each taken 28 wickets for 60 runs. In the last match of the season A takes 1 wicket for 27 runs and B 4 wickets for 36 runs. Which bowler has now the better average ? Why ?

PROBLEM NINE

Classes are of two kinds; those which are members of themselves and those which are not. Instances of classes which are members of themselves are the class of non-humans, since the class of non-humans is itself non-human; and the class of classes, since the class of classes is itself a class. Instances of classes which are not members of themselves are the class of match boxes and the class of beetles, since in these cases the class of match boxes is not a match box and the class of beetles is not a beetle. Is the class of all classes which are not members of themselves, a member of itself or not a member of itself?

PROBLEM TEN

Detect fallacies, if any, in the following:

(a) The unanswerable objection to an unanswerable objection is that it never *is* answered.

(b) It is most unlikely that the earth will ever be destroyed by colliding with a nebula or with another star or planet: it has never done so yet.

(c) Throughout any one day during the war the chances of a man being killed are five to two against. Throughout ten days, therefore, the chances of his being killed are fifty to twenty against. Hence the longer he stays out, the more do the chances of his not being killed exceed the chances of his being killed. Therefore the longer a man is at the front, the less likely he is to be killed.

(d)
$$4 - 10 = 9 - 15$$
$$\therefore 4 - 10 + \frac{25}{4} = 9 - 15 + \frac{25}{4}$$

Take square roots
$$\therefore 2 - \frac{5}{2} = 3 - \frac{5}{2}$$
$$\therefore 2 = 3$$

(e) In a certain village there is a barber; one barber only and no more. He is clean-shaven. The barber shaves all

348

GAMES

those and only those who do not shave themselves. Who shaves the barber?

(f) A stone is thrown full at an approaching engine, and rebounds. Immediately prior to impact the stone is moving in one direction, and immediately subsequent to impact its motion has been reversed. Just at the instant of impact it must have been momentarily at rest. But it was then in contact with the engine. Was the moving engine at rest?

(g) *The Short Proof of Determinism.* It is either true or false *now* that I shall be hanged to-morrow; therefore whether I shall be hanged to-morrow or not hanged to-morrow is already determined.

PROBLEM ELEVEN

How would events upon the earth appear to a person observing them through a telescope stationed upon a planet moving away from the earth (a) with a velocity equal to that of light; (b) with a velocity greater than that of light? Should the answer to (b) suggest that the beginning of a man is a disturbance among worms, speculate upon the significance of this (i) for the law of cause and effect; (ii) for human dignity.

PROBLEM TWELVE

If you go round the world travelling from west to east you gain a day, i.e. 24 hours. (Cp. Phineas Fogg in "Round the World in Eighty Days.") What happens if, taking advantage of the facilities afforded by modern travel, you go round the world (a) in 24 hours; (b) in less than 24 hours? Should the answer to (b) suggest that you get back before you started; speculate upon the significance of this for the reality of time.

TRICKS

The following tricks may beguile the more vacuous moments of the company:

349

GYMNASTIC FEATS

(1) Grasp a stiff stick about five foot long behind the back with the palms of the hands facing forwards. Pass stick over head. Lift right leg and put it round the right arm and through the stick. Without changing your grip pass the left hand over the head and back and step out of stick.

(2) Kneel down putting elbows to knees and palms flat on floor. Place pencil at finger-tips. Then clasp hands behind back and pick up pencil with teeth.

(3) Toe a line, go down on one hand and with the other place coin as far away as possible. Regain erect position in one movement, taking supporting hand cleanly off floor. The next man has to put another coin down further off and so on.

(4) Put a chair on its back, and grasping it by one of the legs on the ground, set it gently on its legs. Then weight the back of the chair with heavy books and repeat.

(5) Place a pin on right hand edge of the seat of a chair, sit down, and then without touching the floor crawl round the back of the chair and remove pin with the teeth.

To make a Cockyolly Bird. An old-fashioned night-gown is necessary. Put the legs through the arms, and the head through the neck, then have the bottom of the night-gown tied up as a tail. This fowl is more charming than it sounds.

MATCH TRICKS

(1) Tear off two book-matches and hold them parallel between index finger and thumb, exhibit them to the audience, pointing out that there is a printed inscription on one side of the matches and not the other.

Now turn them over swiftly rolling them over fast and exhibit the plain surface on both sides.

(2) Strike a match and quickly stick its lately-exploded head into the largest side of the match-box so that the match stands upright, its head lightly buried in the box. Then place one match on the table parallel with the longest side of the box, about four inches in front of it. Rest another

match on this at right angles to it, with the forward and tilted end aimed at the vertical match. Flick it, and you will bring down your target at the first shot.

(3) THE HOLLYWOOD KISS

Take two matches, either book or ordinary wooden safeties. Make a slit in a safety match-box and in it stick one book match vertically, head up, as the lover. Lean the other match—the lady—against the lover so that her head is touching his and light her in the middle. It is an improvement to give the lady legs by slitting her lower end with a knife, but arms always seem to burn away to nothing.

match on this at right angles to it, with the forward and tilted end aimed at the vertical match. Flick it, and you will bring down your target at the first shot.

(3)   THE HOLLYWOOD KISS

Take two matches, either book or ordinary wooden safeties. Make a slit in a safety match-box and in it stick one match vertically, head up, as the lover. Lean the other match—the lady—against the lover so that her head is touching his and light her in the middle. It is an improvement to give the lady legs by slitting her lower end with a knife, but arms always seem to burn away to nothing.

TRAVELS

WITH A DONKEY

I WISDOM DWELL WITH PRUDENCE
AND FIND OUT KNOWLEDGE
OF WITTY INVENTIONS
PROVERBS VIII. 12.

TRAVELS

WITH A DONKEY

I WISDOM DWELL WITH PRUDENCE
AND FIND OUT KNOWLEDGE
OF WITTY INVENTIONS

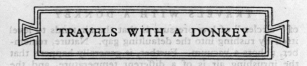

THE WEATHER (SCIENTIFIC)

" Whoso hath but a mouth
Shall ne'er in England suffer drought."

Before making an irrevocable decision to spend the week-end out of doors, the would-be camper is well advised to consult the Weather Forecast which appears in his morning paper, in order to prepare himself against the worst vagaries of the climate.

A distinction must be made, however, between reading any weather forecast and reading the weather chart which appears in *The Times, Daily Telegraph,* etc. The first is almost useless, as third-hand information ; the chart is at second-hand from the minute and accurate records kept at the Government Meteorological Office. It gives a simplified map, of England and parts of Europe, showing the condition of the atmosphere surrounding that part of the earth.

Everybody knows that the atmosphere is constantly in a state of flux, partly because the world goes round, and partly because water (e.g. seas and lakes) is always either condensing or evaporating, owing to the action of the sun's rays. As a result of this changeability, the degree of atmospheric pressure on the earth varies with place and time ; this is shown in the barometric charts made by meteorologists. They have discovered a variety of tricks performed by the atmosphere, each of which has a specific bearing on the weather in the locality in which it is performed. The star turn, so to speak, is the pattern formed by a small circle of low pressure surrounded by several circles of greater and greater pressure. (We speak in terms of the chart, on which areas subject to the same weight of air are linked together by circles, or irregular, but always closed, forms, known as *isobars*. No such pattern exists, of course, actually in the air.) The effect of this condition

355

of " circles " of low pressure is that the air tends to level itself by rushing into the defaulting gap. Nature, remember, abhors a vacuum. Further, it generally happens that the inrushing air is of a different temperature, and the result of the contact is rain. Maxim : avoid an area of low pressure, unless it is forecast that it will move away. For the habit of these meteorological " patterns " is to move about, as well as to widen or to become narrower, to " put out a tongue " or put it in.

Here we arrive at a second point of interest to the chart-reader. Namely, the wider apart the circles of different pressures (isobars) in a low pressure or a high pressure area, the less forceful the wind, whereas the closer the isobars the more violent the wind.

Winds tend to blow along the isobars, with a slight deviation inwards in low pressure, and outwards in high pressure areas. They are often marked on charts by arrows, giving velocity (in miles per hour) in circles attached to the head of the arrow.

Areas of high pressure are (strange to say !) the precise opposite of low pressure ; they consist of a small circle of high pressure surrounded by circles of less and less pressure toward the extreme circumference. There is thus little encouragement to atmospheric movement, and generally fine weather, unless there are unusual conditions of moisture, i.e. prevailing clouds (moisture that will condense on small provocation). The several degrees of pressure are given by figures close to the isobars.

Nobody knows precisely why these patterns happen at the time and place that they do : it seems that they are governed by the movements of the upper air, which is not yet open to systematic study. Only the experienced map-reader can say that, according to his experience of sequences, he expects such and such a change to take place consequent on what he now observes. Therefore, if such a one forecasts that a given atmospheric " pattern " will move in such and such a direction at such and such a pace, trailing sun, wind, or rain in its wake, it is not incumbent on anyone to believe him, but it is more than probable that his experience will stand the test of events.

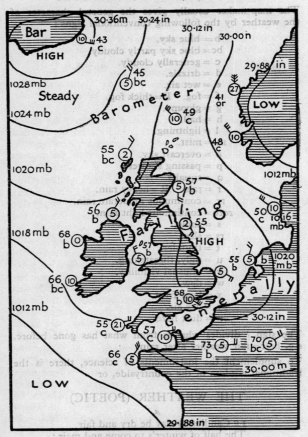

The Weather (Scientific)

The map-maker usually gives the general character of the weather by the following conventional signs :

                b = blue sky.
               bc = blue sky partly cloudy.
                c = generally cloudy.
                d = drizzle.
                e = wet air.
                f = fog.   F = thick fog.
                g = gloomy.
                h = hail.
                l = lightning.
                m = mist.
                o = overcast sky.
                p = passing showers.
                q = squalls.
                r = rain.   R = heavy rain.
               rr = continuous moderate rain.
             roro = continuous light rain.
                s = snow.
               rs = sleet.
                t = thunder.
                u = ugly, threatening.
                v = unusual visibility.
                w = dew.
                x = hoar frost.
                y = dry air.
                z = dust haze.

The sign / divides what is from what has gone before, e.g. bc/r = fair weather after rain.

To supplement the instruments of science, there is the traditional wisdom of the countryside, or

THE WEATHER (POETIC)

> I F Candlemas-day be dry and fair
> The half of winter's to come and mair :
> If Candlemas-day be wet and foul
> The half o' winter's gane at Yule.
>
> (*Candlemas-day is Feb. 2nd*)

358

If the oak be out before the ash
The summer will be but a splash :
If the ash be out before the oak
The summer will be all a soak.

St. Swithin's Day if thou dost rain
For forty days it will remain :
St. Swithin's Day if thou be fair
For forty days 'twill rain nae mair.
(*St. Swithin's Day is July 15th*)

September mild, October gold,
Are followed by November cold.

An air' winter
A sair winter.

Ice in November enough to bear a duck,
All the coming winter will be mud and muck.

A green Christmas makes a full church-yard.

Rain before seven,
Fine before eleven.

Between one and two
See what the day will do.

Red at night is the shepherd's delight.
Red in the morning is the shepherd's warning.

Mackerel skies and mares' tails
Make great ships carry low sails.

359

When the wind is in the East
'Tis neither good for man nor beast :
When the wind is in the North
The skilful fisher goes not forth :
When the wind is in the South
It blows the bait in the fishes' mouth :
When the wind is in the West
Then it is the very best.

OF CAMP EQUIPMENT

If, in spite of the weather-chart, and in spite of the weather (for it has by now become apparent that these are not precisely identical terms), you determine to embark on the preparation of a camping outfit, *Be Prepared* for every emergency of weather and of distance from habitation by making your camping outfit as comprehensive as possible, but as little burdensome and inconvenient *en route*.

THE TENT

is, in England, the primary safeguard of the person, as the mosquito net is in finer and warmer countries. The choice of a tent depends on whether the expedition is one of pedestrians, cyclists or motorists. There is in the types of tents an ascending order of quality, combined, however, with increasing bulkiness and weight, not suitable for the human donkey.

Tents should always be made of special tent fabric : other materials cannot always withstand a heavy shower. The better tents are provided with *fly-sheets* which give ventilation, while not admitting the rain or too much sun. Details of every kind of tent may be had from the Camping Club of Great Britain and Ireland, 2 Greville Street, E.C.2.

THE BED

is a scarcely less important protection to the wary camper than the covering overhead, in spite of all appearances to the contrary. To prevent chills from the damp which never fails in any weather to rise from the ground, a waterproof groundsheet of a light weight mackintosh fabric should be the foundation of the night's rest. It should be of a size to cover the floor of the tent, and may perhaps be spread over with a light ground blanket of cashmere or wool. If the ground sheet is the sole article of bedding, it is a very good plan to make a " *hip hole* " underneath it in the ground, but the hole must be large enough to make sure of not falling out and failing to find it again in the course of the night. Better still, a palliasse case can be carried and filled with straw and grass, or these can simply be spread under the ground sheet and thrown away in the morning, in case of soddenness.

A scout's substitute bed is made by running two poles down the sides of two large canvas bags, placed together lengthwise and slit at their seamed ends. The ends of the poles are placed on logs, and should be wedged apart with a cross-pole to keep the canvas taut.

For the rest, blankets are a heavy burden of superstition. A quilt is far less bulky and gives the warmth of three blankets, and may be rolled around to substitute for a mattress. Incidentally, the eiderdown sleeping-bag, which has the appearance of a long green cocoon fitting closely to the person, is a profitable investment. It is itself an " all round " quilt. When rolled up it occupies the minimum of space, and in an ordinary quality weighs only 1 lb. 15 oz. The wool sleeping-bag weighs from 5 to 8 lbs., is not so easily washable nor so warm. If you use blankets instead of a sleeping-bag, remember that without a mattress you need as many under as over you.

THE KITCHEN

should include a stove, since the incontinence of the climate makes it advisable not to rely for the satisfaction of the appetite on an open camp fire. Of stoves, the very best and easiest to handle is the *Primus* paraffin air-pressure variety, preferably the roarer, which is less easily stopped up, though noisier.

To complete the kitchen outfit, say, for four, there are needed not more than three saucepans, fitting one into the other, a big frying-pan, a kettle with tea-infuser, a milk-can with top, and, for luxury's sake, a toaster. If the fry-pan is provided with a lid, it does duty for baking purposes. The pans should be of aluminium with wire handles (detachable). Paper plates save washing, but paper cups mpart a "mousy" flavour, especially to hot drinks. Lastly, one or two buckets (of canvas) serve for carrying water and washing-up. Cases can be bought containing knife, spoon, fork and tin-opener. In any circumstances, whether cased or no, do not forget the tin-opener. No camper has ever been known to open a tin with his teeth. It is reported that tins can be boiled to such a pitch that the metal becomes soft and pliable, but it seems probable that more of it would be deposited in the food than spooned or wrenched off after this treatment.

Here, however, is a method of opening a bottle without a corkscrew. *Tie round the neck of the bottle a piece of string or other inflammable material, and set it alight. Where the glass is heated it will break in a clean line.*

FOOD QUANTITIES

should be calculated in liberal allowances, seeing that the open air notoriously whips up the sluggard appetite. It is suggested that of the following essential articles one person will require at least the following quantity per day :

Bread ..	1 lb.	Sugar	2 oz.
Butter ..	3 oz.	Meat (adding sausages,	
Jam	⎰ 2 oz.	etc., for breakfast *ad*	
Marmalade	⎱	*lib.*)	10 oz.
Milk ..	¾ pint.	Potatoes	½ lb.

Tea, cocoa, cheese, rolled oats, flour, suet, biscuits, etc. etc., can be kept in tins in quantities which meet the demand for variety. Bacon is a useful stand-by, and its grease will provide fat for cooking. If it is inconvenient to carry or fetch milk, either dried or sweet condensed milk can be made to serve. (Beware of such as have a passion for eating Nestle's milk neat with a table-spoon.)—Similarly, dried eggs suffer no great loss of dietetic value by being treated in this way. They are easy to carry but nasty to eat. One pound of powder represents four dozen eggs.

You can tell the age of a *real* egg, without cracking the shell, by looking at it against the sun or any strong light. If you frame the egg in your hands or any opaque material, the shell will be sufficiently translucent for you to see the size of the air space in the egg. The older the egg, the larger the air space.

ON FINDING THE WAY

When he has provided himself with all his equipment, the camper will require to find his way from place to place by map and compass.

The only way to read with any advantage such maps as are not printed square with the points of the compass is to orientate them so that the North that is marked coincides with the North given by the compass. In the absence of a compass, a watch should be held horizontally with the hour hand pointing at the sun. The South then lies along a line exactly halfway between the hour hand and the figure XII, and the map can be faced South to correspond with this line. Supposing neither sun nor compass is to hand, the only thing to do is to turn towards some well-marked feature of the landscape, and, having identified this feature on the map, set it to give the hill, wood, or whatever it is, in the same direction. You may then pick out the direction of your objective.

The wanderer at night must rely on the somewhat improbable appearance of the stars, and particularly of the Polar, or North Star, to direct him in his paths. The moon is of no assistance whatever.

There is no foundation for the popular belief that one can tell which way London lies by the placing of telegraph posts on one side or other of the road, for they sometimes appear on the left and sometimes on the right going towards London. *But the cross-bars are placed on the London side of the poles.*

ON CAMP SITES

Coming upon a desirable locality, the camper must yet be

practical in the choice of his site. A camp should be pitched in the open, and not under trees, because there may be a visitation of lightning ; and there quite probably will be rain. While trees protect for some time from the rain, after a while they shower heavy drops on the tent, and mixed with these drops is a certain amount of acid which causes canvas to rot much sooner than the hopeful purchaser is led to expect. The camper may, however, protect himself by placing trees between his tent and the wind, the direction of which is easily discovered by watching the bend of boughs or twigs, by lighting a piece of paper to see where its smoke is carried, or by wetting the finger and exposing it.

The best situation of all for a long stay is one open to the South and protected to the North and East. A clay soil should be avoided because it is cold and damp, whereas chalk and, even better, gravel, drain water away. Long grass indicates a place where ground is usually damp, and therefore better left alone ; and even if the weather is undeniably dry, long grass is not a good site for a camp because it is much beloved of things that creep and crawl. Naturally, high ground is better drained than low, and is the wiser choice unless it is unduly exposed.

It is sometimes imagined that the tent should be " ditched " all round, but this is an unnecessary precaution unless there is to be a tropical downpour. Moreover, in that case the ditching would have to be supplemented by a series of channels to carry off the floods. A well-drained site does not give any encouragement to these feats of engineering. A most important precaution, however, is to loosen all guy lines at night, since they shrink considerably in the rain and will otherwise pull a mass of soaking canvas down about the sleeper's ears.

If the soil is not very firm, the pegs to which the ropes are attached can be kept in position by placing logs or stones across them : in a gale the ropes can be attached to logs buried a foot or so deep.

While the tent is packed up the ropes should be rolled round their pegs, otherwise they will become inextricably entangled.

364

ON KNOTS

The following knots will do whatever else is necessary to keep the camp in its place:

The Reef-knot, for joining two ends of equal size.

The Double Sheet Bend, for joining ropes of different thickness.

The Round Turn and two Half Hitches, for fastening a boat, horse, dog, etc., to a horizontal rail.

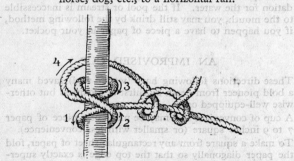

The Clove Hitch and two Half Hitches, for hanging anything from a vertical post.

365

The Bowline, for slinging a hammock, or lowering anything from a height.

OF WATER

Above all, the camp should be pitched near water, if possible, running water. If the purity of the water is at all doubtful, it should be boiled for half an hour, and afterwards strained through a piece of cloth, before drinking. The correct position for drinking from a pool is kneeling on one knee with the other leg stretched behind. Nothing is more uncomfortable than being flat on the stomach, which in this position is incapable of providing proper accommodation for the water. If the pool or stream is inaccessible to the mouth, you may still drink by the following method, if you happen to have a piece of paper in your pocket.

AN IMPROVISED CUP

These directions following have (we are told) saved many a bold pioneer from death by thirst at a cupless but otherwise well-equipped oasis.

A cup of convenient size may be made of a piece of paper 7 to 9 inches square (or smaller with less convenience).

To make a square from any rectangular sheet of paper, fold the paper diagonally so that the top edge is exactly superimposed on the side edge. Cut or tear off neatly that part which is not covered by the folded piece.

366

You then have a square folded about the line A B into two triangles.

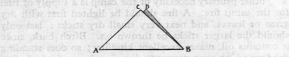

Fold over one corner thus :

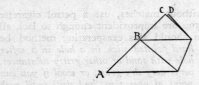

Turn the whole thing round, and fold over the other corner :

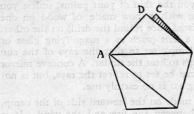

Bend back the flaps, and fold them into the lateral slots. D flap goes into A pocket, and C flap into B pocket :

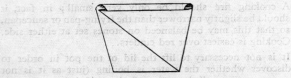

FUEL AND FIRE

The other primary necessity of the camp is a supply of fuel for the camp fire. A fire should be lighted first with dry grass or leaves, and next very small dry sticks : last only should the larger sticks be thrown on. Birch bark, since it contains oil, makes excellent kindling; so does standing dead wood, or even prostrate decaying logs, of which fine dry shavings from the inside are certain to start the fire successfully.

To light a fire without matches, use a petrol cigarette lighter. Only if you are improvident enough to lack all modern appliances should this exasperating method be attempted. *Set a hard pointed stick in a hole in a softer one, first filling the hole with sand or other gritty substances. Set tinder, such as very, very dry grass, or wool if you can find any, near the point of operation, and drill until such sparks as you may bring to life leap onto the tinder and start a blaze.* The operation takes half an hour at least, and will probably cost you the skin of your palms, unless you can do the drilling with a bow made of wood on one side and elastic (twisted once round the drill) on the other. If there is any sun, a lens (such as a magnifying glass or the glass of a cycle lamp), set so that the rays of the sun shine through it helps to heat the tinder. A concave mirror or a lamp reflector can be set to reflect the rays, but is not so effective. Plain glass is no earthly use.

Your fire should be made on the leeward side of the camp, i.e. with the camp between the fire and the wind. It is important in dry weather to cut away all grass, bracken and suchlike surrounding the fire—particularly, of course, on the side to which the wind is driving.

A cooking fire should be only very small ; in fact, it should be slightly narrower than the frying-pan or saucepan, so that this may be balanced on stones set at either side. Cooking is easiest over red cinders.

It is not necessary to lift the lid of the pot in order to discover whether the water is boiling (just as it is not necessary to eat all the peas to find out if they are tender).

368

Hold the end of a stick or a knife to the pot and you will feel it vibrating when the water boils.

Most of your refuse can be burnt; but tins and other non-inflammable remains should be buried in a small pit—*not* thrown into the nearest thicket.

ON RIGHTS OF LAND

The last precaution, which might well be in fact the first, is to make sure of proper permission to use the site you have chosen. *No piece of land* in the British Isles is available for camping without express permission from its owner. Even " common land," so called, is not the property of the world at large ; while paths and rights of way are allowed to be used only for passage. (See Section on The Law.) This is the only general rule that can be made, except that to obtain permission to camp is not such a difficult thing, provided that the landowner, probably the butcher or other strong man of the village, is approached with diplomacy and an order for meat or whatever may be his wares. He will probably, if assured that no damage of any sort will be perpetrated, discourse on the picturesque nature of the situation. However, on almost any of the large commons throughout the southern counties there is little strict observance of the law. It is here that the gipsies camp in large numbers.

Among the gipsies there is an unwritten tradition that they may camp on common land for twenty-four hours if the caravan is placed not more than sixteen yards from the road. Similarly, it is asserted that the police may bring to court only persons who light a fire on the turf. No mention of these provisos is to be found in the Property Acts, but they are said to be a matter of common practice.

The Camping Club of Great Britain and Ireland will provide members of the Club with a list of sites suitably placed, drained and befuelled, according to the descriptions of other members who have camped there. But permission must first be obtained to camp in these, as in any other places.

CHECK–LIST OF EQUIPMENT
Tent.

Ground sheet, quilts or eiderdown sleeping-bags, pillows.

Primus stove (*not forgetting the cleaning needles*), paraffin.

Three saucepans, 1 frying-pan, kettle and tea-infuser, milk-can, cups and plates, 2 canvas buckets, knives, forks, spoons, tin-opener, and corkscrew. (The fun of choosing a really adequate equipment at Woolworth's for next to no money may prove the best part of a rain-sogged holiday !)

Food in sufficient (indeed *more* than sufficient) quantities.

Map and compass.

Rope, axe for fuel, spade, candles or electric torch, matches. And then more matches.

Towels, dish-cloths, soap, soda, dish-mop, wire-brush for frying-pan, Lux for " washing-up " in general, brandy-flask, vaseline for sore extremities.

First Aid Kit (see page 479).

RULE OF THUMB

It is sometimes convenient to be able to measure by rule of thumb—literally. The following figures are those for that elusive character " the average man ":

Span of thumb and index finger	7 inches.
Span of thumb and little finger	9 „
Nail joint of index finger	1 inch.
Wrist to elbow	10 inches.

The average size of a shod foot is presumably a foot.

KITCHEN MEASURES
Liquids.

1 teacupful	$\frac{1}{4}$ pint
1 breakfast-cupful	$\frac{1}{2}$ pint
1 tumbler	$\frac{1}{2}$ pint

WEIGHTS AND MEASURES FROM COINS

Five pennies in a row measure just over 6 inches.

One halfpenny measures 1 inch.

One sixpence measures $\frac{3}{4}$ of an inch.

1 halfpenny and a threepenny piece	$\frac{1}{4}$ oz.
2 halfpennies and a farthing	$\frac{1}{2}$ oz.
3 pennies	1 oz.

CONCLUSION

Be patient with your companions, O travellers. Remember that the donkey with whom you travel may be Apuleius. Therefore lead him into rose-gardens and keep him from low company.

PERPETUAL KALENDAR

TO FIND THE WEEK DAY OF ANY DATE IN THE CHRISTIAN ERA

Add together the following numbers :

1. The number of the year.
2. The quotient (omitting fractions) after dividing the number of the year by 4.
3.* Six times the number of completed centuries.
4.* The quotient (omitting fractions) after dividing the number of completed centuries by 4.
5. The Index number of the month from Table I.
6. The number of the day of the month.

Then divide the total by 7 : the remainder will give the day of the week according to Table II.

* For dates expressed in Old Style (in Great Britain before 14th September, 1752, in France before 20th December, 1582) omit steps 3 and 4 and simply add 5 in all cases.

TABLE I				TABLE II	
Month	Index No.	Month	Index No.	Remainder	Day of Week
January	0	May	1	1	Sunday
January		June	4	2	Monday
(in leap year)	6	July	6	3	Tuesday
February	3	August	2	4	Wednesday
February		September	5	5	Thursday
(in leap year)	2	October	0	6	Friday
March	3	November	3	0	Saturday
April	6	December	5		

NOTE. A year is leap in OLD STYLE if its number is exactly divisible by 4. In NEW STYLE it is leap if its number is

371

divisible by 4, unless its number ends in 00, in which case it is only leap if the preceding figures form a number divisible by 4 exactly (e.g. 1600 and 2000 are leap years ; 1800 and 1900 are common years).

EXAMPLE.   What is the day of the week on 9th July, 1930 ?

1.	Number of the year	1930
2.	Quotient after division by 4	482
3.	Number of completed centuries is	
	19. 6 × 19	114
4.	Quotient after dividing 19 by 4	4
5.	Index No. for July (from Table I)	6
6.	Day of the month	9

Total   7) 2545

Divide by 7   ————

363

Remainder   4

From Table II the day of the week is Wednesday.

TO FIND THE DATE OF EASTER SUNDAY IN ANY YEAR OF THE CHRISTIAN ERA

Divide the number of the year by 4 and call the
remainder   a

Divide the number of the year by 7 and call the
remainder   b

Divide the number of the year by 19 and call the
remainder   c

Divide 19c+P by 30 and call the remainder   d

Divide 2a+4b+6d+Q by 7 and call the remainder   e

where P and Q are quantities to be determined by the method given below.

Then d+e is equal to the number of days that Easter Sunday falls after March 22nd.

Thus if d+e is equal to less than 9 Easter Day is March (22+d+e)th, and if d+e is greater than 9 Easter Day is April (d+e−9)th.

372

SPECIAL CASES :

(1) If d+e=35, Easter Day falls on April 19th (*not* on April 26th).

(2) If d+e=34, and if also d=28 and c is less than 10, Easter Day falls on April 18th (*not* on April 25th).

DETERMINATION OF P AND Q :

For OLD STYLE these are constants : P=15, Q=6.

For NEW STYLE they are constant for a century at a time.

Thus for 1700–1799 : P=23, Q=3.
Thus for 1800–1899 : P=23, Q=4.
Thus for 1900–1999 : P=24, Q=5.
Thus for 2000–2099 : P=24, Q=5.

To determine P and Q for any given century :

Call the hundreds' figure of the year	K
Divide K by 4 and call the quotient (excluding fractions)	L
Divide K−17 by 25 and call the quotient (excluding fractions)	M
Divide K−M by 3 and call the quotient (excluding fractions)	N
Divide 15+K−L−N by 30 and the remainder will be	P
Divide 4+K−L by 7 and the remainder will be	Q

N.B.—Until the year 4200, M=0.

EXAMPLES :

On what day does Easter fall in 1930 ?
(For 1900–1999, P=24, Q=5.)

Remainder after dividing 1930 by 4	a= 2
Remainder after dividing 1930 by 7	b= 5
Remainder after dividing 1930 by 19	c=11

Then 19 × 11 + 24 = 233.

Remainder after dividing 233 by 30	d=23

Then 2 × 2 + 4 × 5 + 6 × 23 + 5 = 167.

Remainder after dividing 167 by 7	e= 6

Then d+e=23+6=29.

Therefore Easter Sunday is April (29−9), i.e. April 20th.

Find P and Q for the hundred years 1900–1999.

	Hundreds' figure	K = 19
	Quotient after dividing 19 by 4	L = 4
(19 − 17 = 2)	Quotient after dividing 2 by 25	M = 0
(19 − 0 = 19)	Quotient after dividing 19 by 3	N = 6

Then $15 + 19 - 4 - 6 = 24$ and $4 + 19 - 4 = 19$.

Remainder after dividing 24 by 30	P = 24
Remainder after dividing 19 by 7	Q = 5

374

BIRD SONG

AT MORNING

YES, I WILL SPEND THE LIVELONG DAY
WITH NATURE IN THIS MONTH OF MAY;
AND SIT BENEATH THE TREES, AND SHARE
MY BREAD WITH BIRDS WHOSE HOMES ARE THERE.

W. H. Davies.

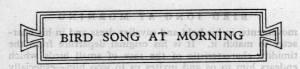
The following pages give a brief description of some of
the birds a week-end visitor to the country is likely to meet.
In so short a space the selection has had to be somewhat
arbitrary. The attempt is confined to taking the stroller
from his roof-tree through the garden, into the woods and
fields and open spaces, but not upon the further adventure
over moors, along rivers, up mountains, or down to the
seashore.

HOME AND GARDEN BIRDS

THE ROBIN, *Redbreast or Ruddock*

There are certain birds which show a preference for the
society of man and take advantage of his curious activities
to make their habitations in the neighbourhood of his own.
Of these the robin is the most intimate. The reason for
the universal recognition of the robin in England is not
merely his friendships or indifference to the presence of
man but his strong personality. He is striking in his way
of coming into the open, in the jubilance and forth-rightness
of his song when other birds are silent, in his staccato

movements, in his bold and cavalier dress and in his character to match it. It is his original departure from the
timidity characteristic of the race of small birds which
endears him to us and invites us to woo him—especially
with the irresistible bait of the meal-worm—to familiarities
we can achieve with no other species. His alarm note is
as explosive as his nature, and sounds like the tocking of
a grandfather clock. The song is unlike that of any other
warbler, and follows no set pattern, being at once ringing,
exultant and full of timbre, but at the same time a kind
of musing recitative, with a beautiful undersong.

The robin nests pretty well anywhere and in anything
from a tin kettle to an orthodox hole in a tree or bank.
Five or six eggs, white in ground colour, with freckles of
light red, are laid in a roughish nest of dead leaves, grass
and moss interwoven with hair and a few feathers. The
bird is easily recognised by his challenging red breast
above white underparts. The rest of his spruce form is
olive brown. Young robins have spotted breasts up to
the first moult and so deceive the uninitiated into thinking
them a different species. There is no difference in the
sexes' colouring, and the length is 5·75 inches.

THE BLACKBIRD, *or Ousel*

The blackbird possesses a quite different emotional
quality from the robin, being full of fears, suspicions and
nervous reactions. He is almost as conspicuous about
human dwelling-places, but never reposes in man the same
degree of confidence. His loud chuck of alarm is sign of
his volatile and unstable temperament : anger, rufflement,
uneasy protest change in a moment to the most taking airs
of gallantry to his brown mate. When the blackbird begins
to sing in February his low fluting is unrivalled for its
pure and mellow tone, and is delivered with a leisureliness
which draws out the full value of each note. But the
artist flies too high and falls, like Icarus, into a jumble of
clacks and chucks and broken jars.

The blackbird builds very early, and his shack is an
untidy affair of grasses, roots, and herbs, lined with finer

378

grasses and mud-plastered within. The eggs are four to six in number, greeny blue in colour, smeared with light

brown. The brown female has not the distinction of the ebony male, with his golden dagger of a bill. Length, 10 inches.

THE SONG THRUSH, *Mavis, or Throstle*

Temperamentally there is much kinship between thrush and blackbird; but the thrush's song is far less moving in musical quality than the blackbird's, being at once more powerful and more strident—so much so that at close quarters it can be very harsh. The melancholy tenderness of the blackbird's flute is quite absent. If one may express it in human terms, the thrush's song seems to represent unreflecting joy and the blackbird's the fulfilment of experience. No singer lives more in his song, for he will persist in repeating, from a bold and commanding perch, old phrases and experimenting with new ones for hours at a stretch and in all months of temperate weather. The nest, which may be found in any imaginable site, is unlike the blackbird's in the use of small twigs and moss and of a final smooth lining of rotten wood for the interior. The eggs, usually four to five in number, and laid two to

three or even four times during the season, are of a fine blue tinged with green and stippled with black spots. Both sexes are alike. Length, 8.5 inches.

THE BLUE TIT, *Tom Tit, Blue-cap, Billy-biter, or Nun*

The blue tit forces his minute presence upon our attention not only because of his slightly supercilious fearlessness of man, his intense vitality and handsome colouring, but from the eccentricity of his ways. There is no other bird in the calendar who so far succeeds in defying the humdrum in movement, performing an endless variety of unnatural postures on branch or twig with such topsy-turvy agility that only the most patient observer is able to record the sight of a bird of this species motionless on his perch. He is the most fantastic among the highly strung race of small birds. In winter (for there is a roaming and gregarious but not a definitely migratory impulse through the dark days) fat or a coco-nut will bring him within arm's length. The blue tit will hiss with anger when disturbed on the nest, and the call note is not unlike the metallic

churring and zeeing of the great tit, or oxeye, his larger
cousin in a very sociable genus. But the blue tit also
possesses a spring song of a very bright and limpid note
repeated many times with great speed—one of the most
familiar and endearing melodies of the awakening year.
As few as five eggs and as many as twenty (pure white with
spots and freckles of vandyke brown) may be laid in a
convenient cavity of a wall or tree or stump or letter-box,
into which he bundles a surprising quantity of moss and
dry grass, with wool, hair and feathers for the lining. The

bird himself is richly and strikingly coloured with a blue
crown rimmed with white, and his cheeks are patterned
with the same chequer, while a fainter blue is suffused into
the wings and tail. The back is olive-green, and the underparts are yellow crossed by yet another dark blue line
Length, 4·5 inches.
Five other species of titmice inhabit our islands, of which
the rarest is the willow tit ; the more confined to solitary
places, the cole and marsh tits ; the most engaging, the
long-tailed tit ; and the most self-advertising the great tit.
The great tit can be distinguished from his relatives by
the long black line which cuts down athwart his primrose-
coloured breast. The cole, marsh and willow tits are
black-capped, while the long-tailed tit sings its own story.

THE CHAFFINCH, *Spink, Shilfa, Scobbey, Skelly, or Shel-apple*

The jovial rattle of the chaffinch is one of the most copious and familiar set songs between February and June, but it is uttered with an air of deliberation. We delight most in what seems to be an unpremeditated melody, when singing seems a tuneful breath of a bird's being, less in the ditty which appears the performance of an appropriate act. The songs of the chaffinch and the yellowhammer, for instance, are similar in texture and in the flourish at

the close, but the latter is an expression of the way the bird lives, the former suggests the accomplishment of a ready professional. The chaffinch frequents human habitations more closely than any other except the house-sparrow, and so is seldom noticed as he really is, a bird of a lustrous and even gawdy display in plumage, suiting the rollick of his song and his mettlesome disposition. His flight conforms to the undulating finch type, but is less volatile than the goldfinch's or the linnet's, though more buoyant than that of the hawfinch or bunting. On the wing he delivers a sibilant double note not unlike the pied wagtail's, and his alarm cry is a sharp "ping." He prefers the ground more than all other finches, except brambling and house-sparrow, and in winter joins the mixed companies of roaming flocks in the fields.

The nest, which is built entirely by the much drabber female, is fashioned perfectly, felted without of mosses, lichens, grasses, wool and other very soft substances deftly woven. It is compacted with cobwebs and lined with hair, feathers and the down of plants. Four to six rather variable eggs, pale bluish green or strong reddish brown in ground colour with streaks and freckles of black or purplish brown are laid twice in a season. The forehead of the male is black and the rest of his crown and nape a greyish sea blue with chestnut pinkily diluted on the cheeks, while the same blend of pink deepening to reddish brown suffuses the underparts which fade into white. The rump is green, the back a warm chestnut, while two bands on the brown wings make a conspicuous recognition mark. Even so the colours are not so pure nor so authentic as the bullfinch's, and fade into commonplace in the winter. Length, 6·5 inches.

Other finches the week-ender is likely to meet are the greenfinch of gardens and copses, with a toy golden sword strapped to his side and constant twittering talk ; the stocky bullfinch of the orchard, with his tender pipe, velvety black head and wonderful rose-madder breast ; the goldfinch " pausing upon his yellow flutterings " ; and the rarer, bulky hawfinch, very shy and very handsomely plumaged, with an adze-like bill.

THE WREN, *Stumpy or Jenny Wren*

The wren is as individual a bird as the robin, and his haunts are much the same, except that the wren's distribution is a little more extensive. You will see a wren creeping mouse-like among the stalks from your window, and you will see the same movements, the same upcocked tail, and hear the same blast of song from the undergrowth of the wildest and most desolate moor, cliff or forest. The quaintness of the wren comes from his exceeding small size, his secret illusive ways in contrast with his vigorous and brave personality. The latter shows itself in his song, a bright clear gush of notes hastening to a trill and wonderfully heartening on grey winter mornings, for the wren is almost as abundant a singer as the robin or the thrush.

It is delivered with extraordinary virility and indifference to the presence of an observer. His excitement note resembles the ticking of a clock sharply anxious to be much faster than other clocks, and when he flies his blunt wings whirr like clockwork, which is all too soon unwound. No bird is so much at home in the densest maze of undergrowth, threading the labyrinth with a dexterity rivalling the most cunning movements of any small mammal, and emerging upon a free spray to sing his song. The bird is as hardy and even more prolific than the golden-crested wren, our

smallest, and yet the mortality is very great, and the birds seem to have no migratory impulse to seek more sheltered and southerly quarters.

The wren's energy is also vented in building more nests than it ever uses, while the regular nest, wedged into holes or crevices in houses or faggots or other odd litter, or woven in bush-tangle, ivy, rock-shelters or heather is larger than that of birds twice his strength. The external structure is domed of moss, dead leaves, lichens or grasses, which usually match its surroundings, though hardly with intent, since wrens' nests are often so conspicuous; and the snuggery within is warm with moss, hair and feathers. From four to nine, or occasionally even thirteen, eggs are laid twice in a season, white lightly and ruddily splashed. The plumage is a warm rufous above, a greyer brown below, and barred and mottled, with a pale streak through the eye. Length, 3·5 inches.

THE SWALLOW

The swallow leads a double life, his own and a symbolic one in human imagination. Not the voices of all the warblers that announce the spring can evoke its presence and banish winter so surely as the sight of the first swallow. The habits of the swallow are so universally known as to

need no description; but the song, delivered in full air or from a gable, stump, telegraph wire, or coign of vantage, is, though a very abundant music, less familiar. For brightness its only rival is the skylark's, but the expression has more warmth, with a perceptible contralto tone which distinguishes this song from all others except those of blackbird and nightingale. When the swallow sings from a perch, he will often conclude his stave by rattling the mandibles together in a self-appreciative clap.

The first swallows arrive on our coasts about the middle of March, but the first clutch of from four to six white eggs, freckled with reddish brown and grey, is rarely laid before early May, though the nesting season may continue until late in October. The beam or joist of a barn is a favourite site, and the saucer of mud is lined with grass

o   385 and feathers. But the swallow occasionally builds a half cup under the eaves in the manner of the house-martin, when it often drops off for lack of buttressing, as the house-martin's never does. Old hats, shrimp-pots on shelves, and even boughs of trees may also become homes for the swallow.

He is a far more brilliantly coloured bird than the house-or the sand-martin, wearing a many-coloured dress of steel-blue above with a rich chestnut on the throat and forehead, a band of blue across the chest, buff underparts and a greenish gloss on the wings and tail. The swallow can always be distinguished from the house-martin, not merely by the greater mastery, rhythm and sweep of the flight, beauty of song and richness of colouring, but by the long pointed wings and the elegance of the extended tail feathers. Length, 7·3 inches.

The brownish sand-martin, that builds in sand-pits, and the house-martin that plasters a mud-saucer under the eaves, are the companions of the swallow in the pathways of the air, but theirs is a flittering beside the swallow's sweep of flight. The black swift belongs to a different family and is easily distinguished from the hirundines by the scythe-shaped wings, the tearing flight through the upper air, and by his wild scream.

THE PIED OR WATER WAGTAIL, or Polly
Wash Dish

The pied wagtail is a duodecimo edition of the magpie, both in the variegated black and white (greyer in winter) of his plumage and the inconsequence of his ways. The term " water wagtail " is far too narrow, for this oddling is even happier in the farmyard, darting about the lawn and hawking flies under the feet of the cattle than by a pond, stream or squelchy tin-can deposit. It is the grey wagtail whose sole haunts are stream and waterfall.

The pied wagtail is never in the same posture for a minute at a time. He trips nimbly to and fro, whirrs round upon himself, leaps into the air, goes tittering across the grass so swiftly that the movements of his feet are lost in a mist, stops dead and then bounds off into a dipping switchback

flight with a double note made up of zzzzzs and ssssssssss.
The pied wagtail will go no way but his own, and so he
has invented two little songs to be uttered, the first in
flight, a rather loud and gleeful warble, the second when
perching and sometimes murmured in chorus with others.
This is his evensong, a sighing breath of music so faint
that it is scarcely to be heard at all.

The nest of the pied wagtail is a hole packed with welded
grass-roots, leaves and other material lined with hair,
wool and feathers. This is the only regular thing about it,
for he will build it in almost any imaginable site, in a bank,

against a wall, among rocks, under a clod, at the roots of
a tree, between railway sleepers, in an old nest of the magpie. The eggs, four to six in number, are correspondingly
variable and capricious in colouring, the more normal
having a bluish white background streaked and flecked
with greys and browns. Some of the birds migrate in
winter. The sexes are more or less alike in plumage.
Length, 7·5 inches, including the long tail.

THE STARLING, *or Stare*

The starling, a bird belonging everywhere, and especially to
buildings, presents on first acquaintance a rough-and-ready
manner and hobbledehoy appearance. Only at close view
and in the spring can his irridescent coat be seen, the
feathers of a beaten-out metallic gleam throwing a lustre
of black, purple, blue and green reflections changing colour
at different angles and in striking tone with the lemon

yellow of his bill. In autumn the tipping of the feathers with buff and white dulls their brilliance. No casual observer, noting the starling's adaptable, quirksome and rather clumsy daily occupations, would guess his mysteries. One of these is his morning and evening song, time-keeper of the dawning and failing light, which, for all its hotchpotch of melodious and instrumental sound, its squeelings, whistlings, chatterings, clickings, smackings and bubblings,

for all its casual mimicries, has a very beautiful and moving effect, especially when uttered in chorus. But the greatest mystery of the starling is his autumn flocking. Thousands, and in favourable places hundreds of thousands, of birds congregate and perform as one bird a number of rapidly changing figures on swift triangular wings. Then as the dusk thickens they fall like hail upon trees or buildings or reed and osier beds and burst into a shrill massive chanting. When these orisons emanate from innumerable throats, as the flocks make clouds in the heavens, the onlooker is in the presence of one of the seven wonders of Britain.

388

The nest is a cavity in a tree, cliff, water-spout, chimney, haystack, ruin, barn, quarry, or spire, and is a mere litter of straw, twigs and grass, lined with soft substances. The eggs are pale blue and from four to seven in number. The female is more spotted than the male. Length, 8·5 inches.

WOODLAND BIRDS

THE WOOD-WREN, or *Wood-Warbler*

The wood-warbler is the most interesting of the trinity of leaf-warblers, though the chiff-chaff and the willow-warbler are the first of the homing warblers in the spring. The three birds are difficult to distinguish in appearance, being similarly built on very slender lines and of a colouring that matches the tender yellow-green of opening beech leaves. But the wood-warbler has longer wings, and frequents the tops of the taller oaks and beeches, from whose mists of foliage he delivers a song entirely dissimilar from the minute threshing-machine sounds of the chiff-chaff and the vanishing cadence of the willow-warbler. The wood-warbler is remarkable for possessing two songs which seem to belong to two different species. The first opens with a shining resonant note repeated more and more rapidly until it merges into a peculiar shiver, and if we are so lucky as to catch sight of the restless and elusive singer we shall see that the wings are quivering in pace with the brisk pattering of the notes. The second song is usually uttered after a short or long interval, and consists of one note repeated with longish pauses and unlike that of any other bird utterance in England. The note has a wonderful lucidity, but its unique quality is derived from the depth of feeling which the human ear seems to hear in it—now close and poignant, now fey and remote.

The wood-warbler builds a domed and oval nest under fronds or tumps of moss or coarse grass, made of moss, grass and dead leaves lined with fine bents and horse hair. Unlike the nests of chiff-chaff and willow-warbler, it has no feathers. The five or six eggs laid late in the season are larger than those of the willow-warbler and of a transparent whiteness thickly speckled or zoned with violet, purple, grey and dark brown flecks. The bird is coloured a delicate yellowish-green with white underparts, and a sulphur yellow dye on the throat and breast, while a stroke of like brightness passes from eye to nape. Length, 5·2 inches.

THE CUCKOO, *or Gowk*

This famed and enigmatic bird looks on the wing something between a disconsolate hawk and a top-heavy pigeon, and his flight, though powerful, is uncertain in direction and unsteady in poise. Poetic associations have invested the male cuckoo with a symbolic romance as the messenger of spring, on account of the soft flute-like major third of his call, first heard on his arrival in mid-April. But the scientific interest is in the female, who diverges from avian custom in her promiscuous mating and in depositing her eggs in the nests of pipits, wagtails, robins, dunnocks and various warblers, sometimes even of magpies and kestrels. It has been discovered that the bird lays her egg on the ground, picks it up in her bill and carries it to the chosen nest, while the nestling, a very ill-conditioned young oaf, has an irritant surface to the hollow of the back which enables it to pitch the other inmates out of the nest onto the ground, where they perish.

The female is also unusually vociferous when calling her paramours, repeating " cuckoo " more clearly than the male, as well as uttering a bubbling cry rather like water poured out of the neck of a bottle, and a strange howling note. Both sexes are very greedy and irritable, and appear

to obey a series of strict conventions in the biological routine of the year, showing that the parasitic habit is not a recent development. Five or six eggs are laid at intervals of several days between each egg, and though these are often similar in size and colouring to those of the species victimized, there is no evidence that the cuckoo deliberately chooses a clutch to match the eggs she lays.

Even more curious than the behaviour of the cuckoo is the apparent willingness of the foster-parents to play the role assigned to them without a hitch. It has been suggested that the young cuckoo has a mesmeric power in its voice. Another point of interest is that the old birds depart for

Africa a month or six weeks earlier than the young. The sexes are alike in their handsome plumage, bluish grey above, lighter on the neck and breast and darker on the wings, whitish on the underparts with dark transverse bars. The feet are yellow, the inside of the mouth is orange (probably a sexual decoration), while the wings are tipped and spotted with white and black. Length, 13 inches.

Other large birds commonly met on a casual visit to the country are the rook, distinguished from the carrion crow by his baldness at the base of the bill, his social organisation and the mellower tone of his call; the magpie, a much-maligned and very beautiful bird in chequered blacks and whites with pink and green irridescences, whose grace and sportiveness are seldom recognised; the blue, white, black and chestnut jay of the woodlands, who is too wary, in spite of his slow and heavy flight, to allow us more than an occasional glimpse of him; the jackdaw, with his grey pate and " amusing " ways and staccato yelp, between the starling and the rook in size; the tawny or wood owl of variegated browns, whose melodious hoot in B flat " makes the darkness deeper and the silence more profound "; the white or barn owl, with his ghostly flight and " fiendish " shrieks, and the curious night or hern-owl with enormous gape, plumage perfectly matched to brown heath and dead bracken where the eggs are laid, and mysterious purring or jarring note without beginning or end, produced by the mandibles.

THE BLACKCAP, or *Northern Nightingale*

The blackcap is a summer warbler of the woodlands, and what Gilbert White describes as his " full, deep, sweet, loud, wild pipe " bursts from the undergrowth about the middle of April. As a rule he leaves us in September, but has been known to winter in the warmer parts of England. His song has been often and justly compared with that of the garden warbler, of whose presence he appears to be intolerant, though having no objection to his own kin. But the difference between the two songs is that the blackcap's is a jet of melody while the garden warbler's is a more continuous stream. The tone is nearer to the black-bird's than any other melodist, but the utterance is very rapid and much more confident. The quality of the song is its freedom from any heavy, flat or discordant element. Shelley's " unbodied joy " fits this beautiful pipe more appropriately than the skylark's.

Like other warblers, the blackcap is perpetually in motion, but is much shyer than any of the leaf warblers. The scold note resembles the whitethroat's grrrrrrrrrrrr. The nest of this very private little bird is wedged into the

darkest shade of a thick bush, usually a bramble, and built up of dry grasses, sedges, roots and bents, with a lining of hair and finer threads. Four or five very variable eggs are laid about a month after the bird's arrival, ruddy in ground colour and very richly mottled and clouded with a mingling of deeper reds and yellowish browns. The rich black hood of the male makes him easily recognisable among other warblers, and the rest of the upper parts are a bluish grey with a faint tinge of olive. The grey passes into ash on the underparts, whiter lower down and under the chin and browner on the flanks. The female differs from the male in having a stronger tone of olive on the back and of buff on the breast. Length, 5·75 inches.

THE NIGHTINGALE

The nightingale, who arrives about the middle of April, is obviously related to the robin—larger and more slender in build, and of a richer brown on the upper parts, but possessing very much the same air, the same habits of feeding on the ground, and the same abrupt, gallant movements. He is very much more restricted in range and is a rare bird north of South Yorkshire, west of the Welsh marches, and beyond the Tamar in the south. The Home Counties are

his headquarters. He also diverges from the behaviour of the robin in preferring thick copses and the more tangled hedgerows on the borders of woodland, especially where there are oaks.

No bird enriched with so classic a fame as a melodist is so little familiar as a genuine singer. The error that the nightingale only sings by night is as widespread as the convention that the song itself is the celebration of a broken heart, and he is constantly confused at twilight with the last thrush, blackbird or robin. Nevertheless, the nightingale, or rather the best nightingales—for the quality of the song differs enormously among individual birds—do deserve their reputation as singers unapproached in power and range by any other warbler. The song is not in the least sorrowful or appealing, but of a triumphant nuptial fire. It is a very broken and varied song, and separated into phrases which plunge into silence and then suddenly burst again into utterance. The notes and even the peculiar timbre of other birds can be distinguished in this "impassioned recitative," but the wonderful crescendo culminating in a high clear throbbing peal is like no other woodland sound in the world. The only melancholy element in the nightingale's voice is his call note, a soft plaint. The alarm cry is a croak.

The nest, of dead oak leaves and a few grass wisps lined with hair and finer grasses, is built low down in the densest litter of a thorn or low-spreading bush on a clay soil or near water, and four to six olive-brown eggs are laid in it rather late in the season. The song ceases as soon as the eggs are hatched, and is not resumed as it often is among other warblers when the young are flown. The fine rich brown of the back deepens into rufous along the tail, and the underparts are of a dull white with an ashy tinge. Both sexes, as is usual among the warblers, are alike. Length, 6·5 inches.

THE YAFFLE, *Rain-bird, Green Woodpecker, Woodspite, High-Hoe, Hew-Hole, or Pick-a-tree*

It is difficult to believe in the yaffle as an English woodland bird, what with his bold tropical colouring, so foreign to the subdued tones of our landscape, his piercing cry, his oddly demoniac appearance, and his superlative animation. The yaffle, digging his trunk-dwelling, will be heard over the length and breadth of the woodland, and his movements seem to match that blithe laugh which, for those who love him, makes him the bird of liberty.

This indeed is true in fact as well as impression, for the yaffle is evolving into a new species under our very eyes, changing from a bird of the woodlands, who seeks his food and builds his nest in trees and flies in huge drooping loops and crests among the pillars, to a bird of the open spaces, getting his livelihood entirely from ants' nests on the ground. As an instance of his change of habit, the yaffle is rarely heard nowadays in deep woods, but chiefly in open parkland and the margins of meadow and woodland. Possibly the same enterprise in passing from old woods to pastures new explains his laborious characteristic of alighting at the foot of a tree, spiralling up it in abrupt jerks and bounds, and then curving off to the next.

The nest is hammered out of a trunk that has begun to decay, though it often gives no visible sign of it. Chips of wood are laid on the floor of the hole as a bedding, and five to seven polished oval white eggs are laid upon them.

The bird's colours are disposed in an abrupt and sharply contrasted manner. His face is black, his crown, moustaches and back of the head are crimson, his rump is bright yellow, his wings have the outer webs barred black and white, his back olive-green, and his underparts run to green with an infusion of yellow. The sexes are alike, though there is a touch more crimson in the male. Length, 12·5 inches. The lesser spotted woodpecker is very rarely seen, being exceedingly shy, no larger than a chaffinch, and seldom descending from the tops of high trees. The greater spotted or barred woodpecker, about the size of a starling and likewise liveried in black and white, has a love-tattoo drummed on a hollow branch and echoing all through the woodland.

The yaffle, being a half-and-half bird, living between woodland and open country, introduces us to a few characteristic species of the latter.

BIRDS OF THE OPEN

THE YELLOWHAMMER, *Yellow Bunting, Yoldring,*
Scribbling Lark, or *Yellow Yowley*

The yellowhammer is a bird of the open uplands, of commons and the tops of incult hedges in their neighbourhood, where he sits for most of the day from February to August uttering his set and wheezy song at the rate of certainly more than a thousand times a week, showing his golden head, bright as a small sun, above the leaf-tangle. His retirement, his Sancho Panza air, his monotonous and yet touching phrase of half a dozen reed-like notes culminating in a high thin cheer (a little bit of bread and NO cheese), make him seem the most complacent of all birds, more so than his shiftless and slatternly cousins, the corn-bunting, the livelier cirl-bunting and the rather drooping reed-bunting.

Like that of other buntings, his flight is slow and cumbersome. In the winter he does not migrate but joins the strolling companies of finches. The large but not unwieldy nest, near to or on the ground in a hedgebank or among bracken, is lined with fibres and horse hair, supported by a structure of thin roots, moss, stalks and dry grass. Three to five eggs, purplish or brownish white in ground tint, and scribbled with runic hieroglyphs, bluish grey or reddish purple in colour, are laid in April, and the nesting season will sometimes continue right on to the end of September. The male's underparts are as glowing as the head, while the back, rump and mantle are a warm chestnut, also with an infusion of orange. Dusky brown streaks splash the head, throat, flanks and back, while the female runs more to browns than yellows. Length, 6·7 inches.

THE KESTREL, *Stonegall, Stannel Hawk, or Windhover*

The kestrel is the only common hawk surviving in our islands, for all other birds of prey have been exterminated or reduced to comparative rarity. The surest way of identifying the kestrel is by his capacity to suspend himself on the wing in a given place as though hanging from an invisible wire. This is achieved in part by a rapid vibration of the wing tips ; but a close watcher will notice that this flickering of the wings only continues for a certain time, and that the bird, by processes as yet unknown, can

maintain itself in mid-air without any perceptible movement even in a high wind. This continues for several
seconds before the wing-fanning is resumed. As soon as
he spies a possible meal, be it rat, vole, or even beetle, the
wings are half furled and the bird drops headlong from the
sky. The flight is easy and graceful, less erratic and dashing
than the sparrow-hawk's, and far less powerful than the
peregrine's, nor can the kestrel's ever reach the mastery
of the buzzard's flight, which takes half a mile on one wing
beat. The call note is a high shrill kee-ee.

The kestrel is not confined to any particular type of country,
and he is very catholic in his choice of nesting sites, which
may be an old building, tower, a high tree, a quarry, an
old nest of magpie or even sparrow-hawk, or even a hollow
in the ground. A nest in a rabbit burrow has been
observed. The eggs are from four to six and of variable
colouring, the normal being a yellowish ground colour
smeared with heavy tawny strokes. As is usual among
birds of prey, the female is the handsomer and larger of
the pair, the upper plumage and tail being a beautiful light
red splashed and barred with dark brown. The male is a
rather sullen grey above and on the breast, while the sides
and thighs are a pale yellowish red with narrow longitudinal
streaks of dark brown. The female is the lighter underneath. Length, 15 inches.

THE LAPWING, *Green Plover, or Peewit*

The lapwing is one of the most beautiful and individual
birds in all the land, and as he is one of the larger of the
plovers and lives entirely in the open on the furrows and
pastures, on downland and in marshy country, is very
easy to recognize. His winter congregations (to which
many foreign immigrants contribute in the autumn) are
mingled with gulls, curlew and other waders on the seashore and tidal flats. In repose, to which he is much
inclined, he is a tall, statuesque bird, with a metallic green
gloss, patches of chestnut and black, white underparts
and an uptilting crest of greenish black. In the air he loses
his stateliness, for the broadly rounded wings, flashing
black and white, give him a sagging, cumbersome gait in

flight. There is a dramatic change when the ardours of courtship take possession of his faculties. He rises in wide circles to a lofty plateau of air and suddenly hurls himself down to earth. At the very moment when it seems that he must dash himself out of life altogether, he checks his headlong descent a foot or two from the ground and comes to rest in an equally dramatic stillness.

These aerial dances are accompanied by a further change in his call from the drawling double mew of normal life to a wild and lovely undulating whistle in the same notation as the liquid cries of his plover and wader relatives. No bird is more practised in the arts of decoying the predatory—human and otherwise—from his nest, feigning wounded wing and broken body to lead the intruder astray. In the autumn flocks he conducts the same collective and aerial manœuvres as do other plovers, though without their power of dashing speed and quickness of turn. The nest, though no more than a casual scrape in grassland or ling or between the furrows, with a few bents or straws for decoration, is yet very difficult to see, the four eggs of olive-green richly mottled in blacks and browns resembling the broken lights and shadows of the ground. The first clutch is usually laid in March, laid and lost to the greed of the gourmet. The sexes are alike except that the female's crest is shorter and wings a little more angular. Length, 12 inches.

THE SKYLARK, *or Laverock*

If the skylark is not merely regarded as a couple of mouthfuls, as he is in Italy, his image as a small black star pouring down continuous rays of song is present to every mind. The bird opens his lyric when a few feet from the ground, and ascends the sky in wide arcs and on trembling wings, the melody growing more powerful as he mounts. The wonder of the song is not its quality, which at a near distance is distinctly harsh and full of grating notes, but its continuity, its vehemence, and the sense of illimitable space which its distance gives. No sooner is the torrent of song suspended than the bird drops plumb to earth. Nor do singing and soaring always go together, since the music

may be uttered on the ground or from a perch, or when
hovering above his mate in her nest among the grasses.
It is heard at all seasons except August, the time of the
moult, and is best on the downs where the purity of the
atmosphere softens and clarifies the more gutteral notes.
Skylarks are widely distributed over all open country,
especially arable land. Though the majority of our home
birds migrate in winter, the sum of skylarks is greatly
increased at that season by immigrants that flock in from
abroad and make winter parties in the fields. The courtship

is prolonged and accompanied by much *brouhaha* and
skirmishing.
The rather simple grassy April nest is placed in a slight
hollow in corn land or in a hay-field, and the four to five
eggs in it are of a greyish tint with dense brown mottlings.
On close inspection the birds present a somewhat stumpy
appearance, though the tail is longer than the woodlark's.
The pale brown eye stripe and slight crest are noticeable
in a plumage of variegated shades of brown copiously
streaked. The underparts are of a paler buff, and dark
and lance-shaped smears of brown continue as far as the
lower breast. The sexes are alike, and may be distinguished
from other brown birds by their somewhat jutting walk and
call notes of a very rough and throaty timbre. Length,
7·75 inches.

BIRDS IN COMPANIES

A sege of herons.
A herd of curlews.
A dopping of sheldrakes.
A spring of teals.
A covert of coots.
A gaggle of geese.
A bevy of quails.
A covey of partridges.
A congregation of plovers.
A wisp of snipe.
A fall of woodcocks.
A murmuration of starlings.
An exaltation of larks.
A watch of nightingales.
A charm of goldfinches.

STARSHINE

AT NIGHT

I STOOD AND STARED; THE SKY WAS LIT,
THE SKY WAS STARS ALL OVER IT,
I STOOD, I KNEW NOT WHY,
WITHOUT A WISH, WITHOUT A WILL,
I STOOD UPON THAT SILENT HILL
AND STARED INTO THE SKY UNTIL
MY EYES WERE BLIND WITH STARS AND STILL
I STARED INTO THE SKY.

Ralph Hodgson.

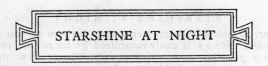

STARSHINE AT NIGHT

It is a distinguishing feature of man's bodily habits that he raises his eyes to the heavens. It is a significant feature of the mind of man that he has the wit and the will to follow the stars in their courses. The purpose of these maps and notes of the firmament of the sky is to duplicate for him the pleasure and the sense of power which he enjoys in recognising, naming and characterising the birds of the air and the wild flowers of the earth.

Naturally, only the most illustrious planets and stars with their particular offices can be described.

THE PLANETS

We will begin with the planets in the order of their brightness. The term "planet" is applied to the spheres which revolve about the sun and which, with this earth and the moon, make up our solar system. The "superior" planets—Mars, Jupiter, Saturn, Uranus and Neptune—are those whose orbits are outside the earth. The "inferior" planets—Mercury and Venus—are those which revolve between the earth and the sun. Only Jupiter, Venus, Mars, Mercury and Saturn can be seen by the unaided eye, though Uranus can occasionally be distinguished by very good eyes. Their constant and elaborate orbital motions make it impossible to identify them by any fixed position in the heavens.*

JUPITER, 1341 times greater than the earth and 483 millions of miles distant from the sun, so far outshines the fixed stars of the first magnitude, being four times brighter than Sirius, the most brilliant of them all, that we cannot fail to recognize it. But VENUS, which plays the double part of the Morning and the Evening Star, outshines even Jupiter after sunset in the west and before sunrise in the east. The ancients, who named it Hesperus in the evening sky and Phosphorus in the morning, did so not knowing that the two luminaries were one and the same. On a

* For precise information concerning the movements and visible positions of the planets, see *Whitaker's Almanack*.

clear, moonless evening, Venus may be seen to cast a shadow. MARS is easily recognized by its reddish tint and a pulsating glow, which is very different from the light of any of the fixed stars. Its movement in the sky is so complex that it requires considerable study to identify it by its place in the heavens. MERCURY is the planet nearest to the sun, its mean distance being only 35,935,000 miles. It is much the smallest of the eight planets, and can only be perceived occasionally in England just after sunset or before sunrise. Like Venus, it was known to the Greeks by two different names—Apollo in the morning and Mercury in the evening. SATURN is at so great a distance from the earth that it appears comparatively insignificant. The bright rings which surround it and have made it the most famous among the planets cannot be seen without a telescope. URANUS is difficult to distinguish from the numerous small stars which encompass it. It is twice as remote as Saturn, and can hardly be identified without a telescope. NEPTUNE, the outermost planet of our solar system, escaped notice till the middle of the last century owing to its size and similarity to the smaller fixed stars. It can be observed only through a telescope.

FIXED STARS

The fixed stars are orbs which shine by their own light and are for the most part millions of times the size of our earth. Each revolves on its own axis, like the sun, and if viewed as closely as our own sun would reveal, in spite of their immensely greater heat, much the same appearance. Some 5000 stars are visible to the unaided eye throughout the year, though the utmost number to be seen on any one night varies from 1500 to 2000. They become more and more numerous as we approach the GALAXY or MILKY WAY, the great stream of starshine which spans the visible firmament. It can be seen every night throughout the year, but is at its faintest during May. In the spring the Milky Way is extended almost parallel with the curve of the horizon between E.N.E. and W.S.W., and so is less conspicuous than at the other seasons. In the summer it traverses mid-heaven from north to south.

In the autumn it has swung back to W.S.W. and E.N.E., but stretches across the sky instead of following the arc of the horizon. In the winter it changes its direction once more, and its furthest ends are anchored to the S.S.E. and N.N.W. limits of the horizon. Again it forms almost the equator of the stellar universe.

No more delusive term than " fixed " could be applied to the stars, since they are in fact travelling at rates varying on an average from 5 to 30 miles a second, while a few plunge through the stellar universe at a pace which is far beyond our power of mental measurement. A R C T U R U S, for instance, reaches the velocity of 257 miles a second. Yet to our eyes Arcturus is always to be found in the same position relative to the other stars. This contra-diction between fixity and inconceivably swift movement is easier to understand when we remember that from the beginning of time our whole solar system has been rushing through space towards the constellation of L Y R A at the rate of a million miles a day, and yet, if Ptolemy were alive to-day, he could discern no change in their appear-ances and positions, nor can the present region of Lyra be attained for at least another million years. This move-ment is not like that of the planets, a revolution round the sun, but a forward flight into space.

Through the revolution of the earth upon its own axis the constellations change their positions to our eyes in a night, whilst the motion of the earth round the sun makes different constellations visible with the changing seasons. The stars reach the same position relative to the north point of the horizon four minutes earlier every evening. If we look up at the same hour every night we shall find that they mark the progress of the months throughout the year. The star nearest to this earth is A L P H A   C E N - T A U R I, almost of the first magnitude and 275,000 times the distance of the sun from us. Its light takes four years to reach us. Stars only faintly seen under the telescope are more than 1000 times the distance of Alpha Centauri.

The stars differ from each other in colour by a regular gradation from blue through yellow to red. These changes indicate difference of surface temperatures, and are connected with differences in their spectra. As a general rule, the redder the star the greater the number and intensity of the dark lines that can be seen in the green and blue parts of its spectrum. The red stars have surface temperatures of 3000° C.; yellow ones like the sun 6000° C.; blue stars like Sirius 12,000° C. This phenomenon means that all the stars are surrounded by atmospheres, hotter than the flame of any surface, but far cooler than the central body of the star. These atmospheres all vary owing to the differences in their elements. The specific gravity or density of some stars is often no greater than that of air, and their intense heat is such that our sun is among the colder and the smaller of the stars. This is the result of their evolution from nebulæ, a process which produces the changes in colour from blue through white and yellow to red, the lines on the spectrum becoming darker and more numerous. Finally, the light of the star fails and it becomes a dark opaque body. Thus we behold stars of all periods in the heavens, from the infant nebula to the star dying of old age.

The twelve brightest stars in the order of their brightness are : SIRIUS, *CANOPUS, *ALPHA of the CENTAUR, VEGA, CAPELLA, ARCTURUS, RIGEL, PROCYON, *ACHERNAR, *BETA of the CENTAUR, ALTAIR and BETELGUESE. (Those marked *, being situate in the southern hemisphere, are not visible from England.) The original method of identifying the stars by linking them together into imaginary pictures is still in use, and the earliest drawings of any of these constellation pictures are recorded upon small engraved stones of Babylonia known as " boundary stones," many of which are more than 3000 years old. The Greek names of the stars and planets were first assigned by Ptolemy in the second century A.D. Our surest means of identifying the most conspicuous among them is to become familiar with the relative positions of the constellations to which they belong. Round about the North celestial Pole, which is almost midway between the zenith and the northern horizon, are stars which in their diurnal revolution round the Pole never set. The stars whose distance from the North Pole is more than 130° are never seen in these latitudes. The stars which

THE AUTUMN SKY

(*See* Map, pp. 418, 419)

The square constellation of PEGASUS, almost overhead, is a convenient landmark for observing the autumn sky. In its north-eastern corner is the Great Nebula of ANDROMEDA, just visible to the eye. By now the Milky Way has made an immense curve across the sky-world until it lies almost due west and east, with Cassiopeia as its central constellation a little to the north of the zenith. The most prominent stars of the autumn sky are Vega, Alpha Cygni or Deneb, and Capella, south-east of which are the PLEIADES, a cluster of six visible stars, the seventh, called the "lost Pleiad," having faded away.

Below the Pleiades flames the great star ALDEBARAN, the eye of TAURUS or the Bull, equal in size to thirty million suns like ours. Now for the first time in the year the constellation of ORION, with SIRIUS, the brightest star in all heaven, comes into view low above the southern horizon.

THE WINTER SKY

(*See* Map, pp. 420, 421)

CAPELLA, the golden star in Auriga, is near the zenith of the winter sky, and the Milky Way has swung round to its fourth quarterly position, spanning the heavens from north to south and separating the Gemini, Procyon, Lyra and the Great and Little Bears from Canis Major, Orion, Taurus, Andromeda and Perseus.

The constellation of Taurus with its fiery red Aldebaran hangs from a branch of the V-shaped cluster of the HYADES (neighbours of the Pleiades), in which the brightest is ALCYONE, once thought to be the central star of the universe. The Hyades—about forty in number —make up the most wonderful family of migrant stars yet discovered. But ORION, with its jewelled belt, is the chiefest glory of the winter sky. Hanging in the south, a tremendous question mark thrown out upon so vast a

411

canvas, this " burning rhetoric " across the heavens has stirred the awe of countless generations of watchers.

East of Orion is Canis Minor, containing S I R I U S, the first heavenly light to draw the speculations of the human mind and fix the divisions of the calendar, for Sirius presided over the agricultural rites of the ancient Egyptians, the founders of civilization. The three stars of the belt of Orion are still known in Provence as "les trois rois " which point to Sirius, "the star of Bethlehem."

COMETS, METEORS, NEBULÆ, AND CLUSTERS

About 3000 comets have been recorded in the last 2000 years, and throughout the whole universe these bodies, according to Kepler, are more numerous than fishes in the sea. Although astronomers have discovered many of the laws which govern these mysterious substances of light, to the lay mind they have been the source of more terrors than any other natural phenomenon. The appearance of Halley's Comet in 1456, when the Turks were sweeping over Europe, caused such widespread consternation that Pope Calixtus issued a Bull in which he anathematised both the Comet and the Turks.

Comets travel in elliptical orbits, their aphelion or remotest positions being so far distant that these strange visitors are completely forgotten long before they reappear. But with the scientific precision which modern astronomers have perfected it is now possible to predict almost to the day and hour when a comet, vanishing into outermost space, will revisit our skies. Thus the return of H A L L E Y 'S C O M E T in 1910, which had been seen last in 1835, was predicted correctly to two days. Though comets move in great sweeping ellipses round the sun, they are also subject to the gravitational attraction of the planets. The group which submits to the pull of Jupiter is known as the " Jovian family of Comets." When a comet draws near to the sun the molecules of atmosphere surrounding its nucleus are first attracted by the central body and a tidal movement is set up. But a repulsive force overcomes the attractive one and the nucleus is swished into a backward stream forming the comet's tail. The tail of Halley's

Comet, photographed at Johannesburg in 1910, extended to 70,000,000 miles in length. The differences in colour between one comet and another are due to the variability in their chemical constitution. Where gaseous elements predominate the comet is bluish in colour, and where its consistency is formed of more solid particles the colour tends to yellow.

Meteors and shooting stars are still believed to mark the extinction of the world. Among the brightest are the PERSEID meteors seen between the 10th and 15th of August, but in some years, notably 1799 and 1833, the LEONID meteors, which come in the middle of November, coursed down the heavens in such flocks as to fill their beholders with terror.

Swarms of meteorites, probably broken fragments of comet-like substances, are found in association with comets which still exist, and are also derived from comets which have now disappeared.

VARIABLE STARS

Between four and five hundred of the stars vary in their brightness, either regularly or irregularly, at different intervals of time. In 1918, for instance, a new star appeared in the constellation of A Q U I L A and so was named N O V A A Q U I L Æ. In a few days it attained almost the brightness of Sirius and then slowly faded away until now it is among the lesser lights of the sky. The variability of BETA LYRÆ can be observed from week to week; MIRA CETI (Omicron Ceti) is at its brightest during two weeks in the year; while ALGOL in Perseus, the most variable of all, is affected by eclipses due to a dark companion. The variations of light in many of these stars is due to the revolution of bright and faint stars round one another.

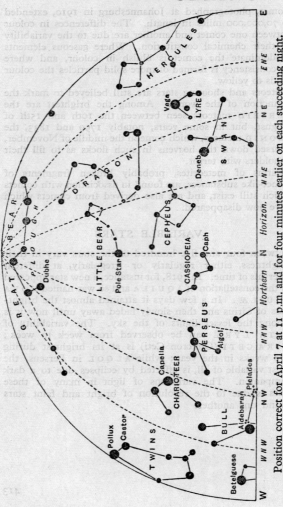

Position correct for April 7 at 11 p.m. and for four minutes earlier on each succeeding night.

STARS

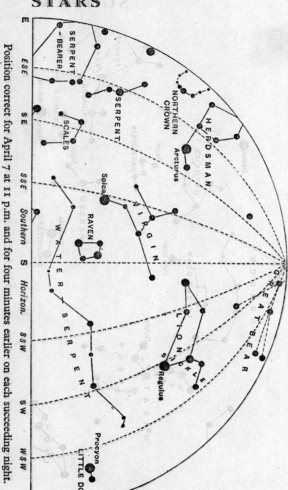

Position correct for April 7 at 11 p.m. and for four minutes earlier on each succeeding night.

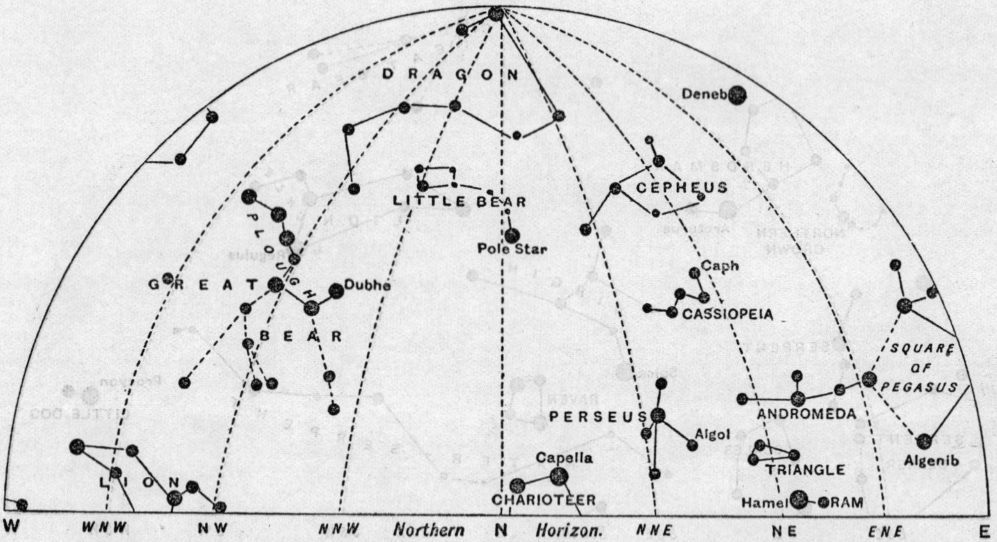

SUMMER

SQUARE OF PEGASUS

Algenib

ANDROMEDA

TRIANGLE

Hamel ○ RAM

Deneb

CEPHEUS

Caph

CASSIOPEIA

PERSEUS

Algol

Capella

CHARIOTEER

DRAGON

LITTLE BEAR

Pole Star

Northern N Horizon.

Oubhe

GREAT BEAR

PLOUGH

LION

Position correct for July 7 at 11 p.m. and for four minutes earlier on each succeeding night.

STARS

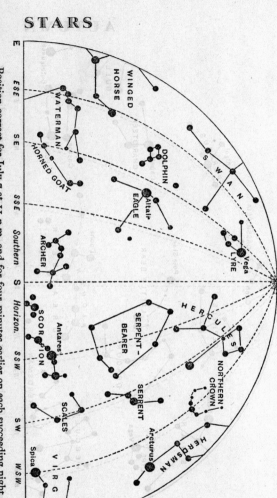

Position correct for July 7 at 11 p.m. and for four minutes earlier on each succeeding night.

E
ESE
SE
SSE
Southern
S
Horizon.
SSW
SW
WSW
W

WINGED HORSE

WATERMAN

HORNED GOAT

DOLPHIN

EAGLE
Altair

ARCHER

SWAN

Vega
LYRE

HERCULES

SCORPION
Antares

SERPENT-BEARER

NORTHERN CROWN

SERPENT

SCALES

Arcturus
HERDSMAN

VIRGIN
Spica

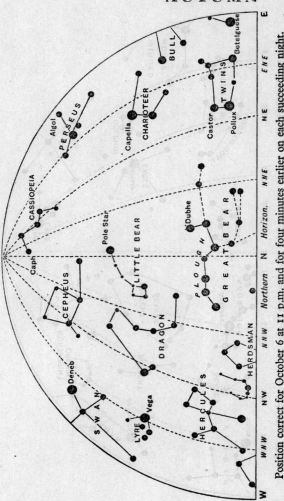

AUTUMN

Position correct for October 6 at 11 p.m. and for four minutes earlier on each succeeding night.

STARS

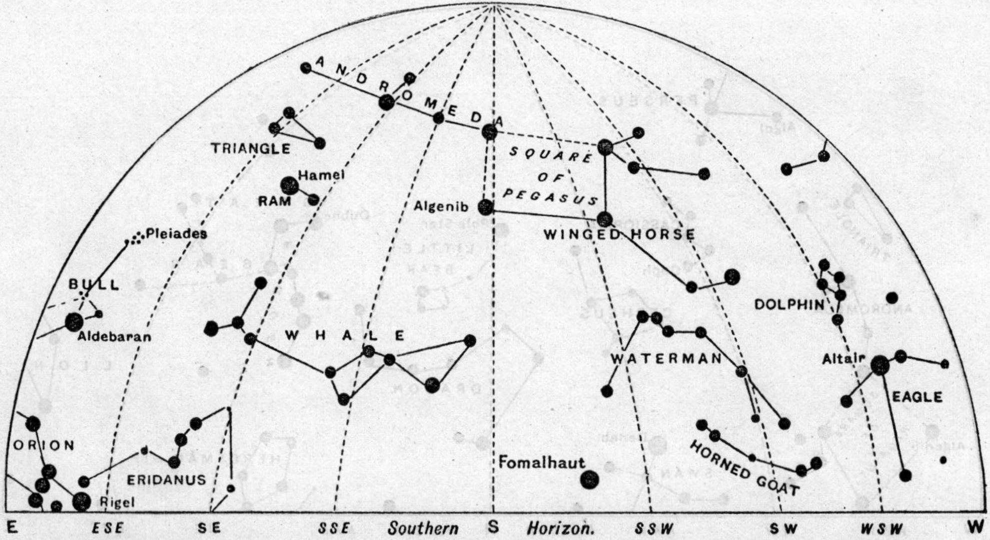

Position correct for October 6 at 11 p.m. and for four minutes earlier on each succeeding night.

E · ESE · SE · SSE · Southern · S · Horizon. · SSW · SW · WSW · W

ORION
Aldebaran
BULL
Rigel
Pleiades
ERIDANUS
TRIANGLE
RAM
Hamel
WHALE
ANDROMEDA
Algenib
SQUARE OF PEGASUS
Fomalhaut
WATERMAN
WINGED HORSE
HORNED GOAT
DOLPHIN
Altair
EAGLE

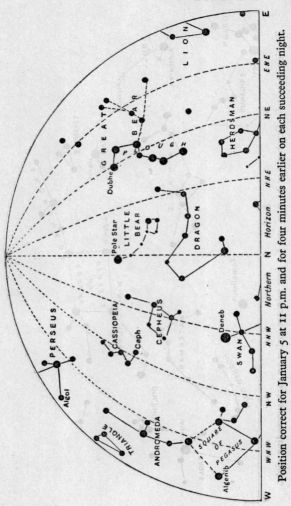

WINTER

Position correct for January 5 at 11 p.m. and for four minutes earlier on each succeeding night.

STARS

Position correct for January 5 at 11 p.m. and for four minutes earlier on each succeeding night.

Labels on chart: E, ESE, SE, SSE, Southern, S, Horizon, SSW, SW, WSW, W

WATER-SERPENT
Regulus
SICKLE
Castor
Pollux
TWINS
LITTLE DOG
Procyon
Sirius
GREAT DOG
Betelguese
ORION
CHARIOTEER
Capella
DOVE
HARE
Rigel
Aldebaran
BULL
ERIDANUS
Pleiades
WHALE
Hamel
RAM

ARCHITECTURE

THE ART PRESERVATIVE OF ALL THE ARTS

ARCHITECTURE

The kinds of building one happens upon most often in country walks, and on week-end visits, are farms and manor houses and parish churches, with an occasional ruined Abbey or Great House by way of grandeur and diversity. For this reason the first place in these short notes will be given to the more modest kinds of architecture. These have a special fascination in that being built by local contractors of local material, they vary in character with every district: for example, the brick or timber houses and flint churches of the Eastern Counties, where stone was an expensive luxury imported by water-carriage from a distance, and by contrast the Cotswolds where almost every kind of building is in stone. Mention of the Cotswolds brings in another interesting aspect of country building: the filtering down into the country of new architectural fashions from London and the big towns, so that one can often find charming simplified variations of smart London architectural features in the attempts of the local builders to keep up-to-date. The Cotswold builders, from among whom came most of the great contractors who executed the masonry of St. Paul's Cathedral, showed the effect of this training under the eye of Sir Christopher Wren in the astonishingly accomplished series of early Georgian houses to be found in almost all the villages of that district. Other local styles are the extravagant timber work of Tudor and Stuart times in Lancashire and Cheshire and the Welsh Border counties, the timber in combination with tile and brick of Surrey, Sussex and Kent, the splendid Georgian brickwork of Buckinghamshire with its extraordinarily high proportion of darker burnt bricks, and the luscious golden stone work of the Ham Hill quarries which is to be found all over Dorset and South Somerset, and, finally, the work of all the good stone-building counties stretching diagonally across England from Somerset, through the Cotswolds, Oxfordshire, Northants, Rutland to Lincolnshire. In all these local styles the determining factor is in the main the materials used in construction, though political and economic conditions appear in some places, as the Peel towers of the Scottish border, where defence was a primary consideration, or the Oast Houses of Kent.

The Georgian architecture of America, called by its owners colonial, though it continued long after the War of Independence, comes intermediate between a regional or local school and a small national school such as that of Ireland or Scotland. There is good Georgian brick building in America, but the most remarkable feature of this group to English eyes is the weather-boarded work. This is found in England, in Surrey especially (there are good examples in Dorking), but in America houses of a size and dignity that would have demanded stone or stucco in England were carried out in weather-boarding. The "Cape Cod House" rather in favour in America, for a week-ending style resembles the simpler and sturdier form of Georgian cottage. Its charms are rather those of atmosphere than architecture. The great majority of old farm-houses are either Tudor or Stuart, that is, late mediæval, for the Middle Ages lingered on in the country till the eighteenth century almost, or what we may call classical, that is, Georgian and early nineteenth century. The typical late mediæval house is like this :

The part between the Porch and the Upper end chambers (sometimes called Parlour and Solar above) was in the earliest examples, that is, before Edward VI (1550 about), all one room open from the ground to the roof—the "baronial" hall in fact—but in the second half of the sixteenth century a floor was often inserted in older houses,

426

providing a big upstairs sitting-room in the roof part of the
old hall, and leaving the hall itself as rather a low-ceilinged,
unimposing room below. This making of a big sitting-room
upstairs was the origin of the grand staircase in larger houses:
in the Middle Ages proper staircases are rarely of much
importance. This division of the hall into two storeys
is the only important change in medium-sized house design
from Plantagenet times down to Cromwell. Various details
do alter, however, and can serve as closer indications of
date. The barge-boards on gables, for example :

EARLY   TUDOR   JACOBEAN

Windows, too, are a good rough guide to date :

TUDOR I   TUDOR II   LATE TUDOR

Most of these examples have been taken from timber-built
houses, but the main forms are the same all over the country.
The Great Houses of Mediæval and Tudor times follow the
same general plan, but in these cases the Upper and Lower
end chambers have grown into long wings which are
returned to form a court like those of the Colleges of
Oxford and Cambridge. Often a second court was formed

427

in front of the house proper out of ranges of farm buildings. These courts were entered through gate-houses over which were sets of rooms, in some cases important enough to be a little annexe to the house.

Simpler examples of gate-houses had a timber-top storey on a brick or stone gate.

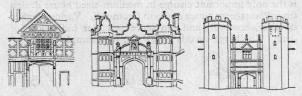

But in Tudor times brick gate-houses with octagonal turrets became popular. They were bright with gilding and diaper patterns, and generally picturesque, and there is a smack of knightly chivalry about them that pleased an age of realistic politicians playing at romance. This taste for pageantry, colouring and a flavour of chivalry in architecture is the first " art " fashion that can be recognized in England. Beside the fondness for gate-houses and turrets and gay colouring, all symptoms of this first fashionable taste, there are the Tudor chimneys, of which a few examples below.

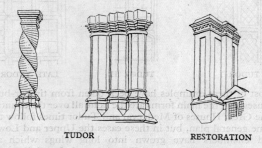

TUDOR   RESTORATION

In the later sixteenth century the " chivalrous " taste is seen rapidly giving place to a " classical," not real classic

428

in the sense of Roman archæologists or even true Italian Renaissance, but a sort of barbarised version of the Italian derived from copybooks printed and engraved in Belgium or Germany. In grand houses the decorative work was often actually done by Flemish and German workmen. Below are instances of typical Flemish ornament in English buildings.

This thoroughly over-decorated Flemish type of architecture was the last word in fashion at the time of Shakespeare,

but as the seventeenth century proceeds the influence of Holland began to supersede that of Belgium and a bolder,

rather less rich and less over-ripe manner began to prevail.
The type of gable shown is found chiefly in the South-East
of England, and is definitely Dutch in origin. It is a sort
of halfway house between the pure barbarity of James I
architecture and the complete Classicism that came in
with the Restoration.

The Restoration and William and Mary to Queen Anne type
of country house is rightly celebrated for the way in which
it is able to combine classical restraint with geniality. The
typical house of the time takes this form :

The roof and chimneys are marked features of the design,
and a sure indication of this period is the heavy ornamental
cornice and wide-spreading eaves. The ornament to
doors is bold and rich.

As the Classic movement became more and more rigid,
large roofs came to be considered barbarous (that is, not
Italian) and this type of house became fashionable during
the reigns of George I and II.

The roof is hidden behind a parapet. (See page opposite.)
Window frames in Classic houses vary considerably and
there is even more variety and freedom of invention shown
in the country than in London, where the tyranny of the
Italian masters was strong.

430

The earliest form of Classic window—it is rare to find
it unaltered—retains the mullion (vertical post) and transom
horizontal crosspiece), relics of the great Tudor windows,
but the window opening has taken on its classic shape.
When sash windows were introduced—the first recorded
is in the sixteen-eighties—many of these early Classic

| TRANSITIONAL | EARLY GEORGIAN | LATER GEORGIAN |

windows were adapted and lost their mullion and transom.
The early Georgian sash windows have very thick glazing
bars, and are often placed flush with the surrounding

431

brickwork. As the eighteenth century went on, however, the tendency was to make the glazing bars more and more thin and elegant, and by the time of George III (1790) they began to assume the thickness we are accustomed to. Many delightful varieties of window were made by local firms during the eighteenth century, as the " Siamese " Twin and the Venetian.

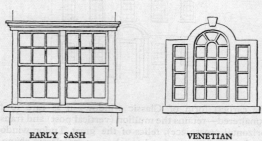

EARLY SASH   VENETIAN

The latter became fashionable with London architects after the return of Lord Burlington (after whom Burlington House is named) from his Italian tour in George I's time, but they do not appear much in country districts till the seventeen thirties and forties. All these types of window are often to be seen inserted into earlier buildings. There is hardly space here to do more than mention the extraordinary variety of types of bow-window, often richly decorated, and of ornamental doorways. It is often possible to recognize the work of one local firm in the windows and doors of a district.

Towards the end of the eighteenth century and in the first quarter of the nineteenth (Regency and George IV), a new type of country house appears.

It is long and low and has a roof of very flat pitch and very far-overhanging eaves. The roof is very often of slate. It is generally severely plain as regards stonework—when it is of brick it is often stuccoed and painted—and the chief ornamental feature often takes the form of a balcony or verandah or porch—sometimes all three—of cast-iron treillage of geometrical design. These are the counterparts of the houses in

Bloomsbury and Phillimore Terrace in London. Cheltenham and Brighton were largely built in this style, and there are many charming examples in South Devon. It prevails in the older seaside resorts such as Sidmouth, which came into fashion after George III was ordered sea bathing for his health. There are a great many pleasant country rectories built in this style.

Of the great houses of the Georgian period the most striking feature is the pillared portico. The earlier Georgian mansions tend to be designed on the scheme of a big four-square central block connected by low passage wings often with arcades or columns to wing pavilions.

In the latter part of the eighteenth century the wings and the connecting arcades tend to disappear, leaving nothing but a

grand square box. The Portico, however, remains the symbol of grandeur to the end. A curious bye-product of the " Great House " architecture of the Regency and George IV periods is to be found in the gamekeepers' cottages and lodges of the time.

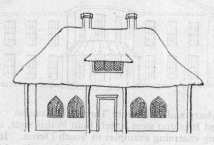

They are the result of the theory of " picturesque beauty " —or " sketchable bits "—that prevailed at that time. Remembering how our great aunts were taught to sketch, and forgetting the works of Gainsborough and Constable, we are apt to scoff at the Picturesque Theory. But our own crazy pavements hardly establish our right to do so. These lodges and cottages anticipate the Babel of styles which characterizes the reign of our late glorious Queen Victoria.

Most people's interest in church architecture, and on country holidays it is generally parish churches that are met with, is confined to spotting the date. But again, spotting the local building character and assessing the good purpose to which it has been put is a considerable improvement on the merely chronological game. Of course, church architecture takes us back so far in time, to the twelfth and eleventh centuries, even, with their echoes of the arts of the heroic age of the Vikings and the early Christian East, that the question of dates so romantically remote overwhelms all other interest : moreover, these survivals from such very early times are hardly plentiful enough

for comparison to establish local building schools. Date
spotting is best done by mouldings :

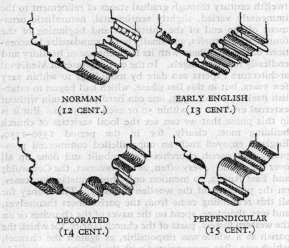

NORMAN
(12 CENT.)

EARLY ENGLISH
(13 CENT.)

DECORATED
(14 CENT.)

PERPENDICULAR
(15 CENT.)

or less safely by windows :

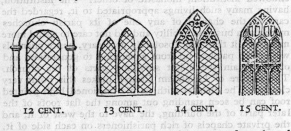

12 CENT.   13 CENT.   14 CENT.   15 CENT.

Windows are not so safe because they were often altered
to give more light and more room for a display of stained
glass, and one often finds windows of the last Phase (called
in the guide-books Perpendicular or Perp.) inserted in

earlier buildings. There are, of course, plenty of other indications of date, for example, the character of the ornament, changing from the primitive barbaric splendour of the twelfth century through gradual stages of refinement to the immensely varied, slightly sentimental, naturalistic ornament of the end of the thirteenth and beginning of the fourteenth centuries, and finally to the standardized decorations of the last Phase with its frequent use of heraldry and endlessly repeated angels. In the earlier phases of Mediæval architecture experts can date by mouldings to within very few years, but in this last phase, which had begun to establish itself by about 1375, one can hardly be certain without external evidence to within 50 or even 100 years. But it is in this phase that we can see the local varieties of church building most clearly, for in the period 1350–1550, England enjoyed such an unparalleled commercial prosperity that parish churches were rebuilt and done up all over the country, very often, as in Somerset, the Cotswolds and East Anglia, to mention only three outstanding cases, on the proceeds of the woollen industry. The money for all this rebuilding came from the parishioners themselves, and was, therefore, spent on the naves of the churches or on the western towers, parts of the church fabrics, for which the parish as a whole was responsible, as against the chancel, which was often appropriated with the living to some richly endowed institution, monastic or other. The institution, having many such livings appropriated to it, regarded the care of the chancel of any one of its parish churches merely as a business liability and did not care to spend more money on it than was absolutely necessary, hence chancels were often patched up from generation to generation, and often contain the oldest surviving parts of the church. The picture of Lavenham Church makes this point very clearly. The chancel with its old-fashioned high-pointed roof can be seen standing out among the flat roofs of the later parts of the building, the nave to the west of it, and the private chapels of rich parishioners on each side of it. In this matter of roofs the flatter pitch gradually tended to supersede the steeper, probably because it was found that the lead sheets were inclined to sag with the heat on a high-pitch roof. Often one can see the line of the older high-pitch roof quite clearly marked on the face of a tower.

The churches we have mentioned so far have western towers. The true cross plan, with a central tower, is to be found at all dates, but is more popular in earlier times, and is related to the Abbey church plan of the great period of monastic building—the twelfth century. Abbey ruins are chiefly of interest to those who week-end in Yorkshire,

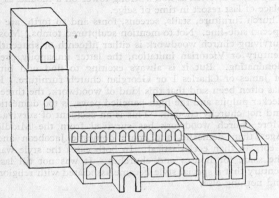

ISOMETRIC VIEW OF LAVENHAM CHURCH

where there are a number of celebrated examples. For date-spotting the rules are the same with Abbeys as with parish churches, except that one should rely on mouldings rather than on window forms, as windows are apt to be altered to meet the increasing desire for more light. On the whole Abbey buildings tend to belong to the earlier periods, for men gradually began to prefer to rebuild their own parish church as something more individual to themselves instead of leaving their money to be swallowed up in the already vast endowments of a monastery. Unless there are special circumstances, a disastrous fire, or a sudden access of wealth from unexpected sources, to occasion the rebuilding of an Abbey church, the later monastic buildings

437

are inclined to be of a domestic character, a gate-house as often as not. While speaking of Abbey ruins and gate-houses, a word should be said of castles. The earliest form often met with has a keep which in some cases is filled up with living-rooms, and even a chapel, but the more usual form relies on its immensely strong outer walls and towers. Within these was a house for the lord, planned like the ordinary mediæval house we have illustrated, and there may be, or as often as not, a strong tower on a mound as a place of last resort in time of seige.

Church furniture, stalls, screens, fonts and so forth, are a special side-line. Not to mention sculptured tombs. Most surviving church woodwork is either fifteenth or sixteenth century or Victorian imitation, the latter unhappily predominating. But it is always exciting to find odd bits of James or Charles I or Georgian church furniture. It has often been said that this kind of woodwork, the three-decker pulpits and the high-panelled pews, is too domestic and not churchy enough. This is an accident of survival. More church woodwork has survived from the Middle Ages than domestic, and more domestic Jacobean and Georgian than ecclesiastical. In both cases the style was the same for houses and churches. It was not till last century that a special style became associated with religion and nothing else.

ON FOOD AND

DRINK

AND COOKS RECORDED FRAMES OF MIND

IN SAD AND SUBTLE CHOPS

G. K. CHESTERTON

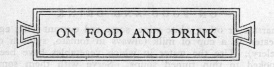

ON FOOD AND DRINK

FOOD AND DRINK

Week-end cookery should be either very quick, a good meal produced in half an hour, or very slow, put on before you go off to tennis or to lazing.

However witty the talk, however shady the garden, however original the cottage and its furnishings, it won't be by these things alone that your week-ends will be judged for repetition, but also by the food you offer.

NOTABLE AND AMUSING FOOD

Serve unusual dishes that will be remembered and spoken of. Settle on a speciality and learn it up, be it the art of devilling, of making fritters, of serving *hors-d'œuvres*, or of compounding a salad. Get an unusual, not a humdrum, cookery book and practice a few dishes between week-ends. Never let any dish be dull. Decorate the commoner foods into jolliness. Your guests eat with their eyes as well as with their palates and noses. Green cherries in grape fruit will be remembered (they can be bought in bottles). Boiled potatoes may be disguised by being mashed, made into balls, and rolled in grated cheese.

TINNED FOODS

Use tinned foods, but disguise them. No one should ever suspect that they are tinned. All tinned foods are improved by additions during the heating up. Never follow the directions on the tin for heating up : few saucepans are large enough to contain the unopened tin ; it takes longer than applying direct heat to the contents ; all but the most agile burn their fingers and spot their clothes when opening a heated tin.

Remember that Campbell's and Heinz's Tomato soups are not the only good soups on the market : there are chicken broths, asparagus soups, clam chowders, pea soups.

S O U P S should have added to them a tablespoonful of

marsala or other white wine, some red currant jelly, egg beaten in a cup of milk (always in tomato, spinach or celery). Use the water in which vegetables have been cooked to thin tinned soups. Serve with them some notable little addition, such as grated parmesan, puffed rice crisped in the oven, or fried cucumber cubes.

Tinned FISH should be wrapped in buttered paper and heated in a covered frying-pan; recooked in crumbs and cheese; rebaked with a good lemon or anchovy sauce; or poached in white wine or broth and served with shrimp, mixed gherkins, chipped olives, minced onion, anchovy paste, or a white sauce containing skinned grapes. (Skinned grapes can be had in tins.)

To recook MEAT: place it on a bed of finely shredded vegetables, top with fried minced onion, pour gravy over, bring to the boil, then simmer, adding herbs, currant jelly, or a touch of vinegar. Some spiced sausages also renew the youth of a tinned stew to be served on a bed of rice or macaroni.

Of tinned VEGETABLES: Baked beans may be baked again in a pie-dish lined and lidded with slices of bacon. Tinned sweet corn and succotash should be heated with additional butter, salt, pepper and sugar. Tinned peas should be drained, washed very thoroughly and treated like sweet corn, with the addition of a sprig of mint.

As for SWEETS, the French fashion of fruit and cake may well replace elaborate creamed puddings or milk baked ones, wearisome even if coloured green or mixed with ginger or praline. Fresh fruit alone, with some white wine and sugar, or with junket, is summer's ideal sweet. Failing that, have a plentiful stock of tinned fruits, to serve as they are or in jelly form.

To make JELLIES: Buy packets of jellies in preference to gelatin by the ounce, and follow the directions on the packets, telling you how to dissolve it in water in a mould. Buy plain in preference to flavoured jellies, so that you are not tied down to the taste of vanilla or lemon, adding your own pet flavouring. For fruit jelly, add berries or cut-up fruit just as the mouldful begins to set. For a sponge jelly, whisk white of egg into the jelly just before it begins to set. For a milk jelly, pour on hot milk in place of water and stir in the mould over very hot water until it dissolves. Go on stirring over cold water until it begins to set.

Tinned cherries and tinned muscats are as nice and less hackneyed than peaches and pineapple. Don't buy the most expensive form of peaches : the cheaper kinds are packed riper. Don't buy pineapple chunks. Only sliced pineapple eliminates the wood-like core of the fruit. Hawaiian brands are the best.

In parenthesis : among untinned sweets, Z A M B A G - L I O N E is simple, memorable and delicious. For eight helpings, take six eggs, two glasses of Marsala, Madeira, or any sweet wine, nine ounces of sugar, and one lemon. Put the yolks, sugar, lemon juice and wine into a thick saucepan. Whip the whites and add them to the rest. Thicken the mixture over an extremely slow heat, beating it furiously and continuously, and remembering that a Zambaglione boiled is a Zambaglione spoiled. When it is really thick, empty it into warmed glasses (to be eaten hot) or turn into a basin and go on beating it until it is cold. Teetotalers may make this dish with fruit juices.

W H E N B U Y I N G T I N N E D F O O D S avoid glass preserves. Rubber is not so durable a seal as solder. Ptomaine forms only when food is left in an open tin, or when the tin is imperfect (a puncture too small to be visible may be detected by rapping several tins with a pencil, when a defective one will ring flatter than others, as a false coin does).

HORS-D'ŒUVRE

T O B E G I N A M E A L : *Hors-d'œuvres* should start a good dinner, unless there is *grape-fruit*. An alternative to grapefruit is to serve an *orange* cut like the grape-fruit and, like it, moistened with maraschino and sugar.

As for the H O R S - D ' Œ U V R E S , don't limit yourself to sardines and tomato in oil. Try anchovy paste on cold egg slices ; tomato slices sprinkled with chopped onion and gherkin ; tomato anchovy and capers on hard-boiled eggs ; or just tomatoes stuffed with sardines or shrimp and

chopped pickle. Cover the oddments with MAYON-
NAISE. The simplest way to make a good mayonnaise is
to buy a bottle, add a trifle of cream to it and pretend you
made it yourself. But in that case remember not to serve it
in the bottle. . . .

Don't buy sardines in anything but olive oil. And buy
your anchovies as anchovy strips, so as to be sure they are
boned.

SHORT TIME COOKERY: THE GRIDIRON

Of all forms of cookery that allow you to get a meal ready
after you come in and before your guests' appetites ruin
their tempers, GRIDIRON COOKERY is the best.
Cutlets, chops, steaks, even fish wrapped in greased paper,
can be cooked between the wires before the fire. Steaks
should first be placed very close to the heat to seal the juice,
then moved to a cooler spot and cooked four minutes or
so on each side, according to thickness. Salt only when
on the dish. Kidneys are first-rate cooked like that, and
then buttered and put on a skewer.

Food is given an unusual taste before grilling by being
MARINATED, that is, steeped in a mixture of oil and
vinegar to which herbs have been added. Steep for some
hours.

Cooked between the wires or on a frying-pan, your steak
or your fish will need a garnish as unusual as possible.
Well-grilled steak dished with watercress and potatoes
fried in deep fat is excellent—once. But next time try
putting on top of your steak or fish a pat of SAVOURY
BUTTER. For this, work the butter with a spoon, season
with pepper, and work in parsley chopped as finely as may
be, or anchovy pulp ; pounded anchovy and sieved capers ;
chopped shrimps ; pounded roes with a half-teaspoonful
of vinegar to two ounces of butter ; or chopped watercress
and gherkin.

As for SAUCES, learn to make a perfect " Mother Sauce,"
and you can vary it as you like. To make a pint of white
mother sauce (the basis for all others), melt two ounces of
butter in a pan over the gentlest possible heat ; work in

an ounce of flour, cook very gently for five minutes, add a pint of milk and water and a saltspoonful of salt. Continue to stir and beat as it cooks. When creamy (in about five minutes' time) remove, and add another ounce of butter. This is the perfect white sauce. You can use pale broth or vegetable water if the milk is not available.

Any good flavour can be added—egg yoke (only do not let a sauce with egg yoke and butter boil) ; egg yoke and lemon juice ; chopped capers ; white wine and tarragon ; nutmeg and onion ; mustard and lemon juice ; mussels ; mushrooms ; tomato purée ; grated parmesan ; mixed herbs and chablis ; pickles and chopped nuts. Lemon, wine, vinegar, pickles or tomato must be added when the sauce has cooled, otherwise it will curdle.

SHORT TIME COOKERY : THE FRYING-PAN

Another form of quick cookery, for those who have neither a coal nor a gas fire suitable for grilling, is CHAFING-DISH COOKERY. This is done in a frying-pan with a cover to it, French fashion. The cover should be domed, so that the pan can be used, not only for frying, but to steam food. This is done by filling little pots, buttered inside and covered with buttered paper, and placing them in water in the covered pan. Fish, anchovy, cheese, or vegetable custards, minced meat and egg, the remains of any food in sauce, quails, made-up cutlets, olives or cucumber in rice and sauce—these are all things to be cooked in this way.

Apart from such poaching, foods are half fried, half steamed in a covered frying-pan with butter, seasoning, and a little liquid. Uncovered it is used for plain frying, to scramble eggs, poach them, make omelettes and sweet pancakes.

The secret of making the best OMELETTES is to withdraw the white of one egg for every six eggs used, and not to beat the eggs for too long. Omelettes containing minced ham, potatoes, pimentoes, mushrooms, asparagus tips, and even fruit or jam, are easy to improvise. Pour the beaten eggs into a pan well covered with smoking lard, and then introduce the other materials. Fold one half of the omelette on the other, and gently slide the whole on to a hot plate.

HOT SANDWICHES also are cooked on your frying-pan. Cut bread slices, butter them and fill with one of these fillings : bacon, tomato and cheese, chopped onion, egg and red pepper, cream cheese, watercress and salad dressing, cinnamon powder in ham paste, bacon, lettuce and mayonnaise, chopped apple, nut and lettuce. These sandwiches may be either buttered all over the outside or dipped in a batter made by stirring one beaten egg into half a pint of milk. They are then fried in margarine until they are a golden colour on both sides.

SLOW COOKING

The BAINMARIE is tremendously useful when food has to be kept hot. It is a shallow dish filled with water and set on an asbestos mat over the flame. In it pans, pots or jam dishes full of food will keep hot without burning.

Big CASSEROLES are ideal for long slow cooking which needs no watching. They may be used in the oven or on an asbestos mat over a flame.

Failing casseroles, slow cooking needs DOUBLE-PAN STEWING, steaming, or jugging, on a plate over a pan of water. For this put your cutlet, steak, fillets of rabbit, cut-up chicken, filleted fish or what it may be on a deep soup plate with broth (or water), diced vegetables and seasoning. Put the plate over a big pan of boiling water, cover it over, and in an hour your food will be cooked. This is not so good as casserole cooking, because the pan of water may dry up. In a casserole in the oven try neck of mutton cut up with sliced onion, celery, parsley and broth covered with sliced potatoes. Or replace the mutton with mixed steak and skirt cut up. Fowl and bacon cook splendidly on a bed of white vegetables. Buttered potatoes, ham and minced onion is a supper dish. Steaks of fish with parsley, tomato, and a touch of salad oil are good. So is rabbit (for those who *can* eat rabbit) with red currant jelly, parsley, gravy, red wine and onion. In the pudding line try apple and breadcrumbs with ginger and milk.

SALADS

Whatever your choice of dishes, serve salad either with the meat or as a separate course.

Green salads may be made of many plants other than lettuce. Chicory, dandelion leaves, sorrel and white cabbage, for instance. They should be perfectly clean, perfectly dry and thickly coated with olive oil, before the dressing is added. The best D R E S S I N G for green salads is vinegar, oil, mustard, pepper, sugar and salt, in proportions varying according to taste, but always very thoroughly mixed.

Waldorf salad is made of equal parts of raw cooking apple and raw celery, sliced, disposed on a bed of lettuce, liberally garnished with half-walnuts, and dressed with a sweetened mayonnaise. Orange and lettuce ; shrimp and lettuce ; watercress and creamed cheese with nuts, are quite as easy to mix as lettuce and beetroot, and much more fun.

SANDWICH SUGGESTIONS

When you go picnicking you will, if a pastry hand, take little pies full of good mixtures, but the average provider of picnic fare trusts to sandwiches, good drinks, (hard and soft), hot coffee in thermos bottles, salted almonds, nuts, and perhaps raw steaks and bacon to be cooked over a camp fire on sticks. This is amusing because the food usually falls in and gets ruined. So be sure that the sandwiches are good.

Here are some fillings to be served, some in white bread, some in brown, some in rye bread, some in water biscuits, and others in split scones : chopped hard-boiled egg and filleted anchovy ; cream cheese and jam (this in a scone) ; peanut butter and chopped olives ; peanut butter and raisins, or dates, or watercress ; Devonshire cream and honey ; " Gentleman's Relish " ; cold minced curry ; tomato ketchup and fresh sliced tomato or lettuce ; chopped boiled beet and grated parmesan ; cream cheese, nuts and shredded pineapple ; cream cheese and olives ; currant jelly and chopped nuts ; chopped dates, cheese and nuts.

Don't butter sandwich bread, but if you like you may mix your filling with creamed butter and spread that. Pack your sandwiches as soon as cut in grease-proof paper. Put hard-boiled eggs in cold water as soon as they come out of the saucepan ; this makes it easy to peel the shells from the meat.

BREAKFASTS

Don't worry about breakfast cooking. Bacon or poached egg on toast does well enough if you get unusual jams, or begin with fruit. Try orange and apple cut up, grated apple in glasses, or summer fruits with lemon juice. To fry crisp bacon, run the fat off and roll it as it cooks. Other breakfast dishes are : mashed potato balls with chopped sausage ; chopped egg and minced ham in white sauce on toast ; any hot sandwich ; scrambled egg and minced onion ; eggs cooked in butter (and cream, if that can be) in individual casseroles for five minutes. Season the butter and cream, break in the egg and bake, with a small spoonful of chopped chicken liver or minced ham or anchovy on top, if you will.

ADVICE TO THOSE WHO ATTEMPT TO SUPPLEMENT THEIR DIET FROM NATURE'S LARDER

FRESHWATER FISH: Trout and salmon should be eaten as soon as possible after being caught, as they are then at their best.
If the other freshwater fish you catch must be eaten, they should be soaked for at least 12 hours in brine. This removes both the slime and the taste of mud. Even carp or tench can in this way be made palatable.
MUSHROOMS AND TOADSTOOLS: Ordinary mushrooms are white on top, with a skin which peels readily, and have pinkish or chocolate gills underneath, according to age. They grow in grass.
PUFFBALLS are round and white, puckered underneath. When young, they are excellent fried. They also grow in grass.
PARASOLLE mushrooms are white with brown flecks

448

on top and with white gills. They are light and elegant in appearance, and grow in grass. Round the stem is a ring or band like the similar band frequently found on the shafts of umbrellas.

There is a BOLETUS TOADSTOOL found in woods which is excellent. It is dark brown on top, like a bun, and white and spongy underneath.

There is another boletus, yellow underneath, which it is also safe to eat.

ALL MUSHROOMS AND TOADSTOOLS are dangerous if they are not eaten fresh; therefore reject all botanist's specimens.

DON'T cook and attempt to eat YOUNG BRACKEN SHOOTS because the Japanese do. What suits the hardy races of the extreme East may not suit you.

DON'T cook YOUNG NETTLES as a substitute for spinach. It is a stringy one.

DON'T eat BOILED RHUBARB LEAVES. This practice caused a large number of deaths during the war.

DON'T take PLOVERS' EGGS from a nest containing four. It is unkind to the parent birds, and at least two of the four will be addled.

DON'T cook things in clay.

N.B.—MICE IN HONEY should be imported from China, not prepared at home.

MENUS

QUICK

Clear soup with sausage rings.

Oiled, grilled herring served in buttered dish covered with butter melted with lemon juice, and cooked just a minute, then sprinkled chopped parsley and salt.

Coffee mousse; (whip cream till stiff; add little sugar and strong coffee made into syrup, with chopped nuts. Serve uncooked and cold).

QUICKISH

Escalopes of veal: season the veal pieces slightly, brown in butter on quick fire, cover pan and simmer ten minutes.

ON FOOD AND DRINK

Add half a cup gravy with lemon juice, cooking until gravy is reduced, only just covering the veal.
Lettuce, nut and olive salad.
Deep-fat-fried potato fingers.
Milk jelly with ginger in it.

VERY QUICK

Slices of cold mutton steeped in olive oil, vinegar and herbs, dipped in breadcrumbs and fried. Served with mint, red currant and orange rind jelly.

Cheesed potato balls and lettuce salad.

Stewed prunes in claret (boil steeped prunes in syrup adding claret ten minutes before removing from fire).

HALF-HOUR

Grape-fruit with green cherries.

Leg of lamb cut into steaks, sprinkled chopped onion, wrapped in cabbage leaves (or bacon), buttered, floured, browned and cooked half an hour in casserole, with little hot water.

Fruit in white wine with cream into which chopped nuts are beaten.

HALF-HOUR AGAIN

Grilled cutlets ; mint jelly on orange rounds.
Tiny mashed potato balls, with bit of olive in centre ; green peas.
Port wine jelly and cream (made beforehand).

FOR A BEGINNER

Tinned spinach soup with egg beaten in.
Rognons en brochettes (kidneys, bacon and sausages grilled on a skewer).
Straw potatoes, deep fat fried.
Cake covered with fruit and cream.

450

ON FOOD AND DRINK

FOR A SUMMER EVENING

Clear soup with tiny diamonds of cheesed toast.
Hake or haddock grilled with capers.
Orange and lettuce salad with mayonnaise.
Strawberries, and cream or claret.

AMBITIOUS

Hors-d'œuvres.
Casserole of duck with orange slices and rind; lettuce,
shredded celery or beetroot.
Pancakes in fruit syrup.

ONE SLOW-COOKING DISH

Orange maraschino cups.
Stuffed steak with tomato, onion and beet; pineapple,
lettuce and tomato salad.
Fruit salad.

DRINK

For hard drinkers, whisky, gin and the vermouths; for
soft drinkers, tea, coffee and ginger-beer are the standard
refreshments supplied at the village pub. But imagination
and bold experiment can break this monotony with many
happy improvisations.

"Ginandit" is the weary walker's counsel of despair.
Any enterprising week-end pub, or cottage, will possess
ingredients from which one or other of the following may
be compounded :

COCKTAILS

EAST INDIAN: Equal parts of French vermouth and
sherry, with a dash of orange bitters.

WEST INDIAN: Two parts rum (preferably Bacardi)
to one part fresh lime or lemon juice, with some sugar
dissolved in it, or failing this, " Kia-ora."

HAWAIIAN: Four parts gin, two parts orange juice and
one part curaçao (or any other of the orange liqueurs).

SIDE-CAR: Equal parts of fresh lemon juice (no

alternative), cointreau (or one of the orange liqueurs) and brandy.

SATAN'S WHISKER (*straight*) : Of Italian vermouth, French vermouth, gin and orange juice, two parts each ; of Grand Marnier one part ; orange bitters.

Ditto (*curled*) : For the Grand Marnier substitute an equal quantity of orange curaçao.

JOHN WOOD: Italian vermouth, four parts ; Irish whisky and lemon juice, two parts each ; Kummel, one part ; Angostura bitters.

MR. SUTTON'S GIN-BLIND (*to be drunk with discretion*) : Six parts gin, three parts curaçao, two parts brandy and a dash of orange bitters.

NOTE ON THE USE OF BITTERS : When cocktails are mixed in bulk, any bitters should be introduced in the proportion of one half to one teaspoonful per pint. In more intimate drinking, delicacy of flavour and economy of material are secured by rinsing each glass with bitters, which are then returned to the bottle, while the glass is filled with a mixture from which bitters have been omitted. If possible, ALL COCKTAILS should stand on ice for at least half an hour before shaking and taking. If you cannot wait so long, you must adulterate your mixture with ice. A large jug, and an egg-whisk (or even a fork) efficiently replace the shaker. The glasses should be as cold as possible before the cocktail is poured out.

ICED DRINKS

GINGER-BEER: (*a*) with gin and lemon or lime juice, preferably fresh, but, if need be, " Kia-ora " or Southwells ; (*b*) (for sweet-tooths) with cointreau and orange juice.

(There is no bottled substitute for orange juice, whatever you may have seen in the shops.)

Strong, cold, black COFFEE with a wineglassful of brandy to a quart and some ice.

For people who can bear to be seen drinking it : Equal parts of GIN and CREME DE MENTHE, with plenty of cracked ice.

452

JOHN COLLINS: The juice of two oranges and one lemon with an equal measure of gin, some soda water and ice.

BAVARIAN CUP: Mix a small wineglassful of cherry brandy (or plain brandy) with a bottle of white wine, and add crushed strawberries and ice *ad lib*.

CIDER CUP: Three large bottles of sparkling cider, a pint of old Marsala, a little sugar, a lot of lemon rind, two bottles of soda water and maraschino or brandy quant: suff:

RAJAH'S PEG: A claret glass of old brandy in a pint of dry champagne.

MINT JULEP: Pack a tumbler as tightly as possible with alternate layers of finely cracked ice and sprigs of mint, freshly picked and bruised ; fill the interstices with whisky (rye if available, otherwise Irish or, if need be, Scotch). This tastes as good as it smells. It is drunk by degrees, as it melts, and through a straw.

CASSIS (black-currant syrup made in France) is obtainable in Soho, and, when mixed with French vermouth, soda-water and ice, makes a delicious " soft " drink. If you can afford the veritable liqueur cassis, it is not altogether " soft."

COLD TEA should be made as follows : Steep the leaves in *cold water* (the same proportion as you use when boiling) for 12 hours and then strain.

HOT DRINKS

TEA with rum, lemon juice and a shaving of lemon peel.

MULLED CLARET (1) *For Boys:* Warm (but do not boil) the wine with nutmeg, cinnamon, cloves, sugar and lemon rind. (2) *For Men:* Ditto, adding dry port one part to six of claret. (3) *For Heroes:* As for boys, adding one part port to three parts claret and as much old brandy as you think the company can stand.

RUM PUNCH: one part rum, one part whisky and two parts (or a trifle less) water, heated with sugar, cinnamon, nutmeg, cloves and dried orange and lemon peel.

453

HANDY PUNCH: to two bottles of whisky and one of rum, add an equal quantity of water. Heat these with a little nutmeg and cinnamon, the juice of two lemons and sugar to taste. When it is very hot, set it alight with a red-hot poker and, after a moment's admiration, blow out the flames.

RED CURRANT TEA is a good hot "soft" drink. It is made by pouring boiling water on plenty of red currant jelly and adding a squeeze of lemon juice. Black currant jam will make BLACK CURRANT TEA.

FOOD AND DRINK

WHY has our poetry eschewed
The rapture and response of food?
What hymns are sung, what praises said
For home-made miracles of bread?
Since what we love has always found
Expression in enduring sound,
Music and verse should be competing
To match the transient joy of eating.
There should be present in our songs
As many tastes as there are tongues;
There should be humbly celebrated
One passion that is never sated.
Let us begin it with the first
Distinction of a conscious thirst
When the collusion of the vine
Uplifted water into wine.
Let us give thanks before we turn
To other things of less concern
For all the poetry of the table:
Clams that parade their silent fable;
Lobsters that have a rock for stable;
Red-faced tomatoes ample as
A countryman's full-bosomed lass;
Plain-spoken turnips; honest beets;
The carnal gusto of red meats;
The insipidity of lamb;
The wood-fire pungence of smoked ham;

454

Young veal that's smooth as natural silk ;
The lavish motherliness of milk ;
Parsley and lemon-butter that add
Spring sweetness unto river shad ;
Thin flakes of halibut and cod,
Pickerel, flounder, snapper, scrod,
And every fish whose veins may be
Charged with the secrets of the sea ;
Sweet-sour carp, beloved by Jews ;
Pot-luck simplicity of stews ;
Crabs, juiciest of Nature's jokes ;
The deep reserve of artichokes ;
Mushrooms, whose taste is texture, loath
To tell of their mysterious growth ;
Quick, mealy comfort glowing in
A baked potato's crackled skin ;
The morning promise, hailed by man,
Of bacon crisping in the pan ;
The sage compound of *Hasenpfeffer*
With dumplings born of flour and zephyr ;
Spinach whose spirit is the soil ;
Anchovies glorified in oil ;
The slow-gold nectar maples yield ;
Pale honey tasting of the field
Where every clover is Hymettus ;
The cooling sanity of lettuce
And every other herbal green
Whose touch is calm, whose heart is clean ;
Succulent bean-sprouts, bamboo-shoots ;
The sapid catalogue of fruits :
Plebeian apple, caustic grape,
Quinces that have no gift for shape,
Dull plums that mind their own affairs,
Incurably bland and blunted pears,
Fantastic passion-fruit, frank lemons
With acid tongues as sharp as women's,
Exotic loquats, sly persimmons,
White currants, amber-fleshed sultanas,
(Miniature and sweetened mannas)
Expansive peaches, suave bananas,
Oranges ripening in crates,

455

Tight-bodied figs, sun-wrinkled dates,
Melons that have their own vagaries ;
The bright astringency of berries ;
Crêpe-satin luxury of cream ;
Wedding-cake that fulfils the dream ;
Pepper, whose satire stings and cuts ;
Raw liberality of nuts ;
Sauces of complex mysteries ;
Proverbial parsnips ; muscular cheese ;
Innocent eggs that scorn disguises ;
Languid molasses ; burning spices
In kitchen-oracles to Isis ;
Thick sauerkraut's fat-bellied savour ;
Anything with a chocolate flavour ;
Large generosity of pies ;
Hot puddings bursting to surprise ;
The smug monotony of rice ;
Raisins that doze in cinnamon buns ;
Kentucky biscuits, Scottish scones ;
Falstaffian tarts that mock the chaste
Rose-elegance of almond-paste ;
Venison steaks that smack of cloisters ;
Goose-liver for the soul that roisters ;
Reticent prawn ; Lucullan oysters ;
Sausages, fragrant link on link ;
The vast ambrosias of drink :
Tea, that domestic mandarin ;
Bucolic cider ; loose-lipped gin ;
Coffee, extract of common sense,
Purgative of the night's pretense ;
Cocoa's prim nursery ; the male
Companionship of crusty ale ;
Cognac as oily as a ferret ;
The faintly iron thrust of claret ;
Episcopal port, aged and austere ;
Rebellious must of grape ; the clear,
Bluff confraternity of beer—

All these are good, all are a part
Of man's imperative needs that start
Not in the palate but the heart.

456

ON FOOD AND DRINK

Thus fat and fibre, root and leaf
Become quick fuel and slow grief.
These, through the chemistry of blood,
Sustain his hungering manhood,
Fulfilling passion, ripening pain,
Steel in his bone, fire at his brain. . . .
So until man abjures the meats
Terrestrial and impermanent sweets,
Growing beyond the things he eats,
Let us be thankful for the good
Beauty and benison of food,
Let us join chiming vowel with vowel
To rhapsodize fish, flesh and fowl,
And let us thank god in our songs
There are as many tastes as tongues.

Louis Untermeyer.

THE LAW AND

HOW YOU BREAK IT

I HAVE NO GREAT REGARD FOR THE LAW

SAMUEL BUTLER

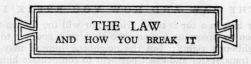

THE LAW
AND HOW YOU BREAK IT

The laws of England are of two kinds : public law and private law.

The P U B L I C L A W S are those which are enforced by the police and the public authorities, and to which the State attaches the sanction of fine or imprisonment, according to the nature of the offence. Such are the laws against theft of all kinds, against murder and breaches of the peace, against disorderly or unseemly conduct, and other offences which shall be nameless. A breach of public law is a crime and renders the offender liable for prosecution. These are the laws with which most people are most familiar.

The P R I V A T E L A W S, on the other hand, are those which govern the rights of individuals *inter se*. These may be either rights common to all citizens, or rights arising between particular persons as the result of some agreement or contract. Private law in general may be roughly out-lined as follows : First : that everyone has a right to pre-serve his property and person inviolate (note well that a footstep on his pasture may be as much a violation of the one as a blow on the nose is of the other) ; second : that, if a binding agreement is made between two people and one breaks it, he must pay for whatever damage the other suffers. To explain what constitutes a binding agreement is a very long story, but two points may be mentioned in passing. First : except in certain special kinds of contract (e.g. trusts) a one-sided promise is not binding ; there must always be a " consideration " in return for any undertaking. That is, an agreement between you and your neighbour, stipulating a certain course of conduct on the part of your neighbour, is not binding unless there is a reciprocal pro-vision, pledging you also to certain performances. Second : an agreement need not, except in certain particular cases, be in writing. It is, however, easier to prove the existence of such a contract if it is.

To break a contract, trespass on someone's land, or run

461

over him in a car is not a crime, nor will the Crown take action to prosecute a man who thus runs counter to his neighbour's rights ; but the neighbour himself may sue the transgressor and exact payment to compensate him for his damages. It is also possible that a driver who is not careful as to the *manner* of his collision with foot passengers or other vehicles may incidentally violate some national or municipal traffic regulation and thus render himself liable to prosecution. Moreover, the result of such a collision sometimes leads to the prosecution of the more active party for manslaughter.

OF ARRESTING AND BEING ARRESTED

The policeman's powers of arrest are wide, and it is unwise to resist his attentions, however inconvenient.

But private persons also may arrest and, on some occasions, it is held by the law to be their duty to do so.

If you wish to prosecute someone, go to the nearest magistrate or justice of the peace and lay your information. The offender will then receive a summons or be arrested, according to the nature of your story. If a serious crime has to your certain knowledge been committed, it may be held to be your duty to prosecute, and failure to do so may render you yourself liable for prosecution as an accessory after the fact.

Anyone arrested without a warrant must be taken as soon as possible before a magistrate. If that is not possible within twenty-four hours, bail must be granted, unless the offence is very serious. Should this misfortune befall you, communicate with your friends, who may or may not be prepared to go bail for you.

OF HIGHWAYS

The term highway comprises all portions of land over which every subject of the Crown has a right to pass. The right of the public on a highway is a right of passing and repassing. Technically a member of the public can only justify *passing along* and not *being in* a highway.

462

Carriages and other vehicles are lawfully in the highway for the purpose of passage only. A learned judge once said, " The king's highway is not to be used as a stableyard." Had he lived to-day he would certainly have opposed its use as a garage.

A highway must be used reasonably and not for purposes for which it is not intended. " Reasonable " use is by wheeled traffic on the road and foot-passengers on the path. It is not reasonable but " excessive " use to drive a car along a footpath, but no ruling has yet decided that to walk even on the most crowded motor roads is " excessive."

It is not permitted to obstruct the highway or footpath by pitching tents or by playing games ; nor to annoy passengers by letting off fireworks or firearms. It is an offence to deposit filth or rubbish within fifteen feet of the centre of the road and to obstruct traffic by lecturing or preaching on any part of the highway or footpath.

OF ACCIDENTS

In traffic accidents motorists driving recklessly or at an excessive pace are responsible for any damage to pedestrians, but if the motorist is not reckless or excessive and if the pedestrian walks carelessly among the traffic, then the pedestrian and not the motorist is guilty of the accident. When a road accident is caused by obstructions, such as a pile of stones or an uncovered drain-pipe, the person who placed the obstruction (or his employer) is liable for damages, provided that the injured person was sober and reasonably careful in his progress.

Whoever carries a pickaxe, a spiked stick, or other dangerous object along the road, is responsible for any damage that may ensue.

So also one is liable for damages who rides or drives an unmanageable horse along the road ; or who leaves any horse unattended in the road ; but if he can prove his ignorance of the intractable character of the horse, he may be held innocent of negligence.

In letting out a horse for riding or driving the owner of the

463

horse implicitly guarantees the horse's roadworthiness, and he is therefore liable for any accidents or breakdowns while it is fairly and prudently used.

Any person who takes money for insecure seats or stands let to spectators at any race meeting, coronation or other public spectacle is liable for injuries caused by the collapse of his structures.

OF RAILWAYS

The purchase of the ticket does not guarantee the purchaser a seat in the train.

A timetable is not a guarantee that a train will run.

The guard can call upon anyone who is disorderly and causing annoyance to the passengers to leave the train, and, if necessary, remove him.

The much vexed question of window up or window down is not dealt with in the bye-laws or by Act of Parliament. In the event of a violent dispute the guard could direct one of the disputants to another compartment.

Each carriage is designed to hold a certain number of passengers. If there are more than this number, a passenger can call upon the guard to reduce the number; and there is a penalty for non-compliance. But this penalty is not paid to the man who lodges the complaint, who has no remedy against the company.

A railway company is responsible for damage or injury caused by sparks falling from its engines.

Those who want more information than is here provided should read the bye-laws of the railway company and the conditions subject to which tickets are issued.

OF COMMONS AND OTHER RIGHTS

Those stretches of uncultivated land which are known as commons are not, as is popularly supposed, common property; nor are they places where anyone is entitled to do as he pleases. The public are usually allowed almost unrestricted use of common land, b███ ██mmon *rights* belong to local tenants and farmers, a███ ██d to the grazing of cattle and such matters where ██ ██visiting public are not interested. There are cer███ ████hts held " by immemorial custom " which entitle t██ ███bitants of some villages to use particular wells or ██ █or to dry their fishing-nets or to erect maypoles and ██████ about them or perform other rustic sports on certai██ ████ces of land. To qualify as immemorial such customs ██ ██ be continuously practised without let or hindrance fo███venty years.

A right of way may be granted by th█ landowner or may be acquired by continuous uncontradi██ed use for twenty years. It may, however, be lost by disuse after an indefinite number of years. If a landlord place an obstruction where there is a right of way any person entitled to this right of way may remove the obstruction; for if all rightful users meekly acquiesce, then after twenty years the right of way is lost.

OF BEACHES

Another place often and wrongly considered public property is the seashore. The beach belongs to someone just as much as the land behind it—probably to the same person. Beach land property is bounded to seaward by high-water mark. Below that the land belongs to the Crown. Thus, unless there is a highway, the beach cannot be reached without trespassing. Even when high-water mark is lawfully reached, it is extremely doubtful whether the public have any *right* to bathe.

In many big watering-places it should be remembered that the foreshore is the property of the town council, who therefore have the right to make any rules they like as to the way people should dress, undress, or otherwise behave themselves before they are permitted to bathe.

OF BATHING

There is one crime which every bather who has forgotten (deliberately or by accident) his bathing costume is in

danger of co   at one time or another, though he
may not be s   nate as to get into trouble for it.

Whatever ope   ges public decency and is injurious
to public mor   misdemeanour. That means your
body, dear rea   Any public exposure of the naked
person is an in   nuisance, and it has been held that
this is so when   s no exposure beyond what is neces-
sarily incidental   athing without a bathing suit. To
constitute the off   it must be an exposure in a public
place before mor   an one spectator, or in view of the
public even thoug   not in a public place. Week-enders
should note that, a though one person does not constitute
the public, exposure before one person (and indeed any
unsuitable conduct) in a public place may be an offence
punishable under the Vagrancy Act.

FLOTSAM, JETSAM AND LIGAN

Goods which float on the sea after a shipwreck are called
" flotsam " ; but if they are thrown out to lighten the
ship they are " jetsam," and if sunk, with a buoy attached,
then " ligan." When it cannot be ascertained who is owner
of such goods, then, if they are found in the sea, they belong
to the finder. But all wrecks and wreckage cast ashore are
in general the perquisites of the Crown, unless the owner of
the land on which they are found has a legitimate " grant
of wreck."

Week-enders (and other persons) who happen to find a
corpse on the shore are obliged to notify the police within
six hours. The reward for fulfilling this obligation is five
shillings.

OF TREASURE TROVE AND OTHER
LOST PROPERTY

Treasure trove is " any gold or silver, in coin, plate or
bullion, found hidden." If the owner cannot be found
the treasure belongs to the Crown and must be delivered
up on pain of fine or imprisonment ; but " the Crown "
customarily rewards the finder by paying him the intrinsic

466

value of his find in money. The coroner decides who is the finder.

All other lost property, if the owner cannot be found, belongs to the finder, who may, if it be subsequently stolen, bring an " action of trover " against the thief. Any person who finds a new-born child must go before the Registrar within seven days and give such information as he has concerning the foundling.

OF MONEY AND KINDRED SUBJECTS

Where there is no agreement to the contrary, a debtor may be compelled to pay his debts in cash and a creditor may be compelled on pain of forfeiting his claim to accept such coin of the realm as his debtor chooses to offer ; subject to the following limitations : copper coins are legal tender only up to the amount of one shilling and silver coins up to the amount of forty shillings. Foreign coins are not legal tender ; but everyone has the right to call upon the Royal Mint to coin for him, free of charge, any gold of standard quality.

An *I.O.U.* is evidence of the existence of a debt and may be produced in support of a legal claim against the debtor. If it is dated, i.e. if it contains the words " to be paid on " such and such a date it becomes a promissory note and must be stamped ; otherwise it is valid without a stamp.

Pawnbrokers may charge interest at the rate of not more than one halfpenny per month for every five shillings on a loan of less than forty shillings ; on loans of more than forty shillings, at a rate not exceeding twenty per cent per annum. Pledges which are not redeemed within twelve calendar months and seven days become the property of the pawnbroker. If a pawnticket is lost, the owner of the pledge must produce evidence of his identity to a magistrate and obtain from him a form of declaration as evidence of his claim to the pledge. Failing this, the pawnbroker is obliged to deliver the pledge to anyone producing the pawnticket. Obtaining a false declaration is equivalent to perjury.

467

OF NEIGHBOURS

Failing any evidence of ownership, the *hedges, walls or fences* between adjoining properties belong equally to the owners of both properties. But if one owner has habitually repaired the dividing structure this constitutes *prima facie* evidence that it belongs to him. When there is a ditch as well as a hedge or fence, the hedge is generally deemed to belong to the owner on whose side of the hedge there is no ditch.

The owner of *fruit trees* which overhang a neighbour's property has a right to any of his fruit which falls upon his neighbour's land, and if the neighbour refuse to give it to him he may (provided that he use no force and cause no damage) go upon his neighbour's land without permission and take it.

Roots and Branches penetrating or overhanging a neighbour's land may be cut by the owner of the land without notice to or permission from the owner of the tree.

OF TRESPASS TO LAND

Every invasion of private property is a trespass, whether the material damage be large, small or non-existent. No man has any right to go upon the land of another except by leave or licence, or where there is a right of way. And, when once the wrong has been done, any cutting of wood, picking of flowers, lighting of fires, or other Arcadian wantonness will but serve to increase the damages payable should the owner choose to enforce his rights by an action at law.

Now some free spirits, remembering how in their youth they treated themselves, at 6s. 8d. a time, to the pleasure of walking across college lawns, may argue that a corresponding damage to a common meadow should cost them but as many pence as formerly they paid shillings to the college authorities. These, in a week-end mood of exuberant rejuvenation, may offer to buy from other landlords a sixpenny right of way. They forget that the costs of an action at law, should the landlord prove implacable, will fall upon the trespasser and will by far exceed sixpennyworth of common grass or even six and eightpence worth of cloistered and historic lawn.

Lest the week-ender in the bonhomie of his heart protest that no landlord in his senses will bring an action for trespass unless considerable material damage has been done, we would remind him that all landowners are not in that enviable state of mind ; and, furthermore, that a pugnacious landlord may lawfully resort to force in removing such trespassers as will not depart peaceably, sixpence or no sixpence. In doing so he may use as much force as is " reasonably necessary," and, if the trespasser feels that the reasonable limit has been overreached, he in turn (if he has been so foolish as to allow this development) can bring an action against the landowner for assault ; and the Court will decide.

Most landowners are amenable to friendliness, argument or money, and it must be left to the genius of the trespasser to choose the right remedy. But there remains one type of landlord for whose injured proprietary instincts no balm can be found : like a powerful nation, he is filled with righteous wrath by the sight of another creature doing something which he is entitled to stop. Prestige must be maintained. Indemnities and apologies are demanded. In fact he should never be spoken to except from the other side of a five-barred gate. A slow but dignified retreat to the highway is the best course to pursue.

OF DOGS

The trespasser has no remedy for misfortunes which may befall him from the savagery of the landowner's animals, domestic or wild. But the righteous man is entitled to security from attack.

Any man who keeps a savage animal does so at his peril, and, if it escape, he must answer for the damage that ensues. Therefore those who take panther-cubs or baboons on week-end rambles do so at their own, as well as at their

469

neighbour's risk. The law does not regard a dog as a savage animal until, by biting someone, the true nature of the animal is betrayed; for, until then, the owner is ignorant of its savage nature and will not be held responsible.

Therefore, if you must be bitten, let it be by an animal that makes a habit of biting and not by a mere amateur. The owner of a dog cannot rely upon his dog's previous good record if cattle are bitten instead of human beings. There is a statute that makes the owner of a dog, however tame, liable for all damage to cattle.

OF CATS

The privilege of being presumed tame until shown to be otherwise (if a recent action at law may be taken as a precedent) is now extended to cats.

OF CATTLE

If you should chance to be gored or trampled by cattle in a private pasture, you have no remedy at law. But if the same mischance befall you on the public highway then you may claim and, perhaps, receive some compensation from the owner of your assailant. But first you will have to prove that such an accident both could and should have been foreseen by the lawful guardians of the animal in question. If it was a bull you will have no difficulty in doing this, but if it was a cow of hitherto unblemished repute, whom the gods suddenly visited with madness, it may happen that your damages will go unsolaced by payment. You may, however, plead that the heat of the noonday sun, or the recent maternity and bereavement of the cow, or some other cause, gave its owner enough warning of impending danger to justify the jury in pronouncing him guilty of wantonly endangering the public safety. And the Court shall decide.

OF NOISE AND OTHER NUISANCES

Any object or occupation which causes noise, smell, dirt or any offence to the senses or health of the surrounding

470

population, may be classified as a nuisance. If the damage is general it is a common nuisance and may be prosecuted by indictment. If it is damage to a particular person, he may bring an action against the offender or he may abate the nuisance himself; and if he goes upon another's land for this purpose (without doing unnecessary damage) it is not trespass.

The noise of children and piano-players is not actionable' unless it is nocturnal and continuous.

When a man has plied a noisy trade without contradiction for twenty years he acquires a prescriptive right to continue; so there should be no unnecessary delay in bringing an action against those who cause such nuisances.

Motor horns and other devices designed to give audible warning, may not be used for other purposes when the car is stationary.

It is not lawful for organ-grinders or other musicians to continue their performances in the streets of London, if any householder within earshot have requested them (for a sufficient reason) to desist.

OF PURIFYING THE PERSON

A magistrate has power to order the cleansing of persons infested with vermin. Any such person may voluntarily and gratuitously make use of the cleansing apparatus belonging to any local authority. To be relieved of parasites in this manner does not count as "relief" under the Poor Law.

OF GAME AND FISHING

All wild swans, whales and sturgeons belong to the King. Game, as defined in various statutes of William IV and Victoria, may not be hunted or killed on Sundays or on Christmas Day. But snipe, woodcock and wildfowl are not game within the meaning of the acts. Nevertheless it would be rash to attempt to correlate the rarity of these birds in England with an anti-sabbatarian tendency during the last century. Game which is started, hunted and killed

471

on one and the same property belongs to the owner of that property. But if it is started on one property and killed on another it belongs to the hunter, although he is liable for trespass to the owners of both properties.

Traps for rabbits or hares must be visited daily on pain of a fine not exceeding £5 Week-enders who have been moved by James Stephens's " The Snare," may find in this law a useful weapon against trappers.

Every British subject has the *right to fish* in British waters and in public navigable rivers. In non-navigable rivers, subject to specially vested rights, the fishing belongs to the riparian owners, each from his bank to mid-stream. *Crabs* measuring less than four and a half inches across the broadest part or carrying spawn, or having cast their shells, or *lobsters* measuring less than eight inches (outstretched) from beak to tail, may not be taken or sold, except for bait.

OF GAMBLING

The playing of cards, or dice, when practised honestly, innocently and for recreation, is not unlawful. There appear to be certain games which are unlawful in themselves though there is no record of anyone being punished for playing them.

These are " Ace of Hearts," " Faro," " Bassett," " Hazard," " Passage " and " Roly-poly."

The laws on the subject are really directed against persons who seek to make a business of gaming. The first of these, under Henry VIII, was aimed at encouraging the more patriotic sport of archery, which was held to be falling into disuse because of the undue popularity of other games.

It is unlawful to keep premises for the purpose of gaming, although the games played are not unlawful in themselves. Gaming in public places is also unlawful. A bar-room or a coffee-room or a railway carriage is a public place within the meaning of the Act.

But the playing of cards or dice when practised honestly, innocently and for recreation, is not illegal.

OF INNS

An Act of Parliament in the reign of James I describes as follows the nature and function of an Inn : " The ancient true and principal use of inns, alehouses and victualling houses was for the receit, relief and lodging of wayfaring people travelling from place to place and for such supply of the wants of such people as are not able by greater quantities to make their provision of victuals. . . ." Unless an establishment lodges wayfaring people it is not an inn. All licensed houses are not inns. All inns are not licensed.

Innkeepers can only refuse admission to *bona fide* travellers when the inn is full. But he is not obliged to allow a traveller to sleep in any living-room if all the bedrooms are occupied. An innkeeper is entitled to payment in advance and there is no liability for refusing admission unless a reasonable sum is tendered.

He is bound to supply what food and drink he can. The lateness of the hour is no ground for refusing admission unless the wayfarer is drunk or disorderly ; or accompanied by (and inseparable from) a large dog ; or is a chimney sweep in working clothes, or in general an object of distaste for other customers.

The wayfarer has no immediate means of enforcing his rights when admission is wrongfully refused. He may, if revengefully disposed, indict the innkeeper and cause him to lose his licence, but he is entitled to no compensation ; and revenge is a poor consolation for a night spent without a bed. A person who orders a meal without having the means to pay for it does not by that action alone become guilty of obtaining goods by false pretences. He may, however, be held to be a debtor obtaining credit on false pretences. But as the penalty for this offence is one year's imprisonment it is not likely to be imposed upon him for the price of a meal.

An innkeeper cannot sue a bar-customer for the price of

473

drinks consumed on the premises unless the debt amounts to twenty shillings or more.

Knowingly to let a room which was previously occupied by some one suffering from an infectious disease and which has not been adequately disinfected is an offence for which the innkeeper may be fined £20.

An innkeeper is responsible for a traveller's goods while in the inn. His liability is limited to £30, unless the loss is due to his wilful default or neglect, or if the goods have been given to him for safe custody.

A visitor staying at an inn at which he had booked rooms would not be a traveller, but a lodger, and would lose the benefit of this protection.

OF JOY-RIDES

To take and use a car belonging to another and afterwards abandon it is not theft, provided that the " borrower " can prove he had not the intention " permanently to deprive the owner thereof." But it is trespass.

OF MASQUERADES

To go about by night with the face disguised, blackened or masked and having the intent to enter any building, is sufficient to make a person guilty of a misdemeanour. Therefore, since it is difficult to establish the innocence of one's intentions, it is imprudent to be found in such a situation.

If one disguise himself for the purpose of impersonating the husband of, and to, any wife other than one's own he may (if successful) be guilty of rape ; and it is not wise to rely upon being able to prove that one's histrionic powers are too poor to deceive an unbiassed audience.

OF RIOTOUS BEHAVIOUR

A *riot* is the assembly of three or more persons with an apparent tendency to violence sufficient to inspire alarm or

474

terror, even if only one person be in fact alarmed. If such an assembly consists of twelve or more persons the ensuing disturbance of the peace is a misdemeanour; and failure to disperse, after the reading of the Riot Act, is a felony.

To collect a crowd to the annoyance of the neighbours is a nuisance.

To join with others, by agreement, in hissing a performance is a conspiracy; but if a consensus of audible censure be not prearranged, it is lawful.

OF CURSING AND SWEARING

Indulgence in profanity by soldiers, sailors and navvies is punishable by a fine of one shilling; for other proletarians the fine is two shillings; but for gentlemen and those of higher station the scale is five shillings. This social injustice can no longer be defended on the ground that religion and morals are not taught in the elementary schools.

IN CONCLUSION

The law may be likened to a whimsical lady. It is an advantage to have a knowledge of her character, but her embraces are to be avoided, for they are apt to be both ill-timed and expensive. Remember, therefore, that, should you be haled before the magistrate, whether for a breach of public law or at the suit of some injured person for an infringement of a private right, it is no defence and will avail you nothing to plead ignorance of the law, for the law presumes that every man has full knowledge of his own duties and of the rights of others.

475

terror, even if only one person be in fact alarmed. If such an assembly consists of twelve or more persons the ensuing disturbance of the peace is a misdemeanour; and failure to disperse, after the reading of the Riot Act, is a felony.

To collect a crowd to the annoyance of the neighbours is a nuisance.

To join with others, by agreement, in hissing a performance is a conspiracy; but if a consensus of audible censure be not prearranged, it is lawful.

OF CURSING AND SWEARING

Indulgence in profanity by soldiers, sailors and navvies is punishable by a fine of one shilling; for other professions the fine is two shillings; but for gentlemen and those of higher station the scale is five shillings. This social injustice can no longer be defended on the ground that religion and morals are not taught in the elementary schools.

IN CONCLUSION

The law may be likened to a whimsical lady. It is an advantage to have a knowledge of her character, but her embraces are to be avoided, for they are apt to be both ill-timed and expensive. Remember, therefore, that should you be haled before the magistrate, whether for a breach of public law or at the suit of some injured person for an infringement of a private right, it is no defence and will avail you nothing to plead ignorance of the law, for the law presumes that every man has full knowledge of his own duties and of the rights of others.

FIRST AID

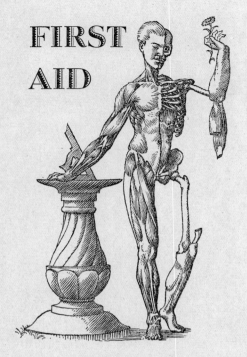

IN DIVERS CRISES

'TIS HIS GREAT HAPPINESS THAT HE IS
DISTEMPERED, THEREBY TO HAVE AN OPPOR-
TUNITY OF EXPERIENCING THE EFFICACY
AND SWEETNESS OF THE REMEDIES WHICH
YOU HAVE SO JUDICIOUSLY PROPOUNDED.
I APPROVE 'EM ALL.   Congreve

FIRST AID

IN DIVERS CRISES

'TIS HIS GREAT HAPPINESS THAT HE IS
DISTEMPERED, THEREBY TO HAVE AN OPPOR-
TUNITY OF EXPERIENCING THE BENEFITS
AND SWEETNESS OF THE REMEDIES WHICH
YOU HAVE SO JUDICIOUSLY PROPOUNDED.
I APPROVE 'EM ALL.   CONTENTS

FIRST AID IN DIVERS CRISES

Now we give you Physic and other Remedies for certain Accidents, Sicknesses and Infirmities which may trouble your week-ends. But should any of the graver mishaps befall you of which we treat hereafter, remember that our advices must be used only to allay the harm and to beguile the time while your Physician is delayed. Remember also that the drugs are occasional drugs, to be used rarely and compounded with discretion. For, though our simples be culled from venerable masters and our compounds be furnished worthily and though your apothecary be scrupulous to the last minim, yet these alone shall not avail to save you.

THE PRUDENT WAYFARER may equip himself against sundry common emergencies with the following armamentarium. Of Tincture of Iodine, two ounces; of Boric Acid, four ounces; of Boric Acid Ointment, two ounces; of Ammonia, four ounces; of Sal Volatile, two ounces; of bandages, absorbent wool, adhesive plaster, safety pins, and packets containing sterile gauze and sterile lint, a small quantity; and of various remedies hereafter described, according to his carrying capacity and his apprehensions.

AGAINST STINGS AND BITES

If Stung by a Bee or Wasp, extract first the sting by pressing on to the puncture with a small key. Now neutralise the Venom by washing the wound with a solution of Ammonia or Potash.

Good against the Sting of all Insects, including Midges and Mosquitoes, is the application, with a pencil of camel's hair, of an analgesic blended of Acid Carbolic gr.v, Tr. Iodidi mx, Potass. Iodidi gr.xx and Aqua dest. ad ℨi. To anticipate an assault apply to vulnerable areas an epithem

479

of Ol. Eucalypti ʒiss, Sp. Camphoræ ʒi and Lin. Saponis ad ʒii; or use as a cosmetic Carmine gr.i, Ol. Eucalypti mxv and Pulv. Cret. Gall. ʒii. Man does not succumb so readily to these as the Harvester, the Midge and the Mosquito.

If the sting is on the tongue, avert the grave mischance of asphyxiation from the swelling, by applying inside the mouth an ice bag, or, lacking this, cold water or dilute ammonia; and hot, well wrung out foments to the surface of the neck. But the physician has remedies that are more effective than these.

To take away the Stinging of Nettles use the above application; but, where there is Dock nearby, apply of this a bruised leaf to the area of stinging and chant the following Cantrap :

> Out Nettle, in Dock :
> Dock shall have a new smock.

To search for Harvesters, dig in the skin with a needle first heated in a candle flame; and afterwards cleanse the spot with iodine.

To search for Fleas, be seated on a white and woolly blanket, for this most readily entangles and makes visible your enemy. But some hold that to clap an open bottle of chloroform or a wet cake of soap upon the spot attacked is better.

HARM BY VENOMOUS SNAKES

Against the Harm by Venomous Snakes take measures to prevent the poison from diffusing itself through the system generally and to destroy what is already in the wound. To achieve the former object a tourniquet may be improvised by tying a handkerchief loosely round the limb between the wound and the heart, placing a short stick in the ring bandage thus formed and twisting this until the limb is tightly compressed. Now withdraw the venom locally by sucking the wound. (This proceeding is dangerous only in that it creates a reputation for courage and presence of mind which is difficult to maintain except

480

in the rare advent of another case of snake bite. It is, however, quite unnecessary to swallow the venom and one may go far to undo the unfortunate impression of heroism by using an antiseptic mouth wash at the earliest possible moment.) It is good to encourage bleeding by bathing the fang apertures with warm water and to extend the wounds down to the subcutaneous tissues with a clean, sharp knife. If the means be available, apply crystals of potassium permanganate or a strong carbolic acid solution to the wound. Give also, to counteract the severe shock, good doses of whisky or brandy, repeated several times if necessary. Some people prefer sal volatile in doses of a teaspoonful to a wineglass of water. No one knows the reason for this.

BURNINGS AND SCALDINGS

Burnings and Scaldings by Fire and Water and Corrosive Substances may, when slight, be treated by pouring over them ordinary Salad Oil, or a mixture of Olive (or Linseed) Oil and Lime Water in equal parts, and then covering with a dressing of lint soaked in oil. Remember that it is necessary to exclude air from the burn as quickly as possible, to administer stimulants, and on no account to break a blister. Severe burns must not be touched by the untutored hand.

BLISTERS

The popular Indulgence of Biting off Blood Blisters is strongly to be deprecated. The proper treatment is to sterilise the skin that covers them with an antiseptic and then to evacuate the blood with a needle which has previously been reddened in a flame.

TO STAUNCH BLOOD

To Staunch Blood that oozes gently or that flows in a continuous stream of dark purple, it is sufficient to apply a pad of lint on which Iodine has been poured and then to fix this by means of a handkerchief, scarf or bandage.
But when the blood is scarlet and issues from the limb in a series of jets, you must act with coolness and promptitude.

Press the thumb or forefinger tightly to the wound, while another improvises a tourniquet, which must be bound to the thigh or upper arm between the bleeding point and the heart. The only modification of the already described tourniquet (vide *Venomous Snakes*) is that now there is included within the folds of the handkerchief a smooth pebble which presses directly upon the artery when the tourniquet has been fixed in position. When the bleeding has been arrested it is good to cleanse the wound and apply a simple Iodine dressing. Unless collapse has occurred it is forbidden to administer stimulants until the Surgeon has taken measures to prevent recurrence of bleeding.

EPISTAXIS (NOSE-BLEED)

When the Nose bleeds do not bow the head over a basin, or you will very soon need another. Sit with the head slightly thrown back and apply Cold Water Compresses to the root of the nose, the face and between the shoulder blades. It is good in moderately severe cases to inhale the Vapour of Turpentine or a Snuff of powdered Alum. Where these methods fail or are not available, it is an emergency measure to plug into the nostrils long, narrow strips of gauze, packing these as far back as possible and continuing until the whole nasal cavity is filled.

EMERGENCY ANTISEPTICS

The following Emergency Antiseptics may be used in any case where sterilisation and antisepsis are indicated :

Methylated Spirits with an equal bulk of water ;
Whisky similarly tampered with ;
Salt, a dessertspoonful dissolved in a tumbler of warm water ;
Vinegar.
Tincture of Iodine should, however, be preferred to any of these.

SYNCOPE

When Syncope (fainting) is imminent, let the sufferer clasp his head between his knees and the crisis may pass. Should unconsciousness supervene, keep the head low, loosen the clothing and hold to the nose smelling salts or burnt feathers. It is pleasant and fitting that the patient celebrate the first moment when he is able to stand upright by partaking of a fluid ounce of brandy or whisky. Sal volatile should not be withheld on grounds of principle.

PERIPALPEBRAL ECCHYMOSIS

Peripalpebral Ecchymosis (black eye). First counteract the swelling and discoloration of this and every other manner of bruise by gently rubbing in the tincture of Arnica Flowers or a solution of Witch Hazel Leaves (Liquor Hamamelidis). Then apply with a moderately tight bandage a compress made of cotton wool or lint steeped in cold water. *When bruised all over* and feeling shaken but not faint there is much relief in a hot bath. This may be followed by the use of an embrocation made from Spr. Vini Rectif. and Liq. Ammon. Acet. of each ʒiss and Aqua Camphoræ ʒviii, which is gently applied to the skin and allowed to evaporate.

FOREIGN BODIES IN EYE

To overcome opposition of the eye to your endeavours to remove from it foreign bodies, practise this manœuvre aimed at exposing the whole conjunctiva of the upper lid : First place the edge of the thumb along the lower lid just below, and the index finger on the upper lid just above the lashes. By artfully pushing up the skin with the index finger you will disengage very slightly the upper lid margin from the eye surface. Now, with the thumb slip the lower lid behind the upper and by a deft follow-through movement evert this lid between the thumb and index finger. The foreign body can now be removed with moistened linen. Do not fear you have failed in your quest if it prove very small. The patient's description of its size as maybe less than a plover's though surely more than a pigeon's egg is usually not correct.

The lower lid can be best explored if the patient looks up while the lid is pulled down.

FOREIGN BODIES IN NOSE

To eject a foreign body from the nose stimulate sneezing with pepper or a paper spill.

R *

FOREIGN BODIES IN EAR

A foreign body in the ear does not constitute an emergency and is not remedied by the introduction of other foreign bodies such as bare bodkins or syringes. It is in such matters as this that the Art of the Physician and Surgeon still avails.

AFTER EXPOSURE

After Exposure to Wind and Rain it is good to seek the *Abortion of Nasal Catarrh*. Take, therefore, immediately on returning home, of Calomel gr. iii and a hot bath. At night, another hot bath should be followed by Pulv. Ipecac. Co. gr.xv. taken in a warmed bed. Take now, for not more than three days, a pill compounded of Quinine Sulphate and Powdered Camphor, of each gr.ss and fluid Extract of Belladonna Root m ¼, four times a day. These things are inimical to the thin rheum.

AFTER EXPOSURE TO LOCAL INFECTIONS it is said that to apply, within one hour, thoroughly, to the very place, an ointment made of calomel thirty-three parts, vaseline ten parts, and lanoline a hundred parts may stave off the affliction. Some say that prophylaxis should begin one hour earlier than this.

TO REMEDY THE TOOTHACHE

Where there is no Doctor or Dentist, but only an Apothecary, *remedy the Toothache and the Gumboil* by applying cotton wool saturated in Tr.Opii, Chloroform, Sp. Camph., and Tr. Pyrethri, of each ʒi, which is a potent analgesic. But if there be a Dentist or a Doctor, shun this like poison (which it is) and go at once to the one or the other ; for only in them is Salvation.

GOOD AGAINST THE MEGRIMS

Good against the Megrims, Neuralgias and all manners of Aches and Pains is a cachet made of Phenacetin gr.v, Aspirin gr.v and Caffein Citrate gr.iii.

484

SEA-SICKNESS

On Becoming Indifferent to the Fate of your Ship, pack the ears firmly with gauze until the pressure on the tympanic membrane can be felt. It is useful to take of Chloretone gr.v in a cachet, repeating two-hourly if necessary three or four times. If Chloretone disagrees, compromise with the semicircular canals by taking of Syr. Chloral ʒii, Pot. Bromid. gr.xxx, and Aqua Chlorof. ad ʒiss, one teaspoonful every five minutes till relief or sleep occurs. It is best to lie on the right side with the knees drawn up to the abdomen.

OF SUN-BATHING

ARSENIC, like sunshine, is good for the blood ; but to partake of an ounce or two, on the ground that " one cannot have too much of a good thing," would be folly. Folly likewise (though not lethal) is it to expose the whole body, pale and unprepared, for hours at a time to the hot sun. Those who do so may expect a red and peeling skin, headache, exhaustion and sickness of the stomach. To savour the pleasures of the sun-bath and rise from it refreshed and vigorous, with a smooth and daily deepening tan, first inure yourself to the rays as follows : the first day, modestly uncover only the feet and ankles and bathe them in the sun for three periods of five minutes each, allowing an interval of ten minutes between them. Then turn the body and expose the equivalent area on the dorsal surface for three similar periods. The second day, uncover to the knees and bathe the whole area for five minutes ; then cover down to the ankles and continue to bathe the area that has already been exposed on the previous day for another five minutes ; making thus ten minutes in all. The third day, bathe up to the hips for five minutes, up to the knees for ten minutes, and up to the ankles for fifteen minutes. The fourth day, bathe up to the navel for five minutes, up to the hips for ten minutes, up to the knees for fifteen minutes, and up to the ankles for twenty minutes. The fifth day, bathe up to the shoulders for five minutes, up to the navel for ten minutes, up to the hips for fifteen minutes, up to the knees for twenty minutes, and up to the ankles for twenty-five minutes. The sixth day, make these times, ten, fifteen, twenty, twenty-five and thirty minutes respectively ;

485

and on the seventh day increase them by yet another increment of five minutes each. Each day you should bathe for three periods with intervals of ten minutes between them, and then repeat the whole process on the dorsal surface of the body.

Those who are habituate, as well as those in training, should bear in mind the following beneficial rules:—If after sunbathing you experience vertigo, fatigue, or great excitement, you have done too much and must expose a smaller area and for a shorter period on the next occasion. Keep the head covered with a wide-brimmed hat and the eyes protected with dark-rimmed glasses. Prefer the morning or late afternoon to noontide when heat-bearing waves preponderate and choose a place in shelter from the winds ; but do not attempt to take a sun-bath under glass, for it is opaque to the more potent rays. Beware of sun-bathing when you are exhausted from exercise (or any other cause) and during the hour that follows the midday meal. If you are debilitated or have the slightest suspicion of Tubercle you must not sun-bathe except under the special guidance of a physician.

Those who sun-bathe for a cosmetic rather than for a therapeutic purpose will anoint themselves with olive-oil.

TO SOOTHE THE FACE

To soothe the Face tormented by the Sun and Wind, use an anodyne compounded of Acid Hydrochlor. mxv, Acid Citric ʒi, Ess. Rosæ alb. mxxx, Glycerin and Sp. rectificat. of each ʒiv and Aqua dest. ad ℥iv.

To withstand the Pigmentation of Freckles, wash in Sour Milk or in Buttermilk ; or from the Apothecary obtain their active principle in the following formula : Acid Lactic (10 per cent) ʒii, Glycerini ʒss. Ess. Rosæ Alb. ʒiss, Tr. Benzoin ʒi and Aqua ad ℥i. This should be dabbed on the face with cotton wool twice each day.

SUNSTROKE

Upon such as are Overcome by the Sun, cold water should be dashed, especially over the head, neck and chest. Apply frequently to the forehead cloths wrung out of iced water ; and ice itself is very good.

486

SPRAINS

Before treating a Sprain of the Ankle or any other Joint remember that there may be a graver injury present ; a dislocation or even fracture of one of the component bones of the joint. But as emergency measures (having transported the victim home, with the limb in the position that gives greatest ease) remove the clothing, put the patient on a couch and, under the guidance of his sensations, rest the limb on cushions, preferably in such a way that it is well elevated. Now try the application of cold compresses ; or, if these fail to relieve pain, of hot fomentations, which should be tightly bandaged over the joint. It is good, if pain is excessive, to apply a teaspoonful of laudanum to the fomentation.

Treat Tennis Elbow and Jumper's Sprain by massaging the injured part and applying a firm bandage. Bathing alternately with hot and cold water is soothing and beneficial.

THE FEET OF THE ITINERANT, VAGRANT AND PILGRIM

The Abrasion, Blister and Callosity torment, and ultimately bring to a standstill, the traveller who ventures on foot without regarding the precepts we now give you.

By these tokens shall you know that you are shod well for the open road. In front of the toes there will be a clearance of one thumb-breadth ; there will be no pressure down on the toes ; the leather grasped across the shoe in the line of the ball will not feel tense nor will it wrinkle under your fingers ; the sole will be thick, the heel low, and the tongue fitting smooth and even.

The Socks will be made of light wool ; they will not be small, cramping the toes, nor yet so large that blisters may form where there is folding ; neither shall they have darn or blemish. They should be washed and stretched every day ; and changing from one foot to the other is good. Do not lubricate the shoe leather too much as this may close the pores and prevent proper evaporation of moisture from the foot.

To harden the feet against prolonged strain, for two weeks

before apply every other day a lotion of formaldehyde, 10 per cent. Cleanse the feet with cold water to which may be added a few drops of ammonia before and after each day's walking. Beware of the skin made sodden and vulnerable by too long immersion in water.

Pressure points liable to abrasion may be protected by application of tincture of iodine followed by boric acid ointment and adhesive plaster. These things may also be used to remedy abrasions that have formed.

Puncture the bases of blisters with a sterile needle, but always precede and follow this operation with the generous application of tincture of iodine. The outer skin should on no account be removed.

To soften and ultimately remove callosities paint on, after cleansing the foot, a preparation of acid. salicyl. gr.xx and collodion flexile up to one ounce. Do this every day till the tissue has a blanched appearance, when the whole callosity can be removed with any small blunt instrument.

TO STAY THE HICQUET

To stay the Hicquet drink water backwards. This art consists in applying the lips to the far side of the glass and bending forward the head and body till drinking becomes possible. As a prophylactic measure it should be practised secretly.

Another method is to sip slowly a glass of water with both ears and nostrils stopped. A few drops of essence of peppermint on sugar are very effective in the case of such patients as cannot take water.

RELIEF OF THE WINDY SPASMS

For the Immediate Relief of the Windy Spasms take on sugar Oil of Cajuput, five minims ; or of Sp. Ætheris Composita thirty minims, repeated every fifteen minutes if necessary.

POISONED FOOD

After Partaking of Poisoned Food it is correct to send for a doctor. (It is good to inform him of the purpose for

488

which he is needed.) Meanwhile provoke vomition by titillating the back of the throat with a finger or by administering, every five minutes until successful, any of the following emetics :

Salt : a tablespoonful to a tumbler of water.

Mustard : a teaspoonful to a tumbler of water ; or Ipecacuanha wine, a teaspoonful.

Meanwhile the patient should be put to bed, hot bottles and hot foments applied to the Abdomen and, if there are signs of collapse, brandy or other stimulants administered. Finally give an ounce of castor oil. These measures are good against Surfeits of Wholesome Meats and Drinks as well as other forms of food poisoning.

BEFORE HOBNAILING THE LIVER

Before Occasions devoted to Hobnailing the Liver it is recommended to take a half to one ounce of Olive Oil. The Parkinson Herbal states that " if one doe eate five or sixe bitter Almonds before he fall into drinking company, it will keepe him from being overtaken more than the rest." On the occasion itself, deal with *Imminent Emergencies* by partaking of the following sedative : Acid Hydrocyan Dil. miv, Tr. Nuc. Vom. mx, Tr. Aurant, mx, Aqua Cinn. ad ℥i. But to such as cannot themselves partake administer a potion of Liq. Ammon. Acet. ℥i and await the event with kindly interest.

THE MORNING AFTER

On the Morning After, comfort the cold and feeble brain by recalling the warning of Mayster Isaac Judæus who saith : " It is unpossyble for them that drinketh overmoche water in theyr youth to come to ye æge that God ordained them."

If it matters little to you whether the age that God ordained be reached or no, drink the following cordial :

Take of Sp. Ammon. Aromat. mx, Sodii Bic. gr.xv, Tr. Capsici miii, Tr. Card. Co. ℥i, Tr. Zingib. Fort.mv, Tr.Cinc. Co.mx, Tr.Nuc.Vom.mx, Sp.Chlorof.mx. and Water of Orange Flowers up to ℥i. Take also of Caffein

Cit. gr.v, Acid Cit. gr.x, Tr. Aurant mv; and Water up to ℥i. Add two tablespoonfuls of the first to two of the second drink and whilst the effervescence lasts.

Some recommend—if only the head suffers—to take of Calcium Lactate, gr.xxx.

WHEN COCKTAILS FAIL

If one be overcome by such *mishap or weariness* that even cocktails fail to cure his apathy, let him try this elixir: Ext. Turneræ liq. (B.P.C.) and Syr. Glycerophosph. Co., of each ℨi, and Decoctum Hordei ad ℥i, and he may still rise to the occasion.

A SOPORIFIC

When you are so exhausted that the effort to sleep is too much, a soporific that is rapid and free from risk can be compounded from paraldehyde ℨij, syr. aromat. ℨj and aqua chlorof. up to ℥j. Let two ounces be made and take one of these on retiring and another in one hour if necessary. Paraldehyde tastes as poisons should; but in such doses it is not poison.

POISONING BY NOXIOUS SUBSTANCES

Each manner of poisoning demands the skilled application of its appropriate remedies and antidotes, so that the noxious substance may be removed from the sufferer, the effects nullified by the administration of appropriate antagonists or neutralising agents, and special symptoms combated by the application of proved procedures and remedies.

At the disposal of the unskilled are *emetics and purgatives* to achieve the first end, though the special contra-indication hereafter mentioned must be carefully studied lest by their use worse disaster befall. The appropriate antagonists may be known only if the nature of the poison is evident or deducible from observation of the special manner of poisoning. And the combating of special symptoms may be attempted, until the physician arrives, in the manner presently to be described.

CORROSIVES

The common corrosive poisons are Spirit of Salts, Oil of Vitriol, Oxalic Acid, Carbolic Acid and Lysol which may be counted as acids ; and Caustic Potash, Caustic Soda, Spirit of Hartshorn (Ammonia) and Washing Soda which are alkaline. It is not reckoned good practice to give any of these substances (as so many do) instead of Syrup of Figs.

If the poison is known to be acid give lime water, saccharated if possible, which is the most fitting alkaline ; or if this is not available, plaster from walls or ceilings may be used.

Neutralise known alkaline corrosives with vinegar or the juice of oranges and lemons.

Copious draughts of water dilute the poisons ; and milk, eggs, oils, and starch and water, soothing mucous surfaces and enveloping the poison, have virtue as demulcents.

IRRITANTS

The irritant poisons, among which are Arsenic, Corrosive Sublimate, Iodine Crystals, Household Liniments and Embrocations, and sundry herbs, berries and flowers, produce severe nausea, vomiting, colick and purgation. Emetics (cited under Poisoned Food) should be given freely and followed later by castor oil.

A BLUNDERBUSS ANTIDOTE

Against unknown poisons or mixtures of known poisons has been devised the following formula : Take of powdered Charcoal two parts, and of Tannic Acid and Magnesia, of each one part ; and give, and repeat frequently, a teaspoonful in a tumbler of water.

But in addition it is good to know the following specific antidotes :

Against *Carbolic Acid*, exhibit Epsom Salt or Glauber's Salt.

Against *Corrosive Sublimate and other mercurials*, white of egg.

Against *Opium*, Potassium Permanganate or Condy's Fluid.

Against *Deadly Nightshade* (Belladonna), strong boiled tea and morphia. Though a prescription is needed for the

491

latter. Against *Strychnine*, Chloroform inhalation and dram doses of Potassium Bromide dissolved in water.

The greater number of *special symptoms* of poisoning can be differentiated and treated only by those skilled in clinical medicine. But the unskilled may treat *shock and collapse* by warmly wrapping up the patient, applying hot-water bottles to the feet and thighs and administering hot coffee and sal volatile ; and they may *avert coma* by applying cold affusions to the head and keeping the patient constantly roused.

ANOTHER

Let no cautious week-ender set forth without good stock of tobacco, for, in the words of an old ballad :

> It helpeth digestion,
> Of that there's no question,
>   The gout, and the toothache, it easeth :
> Be it early, or late,
> 'Tis never out of date,
>   He may safely take it that pleaseth.

> Tobacco prevents
> Infection by scents,
>   That hurt the brain, and are heady ;
> An antidote is,
> Before you're amisse,
>   As well as an after remedy.

> The cold it doth heat,
> Cools them that do sweat,
>   And them that are fat maketh lean :
> The hungry doth feed,
> And, if there be need,
>   Spent spirits restoreth again.

> Tobacco infused,
> May safely be used,
>   For purging, and killing of lice :
> Not so much as the ashes,
> But heals cuts and slashes,
>   And that out of hand, in a trice.
>   *Anon.*, 17th century.

492

Such are the ills that commonly befall those who walk abroad with their fellows to enjoy the pleasures of the country.

Should you ail anything else then " all the Nation are already Physitians, . . . every one you meet, whether man or woman, will prescribe you a medicine for it."

But take their medicine, like ours, with circumspection, Reader.

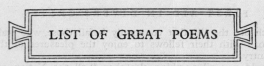

LIST OF GREAT POEMS

WHICH ARE CONTAINED IN MANY MEMORIES AND MOST
ANTHOLOGIES AND ARE THEREFORE OMITTED
FROM THIS BOOK

Psalm 23 . . . The " Great Bible " version.
" The Lord is my Shepherd "

Prothalamion . . . . Edmund Spenser.
" Calm was the day, and through the
trembling air "

Epithalamion . . . . Edmund Spenser.
" Ye learned sisters, which have oftentimes "

O Mistress Mine . . . . W. Shakespeare.
" O mistress mine, where are you
roaming ? "
(And many more by the same author.)

Death . . . . . John Donne.
" Death, be not proud, though some have
callèd thee "

Sweet content . . . . . T. Dekker.
" Art thou poor, yet hast thou golden
slumbers "

Delight in Disorder . . . . R. Herrick.
" A sweet disorder in the dress "

To the virgins to make much of time . R. Herrick.
" Gather ye rosebuds while ye may "

Love . . . . . George Herbert.
" Love bade me welcome, yet my soul
drew back "

Death the Leveller . . . . James Shirley.
" The glories of our blood and state "

Nox nocti indicat scientiam . . W. Habington.
" When I survey the bright "

Go, lovely Rose . . . . Edmund Waller.
" Go, lovely Rose "

Hymn on the Nativity . . . John Milton.
" It was the winter wild "

494

    * Mr. Housman does not, alas, allow his poems to
           appear in anthologies.

ACKNOWLEDGEMENT

THE editors have to thank all living poets whose work is to be found in this book for permission to include their poems. They are similarly indebted to the literary executors of Rupert Brooke, Samuel Butler, James Elroy Flecker, Richard Garnett, George Meredith, Alice Meynell, Walter Raleigh, R. L. Stevenson and Francis Thompson. They further acknowledge with thanks permission from the following publishers to reprint poems appearing in the books here enumerated : *Messrs. G. Bell & Sons :* The Unknown Eros, by Coventry Patmore. *Messrs. Ernest Benn :* The Unknown Goddess, by Mr. Humbert Wolfe ; Beauty the Pilgrim, by Mr. Gerald Gould. *Messrs. Burns Oates & Washbourne :* Poems, by Mr. G. K. Chesterton ; Collected Poems of Alice Meynell ; Collected Works of Francis Thompson ; The Flower of Peace, by Mrs. Tynan Hinkson ; Poems, by J. B. Tabb. *Messrs. Jonathan Cape :* Collected Poems of Mr. W. H. Davies ; Samuel Butler's Notebooks ; Poems, by Miss Muriel Stuart. *Messrs. Chatto & Windus :* Leda, by Mr. Aldous Huxley ; Argonaut and Juggernaut, by Mr. Osbert Sitwell ; Poems, by R. L. Stevenson. *Messrs. Constable :* Collected Works of George Meredith ; Poems by W. Raleigh. *Messrs. Dent :* The Wild Knight, by Mr. G. K. Chesterton. *Messrs. Duckworth :* Sonnets and Verse, by Mr. Hilaire Belloc ; Troy Park, by Miss Edith Sitwell. *Messrs. Elkin Mathews & Marrot :* Poems, by Mary Coleridge. *Messrs. Heinemann :* Selected Poems, by Mr. Robert Frost ; War Poems, by Mr. Siegfried Sassoon ; Collected Poems, by Mr. John Masefield ; Poems, 1914–1926, by Mr. Robert Graves. *Messrs Hodder & Stoughton :* Poems, by Mr. J. C. Squire. *Messrs. Longmans, Green & Co. :* Child's Garden of Verses, by R. L. Stevenson ; Songs of Childhood, by Mr. Walter de la Mare. *Messrs. Macmillan :* Collected Poems of T. E. Brown ; Late Lyrics, by Thomas Hardy ; Poems, by Mr. Ralph Hodgson ; Songs of England, by Alfred Austin ; Songs from the Clay, by

497

ACKNOWLEDGEMENT

Mr. James Stephens ; The Hill of Vision, by Mr. James Stephens ; Later Poems, by Mr. W. B. Yeats ; Collected Poems, by Thomas Hardy. *Messrs. Elkin Mathews :* Poems, by Lionel Johnson. *Messrs. Methuen :* Wine and Water, by Mr. G. K. Chesterton ; Collected Poems, by Mr. W. H. Davies. *Mr. Humphrey Milford* (Oxford University Press): Fifty Poems, by A. D. Godley. *Messrs. Grant Richards :* Little Poems, by Walter Leaf. *The Poetry Bookshop :* Spring Morning, by Mrs. Frances Cornford ; Autumn Midnight, by Mrs. Frances Cornford ; Strange Meetings, by Mr. Harold Monro ; The " Georgian Poetry " anthologies. *Messrs. Elkin Mathews* and *Mr. Martin Secker :* Collected Poems of J. E. Flecker. *Mr. Martin Secker :* Pier Glass, by Mr. Robert Graves ; Verses, by Miss Viola Meynell ; Complete Poems, by Emily Dickinson ; Poems, by Miss Edna St. Vincent Millay. *Messrs. Sidgwick & Jackson :* Collected Poems of Rupert Brooke ; The Dark Fire, by Mr. Walter Turner. The following American permissions to reprint poems are also to be acknowledged : Messrs. Doubleday Doran & Co. : Beauty the Pilgrim, by Mr. Gerald Gould. Messrs. Harper and Brothers : Renascence and other Poems, by Miss Millay (copyright by Edna St. Vincent Millay 1917) ; Second April, by Miss Millay (copyright by Edna St. Vincent Millay 1921). Messrs. Little Brown & Co. : Poems, by Emily Dickenson. Messrs. Longmans, Green & Co. : The Traveller's Curse, by Mr. Robert Graves ; The Fly, by Mr. Walter de la Mare. The Macmillan Co. of New York : Collected Poems, by Thomas Hardy ; Later Lyrics, by Thomas Hardy ; Poems, by Mr. Ralph Hodgson ; The Daniel Jazz and other Poems, by Mr. Nicholas Vachel Lindsay ; Poems, by Mr. John Masefield ; Later Poems, by Mr. W. B. Yeats.

They are also obliged to the following music collectors, editors and publishers for permission to include the songs here enumerated : *Miss Lucy Broadwood :* " The trees they do grow high." *Sir Richard Terry* for " The Chinese Bumboat Man." *Sir Richard Terry* and *Messrs. J. Curwen & Sons :* "Billy Boy" and "Shenandoah," from The Shanty Book. *Miss Kaipeles* (executor of Cecil Sharp) and *Messrs. Novello* for " A-roving." *Messrs.*

498

ACKNOWLEDGEMENT

J. Curwen & Sons: "The Wraggle Taggle Gipsies."
Mr. Hubert Hughes: "The Shan Wan Wocht" and
"The old man that lived near hell." *The Rev. Maunsell
Bacon:* "The Mallard." *Mr. E. J. Moeran:* "Mrs.
Dyer." *Messrs. Erskine Macdonald:* "The Last Long
Mile" and "And when I die," both from More Tommy's
Tunes. *Mr. G. H. Marston:* "The Fire Ship." *Messrs.
Schirmer* of New York: "Chicka hanka." *Messrs. James
Brown & Son* of Glasgow: "Can't you dance the
polka?" from Sea Songs and Shanties. *Messrs. Schott:*
"Marishka," from Hungarian Melodies. *Messrs. Lengnick:*
"The Easter Hymn," from Deutsche Geistliche Lieder;
and further, to *Miss Jane Joseph* for her translation of
"Ideo gloria in excelsis"; to the *Editors of the English
Hymnal* for their arrangement of Bunyan's hymn; to
Messrs. James Brown for the words of "The Rio Grande";
to *Baron Beaverbrook* for "The Jones Boys"; and to
The Oxford University Press for "Michael Finnigan," from
the Oxford Song Book, Vol. II.

THE MANUSCRIPT PAGES

Look, what thy memory cannot contain
Commit to these waste blanks, and thou shalt find
Those children nurs'd, deliver'd from thy brain,
To take a new acquaintance of thy mind.
These offices, so oft as thou wilt look,
Shall profit thee, and much enrich thy book.

Shakespeare.

POEMS

POEMS

POEMS

POEMS

POEMS

POEMS

SONGS

SONGS

GAMES, RECIPES, AND PRESCRIPTIONS

GAMES, RECIPES, AND PRESCRIPTIONS

516

GAMES, RECIPES, AND PRESCRIPTIONS

GAMES, RECIPES, AND PRESCRIPTIONS

QUALITIES THE NEW CONFESSIONS BOOK No one should assess other people before he has assessed himself. Full marks are 20 for each quality. See page 339.	BEAUTY	BRAINS	CHARM	TASTE
_____on_____				
_____on_____				
_____on_____				
_____on_____				
_____on_____				
_____on_____				
_____on_____				
_____on_____				
_____on_____				
_____on_____				
_____on_____				
_____on_____				
_____on_____				
_____on_____				
_____on_____				
_____on_____				
_____on_____				
_____on_____				
_____on_____				
_____on_____				
_____on_____				

DISCRETION	TOLERANCE	WILL-POWER	SENSE OF HUMOUR	MORAL SENSE	COMMON SENSE	SENSIBILITY	SENSUOUSNESS	TACT	SINCERITY	HUMILITY

QUALITIES THE NEW CONFESSIONS BOOK No one should assess other people before he has assessed himself. Full marks are 20 for each quality. See page 339.	BEAUTY	BRAINS	CHARM	TASTE
_on_				
_on_				
_on_				
_on_				
_on_				
_on_				
_on_				
_on_				
_on_				
_on_				
_on_				
_on_				
_on_				
_on_				
_on_				
_on_				
_on_				
_on_				
_on_				
_on_				
_on_				
_on_				

DISCRETION	TOLERANCE	WILL-POWER	SENSE OF HUMOUR	MORAL SENSE	COMMON SENSE	SENSIBILITY	SENSUOUSNESS	TACT	SINCERITY	HUMILITY

QUALITIES THE NEW CONFESSIONS BOOK No one should assess other people before he has assessed himself. Full marks are 20 for each quality. See page 339.	BEAUTY	BRAINS	CHARM	TASTE
on				
on				
on				
on				
on				
on				
on				
on				
on				
on				
on				
on				
on				
on				
on				
on				
on				
on				
on				
on				
on				
on				

DISCRETION	TOLERANCE	WILL-POWER	SENSE OF HUMOUR	MORAL SENSE	COMMON SENSE	SENSIBILITY	SENSUOUSNESS	TACT	SINCERITY	HUMILITY

ADDENDA

530

ADDENDA

ADDENDA